Jelleyman's Thrown a Wobbly

Jelleyman's Thrown a Wobbly

Saturday Afternoons in Front of the Telly

Jeff Stelling

HarperSport

An Imprint of HarperCollins*Publishers*

HarperSport
an imprint of HarperCollins*Publishers*
77-85 Fulham Palace Road,
Hammersmith, London W6 8JB

www.harpercollins.co.uk

First published in paperback 2010

1

Jeff Stelling asserts the moral right to be
identified as the author of this work

A catalogue record of this book is
available from the British Library

ISBN 978-0-00-728126-8

Printed and bound in Great Britain by
Clays Ltd, St Ives plc

Mixed Sources
Product group from well-managed
forests and other controlled sources
www.fsc.org   Cert no. SW-COC-001806
FSC   © 1996 Forest Stewardship Council

FSC is a non-profit international organisation established to promote the
responsible management of the world's forests. Products carrying the FSC
label are independently certified to assure consumers that they come
from forests that are managed to meet the social, economic and
ecological needs of present or future generations.

Find out more about HarperCollins and the environment at
www.harpercollins.co.uk/green

Contents

PART 2 - INTRODUCING THE REAL CRAZY GANG: THE SOCCER SATURDAY PANEL

Foreword

by Chris Kamara

This book is unbelievable, Jeff!

Kammy
A football ground near you, 2010

Acknowledgements

Firstly, a big thanks to Matt Allen, for his assistance in writing this book, and to Emma Wilson, PA, tattooed lady; Caroline Eccles, AP, chairwoman, Neil Mellor Fan Club; Bianca Westwood, reporter/ West Ham fan; Darius Merriman, AP/Spurs; Russ Taylor, AP/Lincoln City; Carly Bassett, co-ordinator/Johnny Depp; Johnny Phillips, reporter/office lothario; Dickie Davis, 'geezer'/reporter; Rob Palmer, reporter/Hull City; Trevor Simmons, stats/Nottingham Forest; Tim Lunn, stats/Leeds United; Dave Todd, egg-swallower/ Colchester United; Caroline Vance, troubleshooter/enforcer/PA; Rob Segal, agent/Spurs (that is tough); Robbie Stelling, son/Chelsea; Matt Stelling, son/Arsenal (I don't know how it works, either); Olivia Stelling, daughter/Blackburn Rovers; Lizzie Stelling, wife/biggest supporter.

Introduction

This is not a rant ...

... But on the sixth day, God created Saturday.

Well, maybe, but during my more reflective moments, I'd like to think He designed it as a reward – something to look forward to during the working weekdays and those soulless evenings on the sofa in front of *Corrie*, *Big Brother* and *Location, Location, Lo*-bloody-*cation*. He stuffed it full of football, goals, drama, dodgy refereeing decisions and penalty appeals to cheer our souls and set our pulses racing. He gave us beer and pies as a refreshing accompaniment. And as an afterthought, He then gave us Sunday to deal with the hangovers and indigestion, while watching even more football and stuffing our faces with more food. Oh, and going to church, of course.

Minor blasphemy aside, though, I figured it would be a fitting way to begin this book by telling you exactly why Saturday is my favourite day of the week, mainly because I'm guessing it's yours, too, otherwise you wouldn't be reading these very pages. Unless you're a judge for the Pulitzer Prize, in which case you're permitted to hate Saturdays as much as you like as long as you look very favourably on these pages. But for most of us here, Saturdays represent a moment of weekly nirvana: twenty-four hours dedicated to superstition, strange rituals, long walks to the train station with siblings, friends and parents. It's about the little details: the rustling sports pages in the newspapers, the TV magazine shows (like my very own), listening to debate programmes on the radio, stumbling into drunken, post-match arguments in the pub, and engaging in long conversations during the late hours, all focused on one subject: football. Sweet, sweet football.

And god, it's great, isn't it? I remember that even as a kid, Saturday always held that extra special holiday quality from the minute I woke up in the morning to the moment my head hit the pillow in the evening. For years it was the bus to Hartlepool's Victoria Park ground, the short walk to the stadium, the smell of police-horse dung in the street, the whiff of frying onions, the first pint of the day in the local pub (after my 18th birthday of course), the first glimpse of the pitch, the ref's whistle, the shouting and the screaming and the ranting and the raving. Then there was the half-time pie and the half-time queue for the toilet. This was topped off with some more ranting and raving and screaming and shouting, before the shrill of the final whistle and the inevitable, crushing, demoralizing sting of defeat and the slow trudge home.

I wouldn't change it for anything else. Even now, the thrill of sitting in the hot seat in the *Soccer Saturday* studio is special. From the moment the first dab of make-up and 'guy-liner' has been stroked onto my face, through to the final results and post-match interviews, I'm usually on the edge of my seat, reacting to every goal, gaffe, sending-off, penalty decision and moment of high drama. Of course, it's not quite the same as sitting at Victoria Park in the wind and the rain from the North Sea, but it's up there.

And, of course, I get to spend my Saturday afternoons with some pretty impressive figures in football (and Paul Merson), among them Matt Le Tissier, Charlie Nicholas, Phil Thompson, Clive Allen, George Best, Rodney Marsh, Paul Walsh, Alan Mullery, Frank McLintock and Tony Cottee. And let's not forget our roving reporter, cult (yes, cult) hero and giggling moustachioed friend, Chris 'Kammy' Kamara. Who wouldn't want to shoulder this cast of football superheroes on a Saturday?

Over the years, the show has picked up quite a following. Hopefully, you're one of the lovely, lovely many who tune in every week. If you're not, the next 200-plus pages are going to be bloody confusing, though you should glean some joy from the nice illustrations. But if you're familiar with the show, hopefully the book will give you a little insight into the madness that goes into making your Saturday afternoons every bit as exciting as mine ...

PART 1

THE CULT OF SOCCER SATURDAY

1

A Short History Of Nearly Everything

(To Do With Soccer Saturday)*

Part I

'You're not even watching football on the telly. You're watching a programme on the telly, where four blokes are watching football ... on the telly!'

Stop for a moment and see yourself meeting someone who has never seen *Soccer Saturday* before. This is difficult I know, but perhaps suspend your disbelief by picturing them as Martians or new Chelsea fans. Then, with this alien concept in mind, imagine explaining the basic idea of the show to these unfortunate souls. Believe me: it's not as easy as it sounds.

You will, of course, start by explaining that this football programme doesn't show any real, actual football. There are no goals, shots or near misses on the telly, so it's a bit like watching Derby

*Apologies to Bill Bryson

County. You'll explain that the closest things to action are the replays of last week's goals in three hours of football analysis, discussion and general messing about that precedes the 90 minutes of match drama on a Saturday afternoon. And that the real drama takes place as the latest scores and events stream onto the TV screen on a computerized videprinter, while four men of varying 'expertise' – all of them former professional footballers – sit in front of TV screens displaying their designated matches, pull on headphones, and relay the afternoon's action with a series of gasps, groans, girly yelps and 'Oh, oh, no, oh, ooooohs!'

You'll probably confuse your enthralled audience further by adding that the roll-call of experts includes a former football playboy ('Champagne' Charlie Nicholas), a one-eyed Liverpool fan and former England captain (Phil 'Thommo' Thompson), a former Southampton legend who dated an Australian soap legend (Matt 'Le Tiss' Le Tissier), and a controversial midfielder who once shared a house with Gazza and could be considered as a football equivalent to Amy Winehouse (Paul 'Merse' Merson).

But hang on a second! Curtail their confusion by explaining that this car crash of information, goals, bookings, red cards, referee blunders and substitutions is held together by 'Jeff's masterful handling of the latest football results' (GQ magazine, apparently – many thanks), as somehow, drawing all this together with a relatively calm head and a prayer to the TV gods, I perch on a precarious chair at the end of a desk as 'anchorman', with some notes and a dossier of information by way of reference while making some semblance of order from the chaos going on around the country.

Sounds strange when explained this way, doesn't it? But bizarrely, in this format, Soccer Saturday has drawn a cult following of fans, which is probably unsurprising given that, between the hours of three o'clock and four forty-five on a Saturday afternoon, it is the only place to receive a continual stream of match-related stats, facts and trivia, without suffering whatever it is Peter Schmeichel is waffling on about on BBC One. And if you haven't got a satellite dish, or even a cheap digital package from the local supermarket (shame on you), then you may have seen my mug gurning from a TV in your local Dixons as you've traipsed around the shops and peered at the half-time scores. This, if you are uninitiated to the programme (and if that's the case, I can only assume that you've been bought this book as a badly-planned present from a none-too-popular auntie), is *Soccer Saturday*. Hopefully you'll enjoy the show, and thanks for watching.

Part II

Calling The Oracle

How the *Soccer Saturday* concept came about now requires a back story of desperate measures, ill-conceived ideas, boozy escapades and Mark Lawrenson's unusual taste in waistcoats. Though by way of a full explanation, it's probably best if I take you back to a time before Sky Sports, when, in the olden days, there was only Ceefax or, if you were really unlucky, Oracle, to deliver live football scores on the telly. For anyone reading this under the age of 25, you may want to imagine Ceefax as a low-tech internet. Visualize a text-based service on your telly, only in colours more garish than a Norwich City away kit and with none of the speed or convenience of broadband, no pictures, no movies and certainly none of the mucky films. Instead, think graphics so big your granny could read them without her NHS specs, delivering the bare bones of a news story all served at a snail's pace. Forget high-speed connections:

if you wanted live football results on a Saturday afternoon, you were probably sitting in front of the telly waiting for the system to scroll through 23 screens of information (the old First Division down to the Scottish lower leagues) with each page turning over every 45 seconds. It was a painful business.

Of course, you could have listened to the radio for results, but this presented another minor headache. In the good old days, the major stations would only focus on the biggest matches of the afternoon, with the odd result from the old Second Division thrown in. So there you were, driving home, listening out for the Crystal Palace versus Grimsby score in Division Two, and instead you're having to listen to a live commentary of Sheffield Wednesday versus Nottingham Forest (like I say, it was a long time ago) in the old Division One. Smart alecs might claim that local radio delivered the more specialized commentary services, but it was unlikely that Hull City's local station would pay much lip service to anyone interested in the scores away from their former stadium, Boothferry Park, so if you had a passing interest in anything happening further up the table, you were in trouble.

Something, clearly, had to give. And that something was dignity ...

Part III
The Big Bang, Crash, Wallop Theory

To anyone with a bit of media savvy, there was clearly a huge audience requiring a wide range of football info in one place, delivered by a dashing anchorman at fast speeds. Somehow, we arrived at the show we all know and love today, though it hasn't always been called *Soccer Saturday*, a football show without any live football to watch. Its predecessor was *Sports Saturday*, a sports show without any sport to watch. This was originally presented by Paul Dempsey, a rather charming man who has now gone to the dark side of Setanta, I believe. Not that I ever watch it, mind. Anyway, my job was to appear on the show once every three weeks as a reserve anchorman, which was a blessing because *Sports Saturday* was a hideous show and would really only pay lip service to football.

When we did mention 'the beautiful game', former Liverpool defender Mark Lawrenson was invited onto the programme as our football expert. For whatever reason, 'Lawro' would usually wear the worst waistcoats you had ever seen. At times it was hard not to imagine that he'd dressed in the dark. In his garish fashions, he would talk in the studio for 20 minutes and discuss the day's big games. Then at four thirty – because there seemed to be an unwritten rule on TV at that time that the football scores should start to appear at four thirty – the results would trickle in.

It was a pretty shoddy service, because nobody had kept in touch with the scores throughout the afternoon. If you were a viewer, you had no idea what was going on in any of the games. If you were a presenter, it was highly possible that you were just as confused. It really was a mind-boggling format. Meanwhile, Sky in those days had very little in the way of live sport, apart from the football on a Sunday, which was their big selling point. As a result we would fill *Sports Saturday* with absolute twaddle or unique features. In fact, some of the so-called 'features' I would have to present are burned in my memory.

For example, one afternoon somebody had the bright idea of inviting a synchronized swimming team into the studio. The brief was for the team of a dozen girls to work through their competitive routines, complete with swimming caps, nose pegs, the works.

Thankfully we were without water, which for safety reasons would have proved disastrous, but the movements and routines were just as disorientating. For anyone in the studio it was like watching the back four of any team managed by Kevin Keegan as they paraded around the floor inelegantly, waving their arms around and pretending to swim. Anyone actually viewing from the safety of their sofas must have thought, 'What the bloody hell is this?' I must admit, I remember shifting uncomfortably in my seat and thinking, 'What the bloody hell is this?' myself.

Later, we ran a feature on the Junior Darts Challenge, which killed a bit of time. We covered the UK Strongman Challenge and the quest for Britain's Best Lady Driver, which was obviously a very short item. During the World Cup we had nothing in the way of live coverage because the TV rights had been cornered by ITV and the Beeb. Instead we laid out a cloth Subbuteo pitch on the studio table and for an hour and half – a full 90 minutes! – fellow easy-on-the-eye presenter Suzanne Dando and I flicked a little plastic ball around, recreating the live match on the other channel.

How anyone could have taken this concept seriously was beyond me. In fact, I remember during the early salvos of our 'match', I actually knelt down and crushed one of Suzanne Dando's players beyond repair. Somewhat embarrassingly, the producer went absolutely crazy off-camera. I later crushed another with my hand. It was a completely innocent accident, but I received a bollocking for not taking our little game seriously. But how could you? It was a bit like Fred Trueman's 1970s show, *Indoor League*, a programme that focused on pub sports in a studio built to look like a pub. Sadly – or maybe brilliantly, however you wanted to look at it – *Sports Saturday* was much, much worse. I think if the programme existed now, it would probably have built a cult following.

I remember one Christmas – and I don't know how we got away with this, what with the rules and regulations that govern TV these days – we took a delivery from the Harrods warehouse, which was conveniently located next to the Sky studios. Very kindly, the store had couriered over a box of toys, all of which would be available from Harrods during the festive season at a very reasonable price, or so we were told. Given our desperate need to fill airtime, we decided to spend a couple of hours on *Sports Saturday* trying out every toy. We even invited former England cricketer Allan Lamb and current panellist Phil Thompson into the studio. Their kids were brought along to try out all the shiny gadgets and, presumably, add some much-needed maturity to the event.

'Harrodsgate' was blatant product placement and probably the lowest point of my broadcasting career, particularly when a Velcro hat appeared from one of the boxes. By all accounts it was one of the must-have toys of the year. It worked on the frankly absurd principle of hurling fuzzy balls onto targets marked on the hat. If a ball stuck, the triumphant thrower would score points. It seemed a stupid concept, but in a moment of TV gold, I donned the hat as former cricket legend and upstanding member of his local community Allan Lamb and various members of the studio crew threw balls at my head. It wasn't a particularly glorious image.

Elsewhere, everything was done on the cheap. Different guests would come in to lend their expertise to different sporting events. We used to drag jockeys into the studio for interviews, even though Sky had no horse racing coverage to speak of. Ex-football managers like Brian Horton would show up for two 20-minute windows (before the kick-off and after the final whistle) and stay for the duration of the show. I don't know what sort of fees were on offer, but it couldn't have been enough.

JELLEYMAN'S THROWN A WOBBLY

Outside broadcasts would take a particularly surreal turn. Allan Lamb and I were once invited to St Moritz in Switzerland where a yearly horse-racing-on-ice event is held by the locals (believe me, I wish I were making this up). Naturally, we weren't going to pass up a free trip to the Swiss Alps, especially when we discovered there was a local cricket team who were planning on playing cricket-on-ice, too. It was hardly the Winter Olympics, but it promised to be a bit of a giggle.

It wasn't until we got to the train that our usually organized party became embroiled in some minor chaos. It was the bloody slow train from Zurich up into the mountains. Everybody got bored and started to drink. Then we did what any right-thinking, slightly tipsy sports nut would do: we started a cricket match in the corridor of the train carriage. Typically, as with all things *Sports Saturday*, we didn't have a bat, stumps or ball, so we made do with bags, a brolly and tomatoes. After four overs, the train was splattered in red and resembled a scene from *The Texas Chainsaw Massacre*. Only a Velcro hat could have lowered the tone.

It came as no surprise when the Swiss train officials took a dim view of our behaviour. We were informed by a particularly disgruntled guard that the police would be waiting for us on our arrival in St Moritz. I remember thinking, 'This will not look good.' By the time we'd arrived everyone had been on their knees cleaning the train. It was spotless and the police were not required, so we'd got off scot-free, which was a relief. Better still, this marked the beginnings of *Soccer Saturday* as we now know it.

Part IV
1997-98 BC (Before Chris Kamara)

I suppose, after the silly clothes, absurd reports and drunken mis-demeanours, it was unsurprising that the show would change. And when some bright spark – I can't remember who exactly, it's been lost in the annals of time – had the idea of plonking four slightly overweight, ex-professional footballers in front of four tellies to report on matches the paying public couldn't see, we seemed to strike gold. It happened in one season, in 1998, and with the show's name changed to *Soccer Saturday*, we were suddenly working on a more football-based programme, which was a blessing because it would mean no more Velcro hats – or tomato-splattered train carriages. Even better, it seemed to capture the public's imagination, though nobody – not even me – really believed the concept had staying power. Who would want to watch four blokes watching football on the telly in a studio? Nevertheless, I began my role as anchorman on the nation's surrealist football magazine show.

Almost immediately it appeared to be good fun. In those days, *Soccer Saturday* started at two o'clock in the afternoon. We'd have an hour-long discussion with a panel, including Clive Allen and Mark Lawrenson, George Best, Rodney Marsh and Frank McLintock. It was principally the same idea as the show's current format, but at three o'clock we might move from football for a brief while to look at the horse racing or rugby. As more and more people began to discover that this was the only place to receive a comprehensive round-up of the day's football events, as and when they happened, the viewing figures began to increase.

Soccer Saturday began to develop into a word-of-mouth success – Sky never really promoted the show and some of our popularity came from the comedy of the afternoon. One idea at this point was for the panel to magically disappear from the studio desk at three o'clock. Each panellist would then sit in a little voice booth in another corner of the building to present telephone reports from their respective games. Why they couldn't stay on the panel and deliver their reports from there was beyond me. And why any right-thinking individual would believe that Frank McLintock had travelled from Middlesex to St James' Park to report on his game in the space of 10 minutes would require a massive leap of imagination.

This surreal situation was given an even stranger twist when our pundits piped their reports into the studio. As I introduced a new match, a picture of Rodney Marsh's face, say, would appear on the telly with his name underneath as he recalled the action at Highbury. Despite their close proximity, the phone lines would sometimes go down and we would lose contact, meaning the studio would be thrown into chaos. It was even less technologically-advanced than 'Andy Townsend's Tactics Truck' on ITV, and slightly more embarrassing. But only slightly.

Somehow, the show survived in this guise for a little while until a producer called Andrew 'Buzz' Hornet suddenly struck upon the idea of *Soccer Saturday* in its modern format. It was blindingly obvious really: rather than moving the panel into phone booths, why not place them in front of TVs on a visible panel so they could relay the match action more visually? With a studio facelift, we were away, and the current format of *Soccer Saturday* was in place. TV viewers were now watching a programme where four men watched live football on the telly. Almost immediately we realized it was a great idea.

I remember thinking the show had made its mark when I stumbled across a magazine interview with actress Patsy Kensit. In it, she began detailing the ins and outs of her marriage to Oasis frontman Liam Gallagher and described his surreal behaviour on a Saturday afternoon. This didn't involve hell-raising lager binges in his local pub, or hotel-trashing drug orgies. Instead, Liam's strangest act was when his wife found him watching Sky Sports on the telly, as four experts in ill-fitting suits watched football ... on the telly. Apparently, she couldn't get her head around it, which was weird because I imagine she'd probably seen some very strange things in the Gallagher household at that time.

'That's where Liam sits on Saturday afternoon,' she explained to the journalist. 'He is mesmerized by that mad programme on Sky where everyone is watching football on tellies you can't see. Honestly, that is the weirdest show I've ever seen and both my husband and my eldest son are riveted to it.'

She wasn't alone. I think a lot of other people felt the same way about *Soccer Saturday* at the time. Thinking about it, they probably still do.

2

Any Given Saturday

noon

← chaos!!! →

6pm

So what really happens when *Soccer Saturday* takes to the air from midday to six o'clock every weekend? Well, dear reader, picture yourself in the following scenario and I shall talk you through a couple of hours of chaos and calamity ...

DATE: A Saturday between the months of August and May.
TIME: Twelve-ish.
LOCATION: The living room. The pub. A shop window of Dixons, Currys, or maybe the electrical goods floor of any popular department store.

Ladies and gentlemen, you are watching Sky Sports.

Welcome to *Soccer Saturday*, a TV magazine of madness, mayhem and general buffoonery that somehow, comprehensively, details the afternoon's football happenings – goals, scorers, bookings, sendings-off, half-time scores and final results – as presented by me, your host, Jeff Stelling. But it's not just a goals and results service. From roughly half past two in the afternoon, when we travel around the grounds for team line-ups and injury updates, until the rundown of final scores at five o'clock and post-match interviews until six, we provide a comprehensive football news-feed. It is, as the *Independent* once argued:

❝ The very next best thing to watching a game in the flesh and an unmissable part of every Saturday afternoon for those who either live on their own, or might be doing so soon if they "don't stop watching that bloody programme". Apart from live football, it is the biggest ratings-puller in the Sky Sports firmament ...

The pitch document must have made quite interesting read-ing, but if you love football this is almost all you need. It is hard-core football pornography and can be accessed on Sky Sports from noon to 6pm every Saturday during the football season and occasionally midweek. ❞

Sounds great, doesn't it? And it is, but of course it's also bloody chaos because while the show does have a structure, this is a very loosely-scheduled timetable and in no way a formalized itinerary of events. It's generally best not to plan too precisely for an after-noon of football action on the telly. As anyone in tune with our award-winning, laugh-a-minute, comprehensive, all-singing, all-dancing show will be aware: it's generally best to expect the un-expected, especially when match reporter and cult hero Chris 'Kammy' Kamara is involved. But more of that later.

TIME: 1:47
THE OUTSIDE BROADCAST

It's at this time that we put our already flimsy reputations into the hands of the goggle-box gods and set up a live interview with one of the many managers making their final preparations around the country. Now, in TV we always say, 'Light, action, sound!' but on *Soccer Saturday* we can get light, action, too much (or too little) sound! I remember we once managed to convince Sir Alex Ferguson to do a live post-match interview with us, which was absolutely unheard of. He never does interviews and we knew we had to be absolutely ready to go when Fergie gave us the green light to talk. Typically, the sound went down as Fergie stepped up to the microphone.

When a manager is talking to us in the studio, they can't actually see anything. They're just standing there, usually helpless, looking into a camera and listening to our questions and comments which are being piped in through their headphones. It's a nightmare for them. Thus Alex couldn't hear anything either, which added to his confusion. I could see he was getting a bit frustrated, and he began flashing us the sort of look usually reserved for card-happy referees. After a while, the technical creases were ironed out and we were away. With our questions in place, I could begin the interview.

'So, we're happy to have Sir Alex Ferguson with us today ...' I said as an ear-shredding PA system at Old Trafford boomed across the stadium for a fire drill. Once again, Sir Alex couldn't hear a thing, which really didn't help his mood. For some reason, this was the moment I chose to ask a question about Wayne Rooney's temperament.

Sir Alex's face started to darken. 'Ach,' he grimaced. 'You usually ask sensible questions, not rubbish like that. Who's telling you to ask these questions?'

I panicked like a frightened schoolboy. 'Er, Charlie Nicholas actually, Sir Alex,' I stammered. It was a blatant lie, and I think Charlie saw the funny side, but Sir Alex certainly didn't.

Then, of course, the pitchside sprinklers tend to get turned on when we go live, soaking cameramen, crew and the already disgruntled Premier League manager. I'm not sure if the ground staff are watching and waiting for their moment, but it happens with a suspicious regularity. I remember Sam Allardyce was spectacularly soaked once (which would serve him right for referring to me as 'Stirling' for a joke, on air). Later, when Gordon Strachan was at Southampton, he was splashed as well. Can you imagine the look on his face? Actually, it's probably best if you don't – you probably won't sleep for a week.

Gordon is difficult to get onto the show at the best of times because I don't think he enjoys doing live interviews. This time, we'd convinced him to talk to us. But as he came onto the camera, the first thing he said was, 'I don't know why I agreed to do this.' Moments later, I could see his point – the sprinkler systems splashed into life and he had to make a dash for the sidelines.

Our old mate Harry Redknapp was actually struck by a football while doing a recorded piece with *Soccer Saturday*. He was at the Southampton training ground. As he spoke to the camera, a ball came out of nowhere and struck him on the back. He was furious. Harry turned around to see who it was and in a heartbeat shouted out, 'No wonder you're in the fucking reserves.' Priceless.

TIME: 2:30
THE PRE-MATCH BUILD-UP

The calm before the storm. This is generally when the team line-ups will come into the studio. At times we'll read these out on air, on other occasions we'll cut to our roving match reporters for a rundown on formations, teamsheets and injury updates. It gives the panel a chance to air their opinions on how various teams will shape up for the afternoon and what they'll be hoping to achieve tactically. It also gives us a chance to speculate on why various players have been included or dropped to the bench.

It's at this point that we'll jump to our superstar roving reporter, Kammy, for the latest news on his designated game. Usually this is where any well-constructed plans are laid to rest, because Kammy is prone to fits of laughter and comical clumsiness. I remember on one occasion he was dispatched to Fulham, where a laughing fit even threatened to reduce the show to tatters. We'd sent him to Craven Cottage with the idea of presenting a pitchside report at around two thirty, hoping he could grab a quick word with either a manager or a player as they came off the field following the warm-up. I remember the big news at the time was that Fulham – who were involved in a relegation scrap – had just signed Sylvain Legwinski, a transfer that had taken place at around the same time as the Bill Clinton and Monica Lewinsky scandal.

'Would you believe it, Jeff,' giggled Kammy. 'His new team-mates are already referring to him as Monica.'

I couldn't help myself. 'That may be so, Kammy, but are Fulham going down as well?'

I knew what was coming. Kammy started to giggle. And he giggled and giggled. The panel began laughing and, within seconds, tears were streaming down his face. I could see in the background that the teams were running off the pitch and he hadn't even spoken to anyone. The piece was ruined, but in the nicest possible way.

TIME: 3:01
THE FIRST HALF

A goal at Selhurst Park.

Another red card for Robbie Savage.

News of a goal at Gillingham.

A flurry of bookings in the game between City and Spurs.

Is that a penalty at Celtic?

Panic over, no goal at Gillingham.

But there is one at Fratton Park. Can we cut to Chris Kamara
for a report?
A shout from Paul Merson in the studio.
Matt Le Tissier texting his friend from behind the desk.
Goal at Anfield!
'And we're going to Portsmouth, where there's been an early
goal: Chris Kamara ...'
'Unbelievable, Jeff!'

Welcome to approximately seven live seconds in the world of *Soccer Saturday*. From the moment the first whistles ring out around the country, the show takes on an element of adrenalized chaos: at times, goals and cards can trickle in at a snail's pace. At others, the action can come in thick and fast. There really is no way of telling.

It's at this stage that the studio takes on an unusual atmosphere. We have three cameramen in front of us and an office where our producer, Ian Condron, and his assistants keep an eye on the scores. It's their job to decide where the show should go in terms of match reports and updates. It's my job at this stage to watch the scores as they come in and update the viewer, while linking the show to match reports, both in and out of the studio.

From here, you never really know how the show is going to pan out. The only guarantee is that it will be bloody exciting. Sometimes, there are moments of intense action when I'll think, 'For god's sake, please don't let anyone score for a few minutes,' just so I can catch up with the scores, scorers and events that are going on in approximately 75 games across the country. Then there are other times when I'll be sitting there wondering if the videprinter is actually working because absolutely nothing has happened for the best part of five minutes. These moments of prolonged calm are the ones I dread the most. You can chat with panellists to pass the time and kill any dead air between goal reports, but it's really a case of keeping the show ticking over in order to maintain the viewer's interest.

Suddenly, there will be a flurry of action: goals, penalty appeals, bookings ... In the back of the mind you know that at any second you could have to deal with 20 goals in two frantic minutes, not to mention a blur of yellow cards and sendings-off (especially if Rob Styles is reffing any of the games that afternoon). This is also the moment when the panel begins its afternoon chorus of yells, squeals and general shouting, which creates a real sense of drama as they watch their games. There's nothing like watching Paul Merson grunting and groaning his way through a Portsmouth match.

Believe it or not, in the early days of the show, panellists were told that they shouldn't be shouting out at all, and even now they're not encouraged to make all that noise, but it just happens naturally, mainly because they become so engrossed in their games. I think it really adds to the atmosphere and sense of occasion for the viewer. There you are, viewer, on your sofa, sandwich or scotch egg in hand, and you'll hear a shout off camera. If it's from one of the panellists commentating on your team, then it can make for a heart-racing moment, especially if the goal has gone your way.

I think Rodney Marsh first brought that sense of excitement and drama to the show, simply by shouting. But then Rodney would shout about just about everything – even if somebody had won a throw-in. At first it was all part of his act, and there was a feeling that he would do it for effect sometimes, but over the course of the last 10 years, it's become one of the show's trademarks.

Meanwhile, my eyes at this stage of the programme are focused almost completely on the videprinter which displays the latest scores and scorers as they happen. This is the most important tool I have at my disposal, because it's my link to the outside world. I've also got a little box on my desk which plays eight different live channels, or games, so I can flick to different matches – if I see or hear that something is happening four seats away in Charlie's chair, then I can flick to TV number four and check on what he's watching. From there, I can instantly see which team is celebrating, who has scored the goal, who has made the mistake that has led to a penalty, and why the ref is incorrectly booking somebody, and so on. It puts me in a position where I can also add comments to the situation if needed. I might get to see a replay of something, but generally I haven't got time to do that and I'll try to get to the relevant commentator as quickly as I can. Everything flies by in a blur.

TIME: 3:21
THE AD BREAK

At last, a breather. Tea and biscuits all round. One of the show's biggest masterstrokes was convincing advertisers to allow us to continually run the latest scores across the screen during the ad break. This was an idea of Vic Wakeling's, the MD of Sky Sports. By maintaining the levels of action and a constant news-feed while the viewers are bombarded with images of tea-drinking chimps (no, not us!) and plutonium-strength deodorants, we've ensured the action rarely lets up in pace. As a result, these are probably the most-watched adverts on the telly. We weren't sure whether the advertisers would go for it when we first suggested the idea, but the one thing we all knew was that ad breaks were the only time that people generally get up and make a cup of tea or turn over. By keeping the scores on-screen, people were guaranteed to watch the adverts as well. It was a little stroke of genius.

TIME: 3:49
HALF-TIME

This is the point where everybody on the show goes out and gets a sandwich and a cup of tea. Sadly, I have to sit there and read out the scores, which can be infuriating, as Matt Le Tissier scoffs more than his fair share of crisps and chocolate – there's never anything for me to eat once he's finished. It's also a worrying time for me, as the half-time break presents the perfect opportunity for Charlie Nicholas to 'redecorate' my car.

This prank started a few seasons ago. While I was dealing with the half-time scores, Charlie decided to wander into the car park to find my beautiful motor (please pretend along with me) before decorating the exterior with leaves, branches and litter bins. There were also one or two road signs and 'Men At Work' notices positioned on the bonnet. This soon became a ritual. Out of consideration for my paintwork, I started to move my car from its regular spot, but Charlie would seek it out and wreak his usual havoc no matter where I parked it. I even went as far as parking it a quarter of a mile up the road, but Charlie would still, somehow, get to his target. Shame he wasn't so proficient when he was playing up front for the Gunners.

Anyway, things got so bad that I had to park in the Tesco's car park, which was located over the road from the Sky Sports studios. On that occasion, Charlie came back after half-time with a face like thunder.

'Where the fuck is it?' he bellowed.

I had a quiet laugh to myself. 'You'll never know, mate, you'll never know.'

He's stopped doing it now, but for a while it became a weekly ritual, much to my despair. It's a terrible feeling knowing that somewhere out in the streets of Middlesex, your newly polished car is being covered in crap, especially when you're reading the scores from Scotland's Second Division.

These pranks might seem somewhat immature to our more sensible viewers, but I guess it's an indication of what life must have been like in the dressing room for a lot of footballers. If his current sense of humour is anything to go by, though, Charlie must have been a right bugger when he was a player. Thank god he didn't play for Wimbledon – I would probably have had my eyebrows shaved by now.

TIME: 4:01
THE SECOND HALF

The only way to deal with the big rush of information that invariably hits the videprinter in the second half is to babble your way through the latest scores and scorers as quickly as possible, desperately hoping that you haven't missed anything out. I always try to make sure to mention at least every goal, even if it's disappeared off the screen – it's awful for a fan to turn their back for a split second or disappear for a cuppa only for their score to flash up. Over the years you develop a sense of how to separate the important news from the trivia, and goals are the most important part of the show.

When they flood in at the business end of the show – which is basically the last 10 minutes of a game – you have to dispense with the gags, puns and banter. There's simply too much information to relay to the viewer. And even if Kenny 'The Good Doctor' Deuchar has scored (a cult *Soccer Saturday* figure, more of which we'll come to later) and you want to make a gag about Granny Mae (likewise), there simply isn't time. You always have to remember that, despite the humour that's so prevalent in the studio for much of the show, it's vital to keep the flow of results going. Making gags only serves as a needless distraction at this stage.

Behind the cameras, it is chaos, but it's organized chaos. The show is orchestrated by two people: Karen Wilmington (Wilma) and Ian Condron, our director and producer respectively. These two have to be absolutely on the ball behind the scenes, watching for scores, deciding which match reporters to cut to and debating where the action is so we can seamlessly switch from report to report. Obviously the tempo and pace of the show increase as we reach the final whistle. My role is to organize everyone on the panel, ordering them to be succinct and straight to the point when they're relaying the information from their TV screens to the viewer. The usual cry from the producers at that time is, 'Walshy be brief! Walshy be brief! Fucking hell, Walshy, be brief!' as panellist Paul Walsh rumbles on through an update. Despite his prolific goal-scoring record for Liverpool and Spurs, he has absolutely no idea what the word 'quick' means.

By this stage of the show, I am in my stride, and shouting and babbling like a madman. If I had to start at this pace from three o'clock, then it would be a bit of a problem, but because the whole show has been building towards these final dramatic minutes, I don't really notice the increased drama or tempo. If there is late drama – which there always is – then the shouting and the cries among Thommo, Charlie or Le Tiss make it so much more exciting. It's brilliant fun and the chaos works really well on air.

At the same time, you have to write all of the information down as it's happening, because later, as you recap, you'll need to know who has scored the goals as the games come to a close. I must say that in the last 10 to 15 minutes, the Scottish Second Division and Third Division fall by the wayside. I'll still pay them lip service and mention the scores, but I won't always catch up with the scorers and events until the final results. Something has to give slightly in the last five minutes.

This part of the show has to be the most entertaining. There are lots of different ways of maintaining excitement, though not all of them are popular with viewers, depending on how your team have done that afternoon. I remember there was a game at Manchester United and I was about to go to Charlie who was commentating, leading in with the words, 'There has been a late penalty at Old Trafford, so you won't need me to tell you who it's gone to.' It's a common complaint that the penalties always go to Man United at Old Trafford, especially in the closing stages of games, so it was our way of acknowledging the fact.

You have to be careful, however. I once got an email from a very angry fan of bottom club Derby who had been enraged by one of my links. After cutting to their game against in-form Spurs, I announced, 'There's been a goal at Pride Park and it might not be the way you'd expect it to go [that is, to Spurs]. But on the other hand it might be.' Derby had conceded and the next day a fan complained that I'd teased him, and demanded a public apology:

❛Jeff Stelling is bang out of order. I'm a Derby fan and he insinuated that we'd scored against Spurs when we hadn't. It was infuriating. He must be reprimanded.❜

I understand it can be bloody irritating to people, but it's only irritating if it's going against you. When the results are going your way, you tend to feel less annoyed about the presentation of facts. And of course, there's a lot more riding on these results than simply pride – football spread betting is so big these days that the number of corners in a game can swing huge amounts of money either way, especially on the panel, all of whom are shameless gamblers. Often, the likes of Charlie and Merse are sitting there with their spread-betting coupons, counting the goals and hanging on my every word – when they should be watching the game in front of them.

It happens outside the studio, too. A friend of mine, Harry Findlay, who is a professional gambler, watches the show religiously every Saturday. He always says to me, 'You do my bloody brains in, because you never know which way the goal has gone when you introduce a match report.' I'm quite proud of that. You have to create some drama to entertain the folks at home.

It can be difficult to keep your composure when the scores of my team, Hartlepool, flash up on the videprinter. I might be reading out another result and then see their name appear at the bottom of the screen. It takes all my concentration to remain focused, because like any fan, I want to know how they are doing on a Saturday afternoon. Off-screen, I'll be punching the air or, more than likely, looking like a picture of doom and gloom.

The other distraction I face is that, as the excitement builds during the afternoon, my vocal cords are put under a tremendous strain. There's a lot of shouting going on, but so far I've managed to maintain my voice, though there have been some close calls. I had one email after a particularly hoarse afternoon saying, 'Jeff, mate, you sound like Rod Stewart after eating a bale of hay, man! Get someone to the chemist's to get you a bottle of Sanderson's throat specific mixture, it'll have you singing like Chris Kamara during a 10-goal thriller. Get well soon, from Leon the Burnley fan.'

I'm not like Mariah Carey or Whitney Houston – I'm not one for drinking milk-and-honey concoctions before I go on air, though I do treat my body like a temple the night before and try not drink too much alcohol.

TIME: 4:45-ish
THE FULL-TIME SCORES/POST-MATCH ANALYSIS

It's a job to keep your concentration at this point. The panel are a constant distraction. Because they've finished for the afternoon, they're often talking and messing around, but generally they know not to push it too far. Still, there have been times when I've had to say, 'Look guys, will you shut the fuck up?' Off-mic, of course. Former Villa striker Alan McInally is the worst, because he's a right old woman. He'll be sitting there with the other maids – John Salako (former Palace midfielder) and Paul Walsh – gossiping away. I always think, 'Do you mind?'

Sometimes you can hear the research team working away in the Sky Sports studio behind us. I remember Rodney would often stand up – sometimes we would even be live – and shout, 'Will you lot shut up?!' Then he'd carry on as if nothing had happened. So it can be distracting, yes, but I use all of my professional experience and charm to remain composed.

TIME: 5:17
POST-MATCH INTERVIEWS

This is the most difficult part of the day in many respects, mainly because it feels like the calm after the storm. During the first part of the show you're building up to kick-off. There are a lot of laughs, the adrenaline is racing and it's really good fun. When the games start, the show and my job increase in tempo until I almost hit fever pitch at four-thirty. The pace doesn't relent until around five o'clock, give or take a few needless minutes of injury time (at Old Trafford usually) and delayed kick-offs.

After this rush and the reading of the final scores, there's a natural lull. It's important to keep some sense of momentum going, but that really depends on the post-match interviews we're picking up from around the grounds and the assessment you get from the guys on the panel. When it comes to evaluating the games, what we don't want from the likes of Charlie and Thommo is, 'Well, in the 10th minute, this happened. In the 32nd minute, this happened ...' and so on and so forth. What we need is a succinct evaluation of the game and some recurring themes – poor defending, exposure at set pieces, the form of one or two particular players – to summarize the results. We don't want lists. We want interpretations of what has happened, just like every watching fan.

You hope these summaries are lit up by some entertaining post-match interviews. Gordon Strachan was always a dream to get on the show when he was the manager at Southampton and Coventry City. I remember one reporter asked him if he could have a 'quick word'. In a flash, Gordon responded, 'Yes. Velocity,' before turning on his heels and walking away. It was fantastic moment. In another one of his post-match press conferences, a hapless journalist asked, 'Gordon, do you think you're the right man for the job?' He sighed. 'No, of course I'm not. I'm nothing like the best man for the job, but I'm the best they could get at that moment in time.'

If you ask Strach a stupid question, you're going to get murdered, but it makes for great telly. One of our guys even asked whether he became depressed after losses and poor performances. 'Depressed?' snapped Strach. 'Depressed?! I get suicidal. I'm going to go home and lock myself in a dark room, I'm not going to come out. Not ever.'

This turned into a five-minute rant on what he was going to do when he got home and brightened what was an otherwise dull close to the evening. You can also rely on the likes of Fergie, Arsène Wenger and Paul Jewell to deliver good interviews. Martin Jol was very good when he was in charge at Spurs. And, of course, there was the Special One, Jose Mourinho. He was a godsend. But again, he could be miserable. During one interview he answered every question with the words, 'Yes, no, yes, no ...' much to the despair of the Sky crew at work. Eventually Mourinho said, 'Have you got any more of these questions?' before walking off. But even though he was being rude to a reporter (who I believe was making his Sky debut), it was great to watch.

Managers and players can be difficult at the best of times, and even more so at the worst – when they've lost. I can understand why it's difficult for footballers to articulate their art minutes after swapping shirts and applauding the fans. They must be knackered. It's also worth noting that a TV crew would never grab Phil Collins as he walked off stage from a Genesis gig (my guilty pleasure, I apologize) to talk a live audience through a particularly powerful drum solo. So, put in that context it seems absurd to quiz a player on things they probably can't even remember. Then, of course, there is the political implications of giving a controversial answer: criticizing a referee or team-mate can land you in hot water with the club or the FA. Having said that, players and coaches are celebrities – without the public interest, they wouldn't be in the privileged financial position they find themselves in today, so they should just grin and bear it.

If it's any consolation, it's also bloody tough on our side of the cameras. I remember a radio interview I did at Arsenal when I was a reporter for LBC in London. You used to grab players as they walked through the marble halls at Highbury and I remember I'd been asked to talk to two young players who had just made their debuts – Paul Davies and Chris White. I approached Paul as he came out of the dressing rooms and convinced him to do a live link.

I said, 'Well Paul, you must have been pleased with your contribution there ...'

He looked confused. 'Well, er, yeah ...'

'And you nearly came close a couple of times ...'

'Well, not that much, but I'm still pleased.'

'And how do you think you teamed up with X, Y and Z in midfield?'

'Well, OK, but it's not really my role.'

'Well, thanks, Paul.'

'No problem, but why do you keep calling me Paul? My name's Chris White.'

So I understand, painfully, the difficulties of interviewing players under pressure – that was probably one of the most embarrassing moments of my career. That said, I, more than anyone, can become frustrated at the interviewing techniques of many football reporters. It really should be a simple business, but sometimes they will answer their own questions before the interviewee has had a chance to open his gob, which is really infuriating. For example, someone will thrust a mic in front of Rafa Benitez and say, 'So great result today ... well done, the way you set out your side with so and so on the left and so and so on the right, it was perfect, absolutely perfect ... it worked a treat.'

And all the manager can say to that is, 'Thanks.'

Crikey, it's hardly Sir David Frost taking down former US president Richard Nixon, is it? So generally, after the dramas, the highs, the lows, the shouting and the screaming of a *Soccer Saturday* afternoon, it can be a low-key end.

TIME: 6:00
AFTER THE SHOW

With the show over, we'll sort out the various bets which have been laid before the programme began. At this point, the two real challenges are to get Charlie Nicholas to pay up in something other than Scottish notes and to get any sort of cash out of Paul Walsh. He never has any! By this point, I am absolutely exhausted. I'll just drive home to Winchester and watch *Ant and Dec's Saturday Night Takeaway*. The likes of Charlie and Thommo get a plane home. Sometimes they'll bump into people who have been involved in the games. Referee Mark Clattenburg will often run into them. When he sees the boys, he'll often say, 'How did I do today?' And they'll reply, 'Crap.'

I'm absolutely spent afterwards. I remember when Big Sam Allardyce came onto the show, he found that he enjoyed it, but he reckoned it was a long haul. And it is, especially for the boys: once they've done their match reports, they have very little to do apart from twiddle their thumbs and sit quietly. Me, I'm dreaming of my sofa in Winchester and a pint of nice, ice cold Hoegaarden.

3

Motorway Service Stations, Wimpy Burgers And Medium Lattes
(Full Fat, Please): Preparing for Soccer Saturday

To the untrained eye, Winchester's motorway service station, positioned as it is on the M3, is just a run-of-the-mill stop-off point: a
loo break for passing travellers; a lunch haven for weary truckers
travelling towards the south coast with a consignment of Kerry
Katona-endorsed frozen lasagnes. Inside, there's not much more
to pass the time than a Wimpy, some fruit machines, a WHSmith's
and, in one corner, a modest branch of Costa Coffee. But despite
these modest surroundings, it's from this very spot that most of
my research for the well-oiled *Soccer Saturday* fact machine takes
place.

MOTORWAY SERVICE STATIONS

Every week, with a stack of newspaper cuttings, stat packs and material downloaded from the World Wide Web (no, not that kind – not unless I'm researching a piece on Dwight Yorke's ex-girlfriends anyway), I'll load up on caffeine and absorb reams of info, figures and snippets of useless trivia. This is quite a down-at-heel environment in which to work, I know, and this revelation may come as a shock to some fans of the show, who, for reasons I cannot fathom, seem to think that I have a glamorous office at home, surrounded by up-to-the-minute data and TV screens playing sports bulletins and non-stop football. I wish. In fact, I have fantasized on many occasions about 'The Stellodrome' – an underground compound similar to the one used by Robert Downey Jr in *Iron Man*, its high-tech interior consisting of a cavern of HD plasma-screen TVs, with banks of blinking computers downloading the latest Opta Index stats. In one corner, a 'Bat Phone'-style communications link even patches me through to the offices of Sir Alex Ferguson, Fabio Capello and Chris Kamara. Well, Chris Kamara at the very least.

The truth is far less glamorous. I can usually be found staring dolefully into a car park, the rain drizzling down the service station windows, as my latte turns cold. Kammy might ring on the mobile, and sometimes, if I'm feeling racy, I'll head into Winchester and take a corner in Caffè Nero. But generally much of the studio magic and preparation takes place from a plastic table in the corner of a food court, my thoughts interrupted only by the sound of a jackpot on the nearby 'fruity'.

Why a service station, I hear you ask? Well, firstly, I live nearby, which means I can take a drive out there whenever I want, but I mainly visit this modest spot for a bit of peace and quiet. When I first started working on the show, my kids weren't quite school age and so doing any homework became problematic, especially as I found much of my research screwed into paper footballs and covered in a charming shade of pink crayon when my back was turned. Since then, Winchester Services has become a rather familiar makeshift office, though any 'Stelling-ettes' planning on mobbing me as I scan the sports pages of the *South London Press* should note that I tend to switch between the northbound and southbound stations, just to keep the stalkers on their toes.

Generally, I'm left to my own devices. Well, who would want to approach a man surrounded by bags stuffed with local newspapers and magazines? Occasionally people will recognize me, but they'll usually pass me off as 'someone who looks like that bloke from the football show on the telly, only he's a lot shorter', which suits me fine. I have a week's worth of news to go through, not to mention all the results, league tables and goalscorers from the previous weekend, so the less hassle the better.

In reality, this is probably the hardest part of the job – I get the groundwork done in the week so I have all the info at hand when it comes to Saturday afternoon. A lot of people have asked me whether I memorize the stats and information I present on the show, but the truth is that, while I do have a certain amount of knowledge that I can bring to *Soccer Saturday* without any assistance, I also have a set of papers positioned discreetly on my desk, so I can refer to them at all times. Each sheet has statistical info on all the games being played that day, along with interesting facts and figures on the teams involved, and all the vital info including league positions, numbers of games won and top goalscorers.

OK, I think I know what you're thinking at this point: 'Oh, I thought he properly memorized all that stuff. What a disappointment. To the BBC and *Final Score*!' But hang on, no anchorman worth his salt could memorize all that info. And as they say in showbiz, it's not what you say, it's the way that you say it. So yes, I'll have the basic facts and figures to hand, but I'll also research pages of human interest stories and funny news to throw out to the panel. How else would we have covered The Good Doctor and Granny Mae (see Chapter Four), or uncovered Total Network Solutions in the Welsh Premier League?

Now, managing all of this on a regular League day can be a tricky business. Handling this data during the closing weeks of the season, when champions are crowned and teams are promoted and relegated, can be a bloody nightmare. Throw in UEFA Cup and Champions League qualification and you have yourself a plate-spinning act that even Paul Daniels would struggle to orchestrate.

Then, of course, some clubs are hoping for an Intertoto place or looking to sneak into Europe with an exemplary disciplinary record. Others are chasing the play-offs, so you have to be aware of all the possible combinations of results and their implications. So, for example, on the last day of 2007/08 a lot of interest focused on Bournemouth. They needed to win to stay up and would have done so, just as long as Gillingham didn't win. Obviously, I mentioned those facts. But I also looked for human interest stories to liven up the show – in this case, Bournemouth were in financial trouble at the time and their players had been on half pay, but they still managed to win their last six games under manager Kevin Bond, which was their best run since 1971 when John Bond – Kevin's dad – was their manager. Phew! I'm getting flustered just thinking about it now.

It's a tricky business to manage all this information, so I guess it can be a blessing that Scotland has usually closed for business by the end of the season. Before the Sky mail office starts getting bombarded with angry letters from north of the border, remember that many of the champions and relegated teams have been decided long before the season's close. Still, you try to pay the Scottish leagues lip service, but the relevant stats are more of a challenge than the English ones because very few websites feature the names of first-team players, let alone squad players. A lot of the teams outside of the Premier League will even have A. Trialist and B. Trialist on their books, unnamed players who are literally trying out for the team. I remember when one team even had 'A. Trialist' and 'B. Trialist' on the scoresheet, though I don't think they were related.

Generally I collate my own figures, but we also have a stats man from Sky who will give me an info package. There's a lot of stuff on these weighty stacks of paper – some of which I'll use, some of which I won't use, but I'll never take these stats packs into the studio because there's simply too much info on there. I'll sift through them during the week and maybe pick out anything I'm interested in. The fact, for example, that at one stage during the 2007/08 season Aston Villa scored 46 of their 69 goals in the second half of games might come in handy at some point, though I can't imagine when.

When I'm not at the Winchester services, the remainder of my research takes place in the office at Sky. On a Friday, I'll trawl the websites for new information and news stories. I'll keep up to date with injury news, transfer speculation, and all the topical information at each club. I'll also go through the papers again. From Sunday through to Friday I'll always read a handful of publications to grab a cross-reference of stories – *The Times*, the *Sun* and the *Mail* for news, the *Racing Post* because it's great for statistical information, and the *Daily Record* for Scottish stories.

When it comes to websites I'll look at the reputable ones. I won't bother with official club pages because they tend to be a bit too politically obtuse – they certainly won't give the gory details on any negative stories. I remember for the Aston Villa versus Wigan game at the end of 2007/08, the big talking point was whether Gareth Barry was going to Liverpool. The news sites were full of quotes and comment, but the official websites for both Liverpool and Villa were bereft of any info. Still, by going through all the available sources, I can throw the subject open to the panel on the Saturday for a serious debate and enter my own opinion, if necessary.

Generally, this is the way I plan the conversations for the show's build-up – the first three hours before the games kick-off. I'll decide where we want to go in terms of discussions and I'll warn the pundits before the show begins, usually in the hotel bar on the Friday night where the *Soccer Saturday* crew drink wildly, I mean, prepare for the next day.

Do I get inside info on any clubs or players? Not really. There are certain clubs that, for one reason or another, I've built up a good relationship with, but it's generally teams like Gretna and The New Saints rather than Liverpool or Chelsea. A lot of that info comes from people we meet in the week or even managers and players we've bumped into on a Friday night when we're staying in the hotel.

On other occasions, I'll rely on the pundits for that info. A lot of them still have great links with their former clubs. Matt Le Tissier never has his mobile phone switched off in the studio (which he should have, by the way). Just before last season's transfer window, James Beattie had been in tremendous form for Southampton. Matt and Beats are good friends and, during the show, Le Tiss texted him, saying, 'We're talking about whether you're going to move or not, mate, what should I tell them?'

Later his phone bleeped and, off-camera, Matt showed me the reply, which was, 'Tell them, "Fuck all."'

So we get info that way, and most of the lads are still well connected. Thommo still has his links with Liverpool and chats regularly to Steven Gerrard. He'd never quote him directly, but it gives him an idea of what's going on at Anfield. Le Tiss is still in touch with Southampton. Merse has contacts here, there and everywhere, though he doesn't talk about Walsall (where he had a stab at management) that often, mainly because the fans can't stand him. Charlie is very much 'in' with a number of football agents, and my own agent looks after a lot of players. If I'm ever struggling for info I'll call him and say 'Am I on the right track with this story?' He'll ring back and say, 'No Jeff, you're miles away.'

Do I get info that I'm privy to that I can't reveal? There have been instances. When Steve Bruce left Birmingham, we had a pretty good idea on why he went, though we couldn't mention it on air, because it happened for financial reasons. It was also a mathematical conundrum so complicated that Carol Vorderman would have struggled to understand its intricacies. But then, our info on Steve Bruce was always pretty good, because his daughter, Amy, worked on the programme. I remember she came in one morning and told us that her dad had been to see *Mamma Mia* the previous evening, which we gleefully reported on the show. Of course we refused to let it go. 'Have they met their Waterloo?' 'Will the winner take it all?' That sort of standard. Sadly Amy has left now. Steve can now sleep on Friday nights knowing that his best-kept secrets will remain just that.

Sometimes you'll go to a dinner or an event and bump into someone interesting. I remember being sat next to Rick Parry at a function and he was telling me about the events taking place behind the scenes at Liverpool. These details weren't for public broadcast because they were confidential, but it gave me an understanding of what was going on at Anfield. In those situations you have to remain discreet. I certainly wouldn't say, 'Well, Rick Parry mentioned this to me the other night.' I was told in confidence, so that's how it remains.

As you can see, it's a lot to handle. When it comes to six o'clock on a Saturday evening and the show is over, I can't remember a thing. Absolutely nothing. I guess your brain is like a sponge. It soaks up all the information, you squeeze it all out during the show, and then it's completely dry again, which means I'm absolutely rubbish at pub quizzes. People are forever inviting me, but I always tell them that I'm hopeless. They never believe me, and it's only after four or five questions that they'll realize that I really am bloody rubbish. In reality, I don't have a big library, or a towering stockpile of books and encyclopaedias. I don't have an army of researchers. I'm not a 'statto'. I am a football fan with a few local newspapers, a laptop, a mobile phone and a Wimpy in a motorway service station. But as you can tell from my svelte figure, I hardly ever use it.

4

You Can Say That Again

The Catchphrases Of Soccer Saturday

A few years ago, while buying a sandwich (from the aforementioned motorway service station café in fact), I was approached by a group of Forest fans who wanted to talk about The Good Doctor, or Kenny Deuchar, the one time Gretna and Northampton striker who was also a practising doctor. Like a handful of characters in the game, I'd made a point of referring to his trade whenever he scored – he was a man of medical science, after all – and given his quick thinking in front of goal, I found I was mentioning him quite a lot. It was apparent by the reaction of these lads that, purely by accident, I had created a cult hero.

But The Good Doctor wasn't the only one. Over the years I have name-checked the previously anonymous Adam Stansfield ('Sister Lisa will be pleased') of Exeter City, and Arbroath's Kevin Webster ('Sally will be pleased'), not to mention Hartlepool wonderkid, James 'I Feel Good' Brown, who gets a mention – and a song – whenever he hits the back of the net. For those of you currently scratching your heads at these 'gags', you will be pleased to know that you're about to receive a thorough explanation of each one over the next few pages.

Anyway, I have to admit that in writing this book I've been forced to think of the impact of my jokes as 'the incomparable ringmaster of Sky's six-hour slog, *Soccer Saturday*' (the *Independent*) and 'Ranting Jeff' (the *Northern Echo*). Unlike broadcasting doyens such as Kenneth 'They think it's all over ...' Wolstenholme and Les 'If it's up there I'll give you the money myself' Dennis, I don't have one single catchphrase to hinge my public image on, which is probably a blessing because on the rare occasions I am asked to sign autographs I can stick to a simple, 'All the best, Jeff.'

Instead, I've amassed an armoury of silly quips, throwaway gags and ill-advised rants. Some of them have gathered a small amount of cult interest over the years. They also tend to appear on YouTube quite a lot. Maybe it's about time I explained the methods behind the apparent madness ...

'Lisa will be pleased, Adam Stansfield has scored!'

This was one of the first catchphrases that I ever delivered on the show. Adam Stansfield was playing at Yeovil Town, though he later moved on to the mighty Exeter City. I said it as an aside one afternoon, the link being a reference to 90s pop sensation Lisa Stansfield. Well, we'll use the term 'sensation' in the same way that the press refer to Robert Earnshaw as a 'goalscoring sensation', that is, a bit hit-and-miss. Of course, they're not really related, but for quite a while people were approaching Adam and asking about the wellbeing of Lisa. Funnier still, the catchphrase threatened to get out of hand. A local newspaper even ran a story revealing how the pair were not really siblings, such was the interest surrounding the *Soccer Saturday* reference.

Since then, there are a number of variations on the gag: Kevin Webster of Arbroath fame is linked to Sally because of the fictional couple in *Corrie*; Fulham keeper Tony Warner was linked to his non-existent brothers, after the movie company Warner Bros (do keep up at the back), and Kevin Nolan of Bolton is referred to in the same breath as The Nolan Sisters whenever he scores ('Kevin Nolan has scored for Bolton, his sisters will be dancing'). I once received a very nice message from Kevin explaining that he doesn't actually have any sisters. He then went on to point out that he does have a lot of brothers, though they're not as easy on the eye as the girl group, I'd imagine. In hindsight, I guess this revelation could have been considered as something of a threat.

'The Good Doctor'

While flicking through one of the many mountains of local papers I have to absorb every week (by way of research rather than any onset of OCD) I began reading about Kenny Deuchar, a prolific striker for Gretna. According to one report, he was a qualified doctor and still practised in his local hospital from time to time. This was remarkable by any footballer's standards. Can you imagine Cristiano Ronaldo even applying a Band-Aid to a stricken Page Three model, let alone practising lifesaving techniques at his local A&E? Given his worthy day job, I figured Deuchar was somebody who deserved some recognition, so I began referring to him as 'The Good Doctor' whenever he scored, which, to his credit, was quite a lot. I even got a very nice letter from him one day thanking me for the publicity.

His biggest fan was Granny Mae, his, er, grandmother. By all accounts, she was an avid viewer of the show and was bowled over by the regular mentions of her grandson on digital telly. In time, I began to mention her, too, and the pair became a bit of a fixture in the cache of *Soccer Saturday* catchphrases. One day we even went up to Scotland to do a piece on Granny Mae as she watched the show from her living room. Of course, The Good Doctor did what he always did best and popped up with a goal or two, which made for a really nice afternoon. I think Granny Mae was beside herself.

I guess the show is good at bringing out characters like Deuchar. He was a player that wouldn't have got any publicity if it hadn't been for us, and to bring personalities to life like that is a vital part of *Soccer Saturday*. After all, the show would be pretty boring if the only coverage we dedicated to the lower leagues was the results and goalscorers. It really raised his profile – he even got a loan move to Northampton – though the fact he was quite handy in the box must have helped, too. He went to play in the States with Real Salt Lake (only in America) against the likes of David Beckham. God knows what Granny Mae must have made of that, but he's back in Scotland with Hamilton Academical now.

'They'll be dancing in the streets of Total Network Solutions!'

This was a play on the famous phrase, 'They'll be dancing in the streets of Raith Rovers tonight' which came from TV commentator Sam Leitch in the 1960s. I remember seeing the team name Total Network Solutions on the screen one afternoon and thinking, 'What the hell is this?' They happened to be a real team, of course, and a very good one at that – they were based in

Llansantffraid-ym-Mechain (thank god they play under a different name) in the Welsh Premier League and tended to score a lot of goals. The more they won, the more their name lent itself to some form of acknowledgement. After yet another TNS goal, and in a flash of quick-witted humour that only a man with several O-levels could deliver, I yelled, 'And they'll be dancing in the streets of Total Network Solutions tonight!' It soon became compulsory to throw in the phrase with every TNS win.

It wasn't long before Mike Harris, the managing director of Total Network Solutions, began sending me a pack of TNS-related goodies every year, which included a Total Network Solutions T-shirt, but I've yet to parade this around the high-fashion emporia of Winchester. The club even invited me to their European games in the UEFA Cup, but the journey to Llansantffraid-ym-Mechain always seemed to be a trip too far.

Still, the name is an indication of how football has changed. The club flogged off their real title (Llansantffraid) to a sponsor for £250,000 when they qualified for the European Cup Winners' Cup in 1996, but they weren't the first – Dutch giants PSV are named after a company. But according to the excellent book *Prawns In The Game: How Football Got Where It Is Today!* by Paul French, which details the state of modern football, 'Total Network Solutions are the most successful example of a sponsored team ... thanks to Jeff Stelling'. That wasn't intended, of course, and I was gutted when they changed their name to The New Saints. It just didn't carry the same punch.

'Guylain Ndumbu-Nsungu – local boy made good!'

In the modern age, there are so many foreign players plying their trade across the country, but when an exotic-sounding player ends up in an unlikely location, like Rotherham for example, or Sheffield Wednesday in Guylain Ndumbu-Nsungu's case, it adds extra comedy spice. Some of these player-pronunciations are a real mouthful, and, to be honest, you get through it with trial and error. I think that when players come to this country we tend to anglicize their names, which is fair enough. Sometimes the players even do it themselves. For example, we pronounce the name of the crack German side as Bayern Munich, not Bayern München, which is the correct title. And if we pronounced Dirk Kuyt correctly, we'd run the risk of offending every member of the parish, given it sounds uncannily like a swear word Tony Soprano has only ever used once on the telly.

I know the BBC have a pronunciation guide, but crikey, if we stuck to the official pronunciations on *Soccer Saturday*, the viewers wouldn't have a clue who we were talking about half the time. Anyone who can understand former Evertonian and ex-panellist Peter Reid's scouse dialect would probably have a distinct advantage, however.

'I Feel Good!'

For those of you unfamiliar with the Hartlepool United squad – and shame on you for not knowing – James Brown is a hotshot striker and a hell of a good player at Victoria Park. Being a bit of a music fan myself – and a pretty appalling karaoke singer to boot

- I figured it might be an idea to pay my respects to his goalscoring feats with a rendition of his namesake's hit single 'I Feel Good' every time he hit the back of the net. It was funny for us, but I'd imagine Mr Brown must be absolutely sick of hearing about me terrorizing the nation's dogs with my tuneless singing. It's got to the stage where everybody on the panel looks forward to James Brown scoring. The boys even join in sometimes, but we often have to apologize to the sound crew afterwards.

I did take the joke too far on one occasion when, at the 2007/08 PFA Awards, I was asked to host the ceremony. Among a crowd of football stars and dignitaries, I knew there was a big Hartlepool contingent in attendance so I began singing 'I feeeeeeeeeel gooooood!' by way of an introduction. My vocal gymnastics were followed by a crashing silence. Clearly, people were thinking, 'What the hell is he doing?' God knows what a watching Fabio Capello must have thought. I'm not sure whether he left in disgust or not, but in one small enclave in a faraway corner, a dozen Hartlepool players were going absolutely mental, so it was worth it.

Then along came the doll. You may have seen it – a two-foot-high James Brown replica that sings and dances to the tune of 'I Feel Good' and was given its debut on the show on the opening day of the 2008/09 season. I'd just been to open a children's centre in Hartlepool and a guy had waited outside for three hours to give it to me. As he handed it over he said, 'Please have this for the show and use it when James Brown scores. It'll put a smile back on the face of football.' Anyway, when I turned it on and it started singing 'I feeeeeel good!' I laughed my cap off.

I'd kept this doll completely to myself through the pre-season of 2008/09, but I was determined to use it on the show. Lo and behold on the first day of the campaign, Hartlepool's James Brown scored and the doll made its first appearance. Alan McInally looked completely bewildered as I put it on the desk. But then moments later, James Brown scored again! I remember saying, 'How sick are you going to be of this by the end of the season?'

The only problem was that James Brown suddenly stopped scoring for Hartlepool. I put the doll in mothballs in a Sainsbury's carrier bag behind my bed. When he hit the back of the net again, the doll was at home and we had to rely on my vocal chords, which felt a bit second-best, it has to be said.

'It looks like Jelleyman's Thrown A Wobbly!'

I'd noticed Mansfield's Gareth Jelleyman in a match report one week and thought, 'What a name! Wouldn't it be great if he was sent off one week.' I wouldn't wish misfortune on any player, but there was clearly a great gag to be made about him 'throwing a wobbly'. Jelleyman was also a defender, so I figured he was likely to score a red card during the course of a season, but when I looked through his records, blow me if he hadn't been sent off once in six seasons. Worse, or better depending on your point of view, he'd only picked up nine yellow cards in his entire career. Regardless, I had him in my mind just in case.

Then, it happened. In 2005/06, Mansfield Town were winning at home against Cheltenham by a couple of goals. At the end of the afternoon, when the results were coming in, when there's a furious flurry of goals on-screen and when there isn't the time for joking around, up pops the glorious news in red letters at the bottom of the screen: 'Off: Gareth Jelleyman'. I thought, 'Yessss! You beauty!' I dropped everything. 'Bugger the scores,' I thought. 'Ladies and gentlemen, Gareth Jelleyman's been sent off! It looks like he's thrown a wobbly!'

It was a cheap gag, but I'd waited a long time for that one to come up. Normally I won't plan the gags in advance, but this time it came to me and seemed to make perfect sense. In a strange twist, Gareth was sent off about three months later, so we had a reprise of the gag. I do hope I wasn't responsible for his bad behaviour.

'He's scored a rocket!'

Used whenever Ayr's Ryan Stevenson scores and a reference to George Stephenson's *Rocket* steam engine. (Yes, I know – a bit of artistic licence taken with the spelling of the surname.) Ryan scored 17 during the 2007/08 season, so there were plenty of trains during the year. Which is more than can be said for much of the country.

'One size Fitz Hall'

One of our earlier jokes, which focused on QPR player Fitz Hall. In fact, this gag didn't come from us and it had been mentioned earlier in the press, but we were the first to use it on national TV. Apparently it was something that everybody in the dressing room called him. People would ask, 'Why is he called One Size?' His teammates would respond, 'Well, because One Size Fitz Hall'. It was a lovely gag and it just ran and ran and ran. A bit like One Size himself.

'Fuck!'

One of the rare moments I lost my cool on camera. During the 2007/08 season I actually swore under my breath when I'd thought, wrongly of course, that the cameras weren't on me. The trouble stemmed from a match between Hartlepool and Barnet – it's always the ones nearest to you that cause you the most trouble, isn't it? We were in the middle of a very good run, unbeaten in 23 games in fact, and the last team to beat us were Barnet away.

Anyway, the day before the game I'd spoken to a few of the Hartlepool boys on the phone and they'd told me that Barnet were the worst team they had played all season. In fact, one player actually said, 'How they beat us when we played them, we'll never know.' Of course, in typical Hartlepool fashion, we went one down on the day. Luckily we managed to equalize in the 80th minute, and I was just about to go to the reporter at Barnet for news of this fantastic goal when I heard something in my earpiece. It wasn't meant for me, but in the background a doom-laden voice shouted, 'There's been another goal! It's Barnet two, Hartlepool one.' Imagine my frustration. I now had to throw over to the match reporter with the words, 'It's not just news of one goal, but two at Underhill.'

Thinking that the screen would have changed to the match statistics, I mouthed the word 'Fuck' under my breath, not knowing I was still flashed across telly screens in electrical goods shops up and down the country. On Monday morning I was busted. I took a phone call from the producer asking me if I'd sworn on TV. Vic Wakeling had even received word that I'd lost my cool. I was completely taken aback. The tape was checked and my blunder was discovered. There weren't any complaints – it was hardly a repeat of Russell Brand and Jonathan Ross's misdemeanours of 2008 – and I was only showing a bit of passion after all, but the footage was plastered all over YouTube. Of course, one should be professional about these things, and it won't happen again, I promise. Unless we lose to 'the worst team we've played all season'. Again.

'How did Agger do-do-do?'

This is a personal tribute to Liverpool player Daniel Agger and 1980s pop group Black Lace, who released the single 'Agadoo'. Sadly, he'd been out of action for over a year, but at the beginning of the 2008/09 campaign he made his Premier League comeback. Charlie Nicholas was covering the Liverpool game and I couldn't help but ask, 'How did Daniel Agger do-do-do?' Cue mass groaning from the panel. I think they thought it had gone away forever, but oh no.

Look, this is not a rant, but ...

6 There was a recent poll which claimed that Middlesbrough was the worst place to live in England, with Hartlepool in 20th place. I thought the list was upside down, to be honest with you. Look, this is not a rant, but the people who compile this tosh – no disrespect – are the type who go north of Rickmansworth only when they go to the Edinburgh Fringe Festival and think that everyone in the north lives in *Coronation Street*-style terraces; they're the type who buy skinny lattes and call their mushy peas guacamole; [Phil Thompson: 'Go on, Jeff!'] they're the sort who go out to the Ganges on holiday so some bearded bloke can sit them cross-legged and teach them to relax; they're the sort who use their Blackberrys in the silent carriages on British Rail and have Babyshambles as their ringtone.

[Charlie Nicholas: 'Go on, Jeff!'] 'They're the type who think that *Little Britain* was funnier than *The Likely Lads*. They've never been to Middlesbrough. They don't know about the things we've done [Panel: 'Go on, Jeff!']. They've never visited Captain Cook's monument, they've never been to the Institute of Modern Art with all its Picassos, they've never been to the beaches, they don't know about the River Tees, they don't know about Yarm Village, they've never seen the historic Transporter Bridge, for goodness sake! They've never visited the Riverside Stadium. I bet they don't know that the Sydney Harbour Bridge was built by a Middlesbrough company, Dorman Long.

'And what about the famous sons and daughters of Middlesbrough? Brian Clough, born at number 11 Valley Road, Middlesbrough, 21 April 1935: they ignore him! What about Rory Underwood, Ray Mallen, Jonathan Woodgate, Chris Tomlinson, Chris Kamara – unbelievable! They've forgotten about Paul Daniels, Roy Chubby Brown, Liz Dawn – alias Vera Duckworth, to you and me – and Journey South. They've never heard Chris Rea and they've never tasted his family's wonderful, wonderful ice cream. Okay, it's not quite as nice as Hartlepool, but I'm telling you, Middlesbrough is a darn good place to live ... [My voice fades out and a two-minute ad break begins.]

[The show restarts] '... And surveys put together by wheat-free, cake-eating, *Guardian*-reading ... Sorry, there's a goal to tell you about at Goodison Park! Here's Alan Smith.

Fancy TV housing show *Location, Location, Location* had voted Middlesbrough as the worst place to live in England during a so-called poll. Who they had actually 'polled' remains a mystery, but they even had the cheek to then claim that Hartlepool was the 20th worst place to live in the country. Clearly they hadn't bothered to ask anyone from the north-east. Most people in that neck of the woods probably would have voted for London.

I guess shows throw out rubbish like this to generate publicity, but people in Middlesbrough were understandably unhappy about the whole affair. The mayor was up in arms and even went as far as to make a complaint to the programme-makers. Being familiar with the area, I was pretty miffed about it, too, so when the opportunity arose to talk about Boro on the show, I decided to let off steam and defend the area.

One of the main reasons I did it was because, in the past, we'd made many tongue-in-cheek comments about why footballers wouldn't go to the north-east to play. Matt Le Tissier would always argue that a lot of players are turned off by the area. I reminded him that there are some beautiful beaches up there and he would respond, 'What's the point of having beautiful beaches if it's minus-10 degrees in the sun?'

So, people had taken cheap shots in the past and I was quite keen to redress the balance. In fact, I felt we owed the Middlesbrough people something – we'd been as guilty as anyone of featuring stereotypical imagery of the town, such as smoking chimneys and the Transporter Bridge. For some reason we never showed the lovely, rolling countryside behind.

Anyway, the night before the infamous rant (which is now featured all over the internet if you ever have a spare two minutes and the boss isn't looking at work), I gathered some thoughts into my head about the *Location, Location, Location* poll. It gave me quite a sleepless night. Sometimes you just go to bed thinking of things, and I had gone to bed – unlike most TV property dandies, by the sounds of things – thinking of Middlesbrough.

Plagued by creative insomnia, I began writing down everything I loved about the area – the River Tees, the beautiful hills, the beautiful beaches, the monuments and statues, Captain Cook's monument, the Picasso museum. Then I made a list of famous people from the area: Brian Clough, Chris Kamara, Chris Rea, and a few others. I thought about famous events such as the building of the Sydney Harbour Bridge, which took place there. When I got into the office I added two or three more. Paul Daniels came to mind, the band Journey South were Middlesbrough boys. In the end, I had quite a varied case for the defence.

When the subject of Middlesbrough's game came up on the show that lunchtime, I really didn't know how far this rant was going to go, but I was determined to go through with it. Looking back, I know I was pretty fired up. I began with the words, 'This is not a rant', which is always a sign that somebody is about to go on a rant, and I claimed that *Location, Location, Location*'s poll was upside down. Suddenly all this pent-up rage was released as the list began to tumble from my mouth. The reaction from the boys was great. They were on their feet, egging me on. The more they urged me on, the more I kept going. Then the ad break came, and in the sort of televisual theatre that has made Derren Brown very famous, we created the illusion that I'd been ranting through-out the break by picking up just where I left off. I couldn't help myself.

The reaction afterwards was sensational. Days later, the local council called the office and the local tourist board were in touch to thank me. There were calls from magazines and newspapers; interview requests from local radio stations and Tyne Tees tele-vision. During my diatribe, I added that Brian Clough had been born in Middlesbrough and added the date of his birth. A Middlesbrough councillor told me that 10 commemorative busts had been made of Brian Clough. Nine of them had been sold and auctioned for charity, but there was one left, a real collector's item and a lovely piece, and they wanted to present it to me as a thankyou present. It was amazing.

YOU CAN SAY THAT AGAIN

I think a lot of what I said was true and some of it was said to make a point and have a bit of fun, but it worked out better than I could have imagined. On Valentine's Day I even got flowers from the Middlesbrough Tourist Board. The card inside read, 'To Jeff, Happy Valentine's Day, Middlesbrough loves you.' I doubt if the producers of *Location, Location, Location* will ever receive one of those.

5

The Jeff Stelling Drinking Game

There are many ways to watch *Soccer Saturday* on an afternoon: at home on the sofa with friends and family; in the local pub nursing a pint and a packet of pork scratchings; or alone in a dark room, curtains drawn, stark naked, save for a pair of Macclesfield Town underpants (beware: these people are to be avoided in public at all costs). Then, of course, there is the alcoholically-charged 'experience' enjoyed by the hardier elements of our watching audience. A marathon, *Soccer Saturday*-related boozing session called The Jeff Stelling Drinking Game that takes place during the 90 minutes of televised commentary and involves a series of convoluted rules, regulations and drinking rituals that nobody really understands. Think of it as being a bit like the offside rule, but a lot more fun for everyone involved.

First invented by a group of students from Sheffield Hallam University a couple of years ago, the game has since taken on a life of its own. A number of variations have recently been posted online in social networking forums such as Facebook. There's even a simmering rivalry between some of the game's organizers. The Jeff

Stelling Fanclub, for example, recently posted a damning criticism of the Drinking Game's inventors, referring to them as 'a lightweight bunch of girls who, if they ever bothered to take part, would probably be hospitalized'. It's all pretty scary stuff.

When trawling the internet, however, this behaviour is really just the tip of the iceberg. The aforementioned Jeff Stelling Fanclub (www.jeffstellingfanclub.com), to whom I'm eternally grateful for their support (please don't come to my house), hold an AGM in my honour every year. God knows what the minutes must involve, but a group of grown adults who should know better have held meetings in places such as Lancaster where, according to their slightly unnerving blog, members 'went to the Walkabout bar to watch the [FA Cup Final] and they had terraces and chicken in a basket. The clumsiest man in the world threw beer over everyone, Chelsea won the cup in extra time and afterwards everyone said the game was really boring but we really enjoyed it! In the evening we danced to 80s music and went to a gay bar. A very confused-looking man pulled Barrow-in-Furness out of the hat for next year's AGM.'

But that's not all. Follow the relevant links from the website of the JSFC (as I like to call them) and you'll discover that a poet named P. Maguire has even posted a rambling whimsy in tribute to the show. According to experts it is 'a bit crap', but make up your own mind:

'The Name's Stelling, Jeff Stelling!'

Jeff Stelling, Jeff Stelling
Is really compelling,
Like James Bond,
As slick and as smooth.
Kamara has passion,
McQueen now in fashion,
And Thommo is biased, it's true!

Jeff Stelling, Jeff Stelling,
His name I love spelling,
Like James Bond,
As smart and as cool.
Charlie Nicholas is charming,
Le Tiss is disarming,
But Cottee is not quite as cute!

Jeff Stelling, Jeff Stelling,
This love never quelling.
Like yours for your
Dear Hartlepool.
The goals you announce
As like leopards we pounce,
'Cos you never say where or for who!

Elsewhere, another internet site called www.dangerhere.com – how very apt – has devised a series of spoofed James Bond movie posters, with the finely-chiselled mugs of Roger Moore, Sean Connery, Pierce Brosnan, Timothy Dalton and Daniel Craig replaced by mine. They've even devised movie plots for each imaginary flick:

Dyer Another Day: On his own initiative, 007 (Stelling, Jeff Stelling) makes the long trip from Hartlepool to Newcastle to have a word with wayward Mag Kieron Dyer, whose camcorder constantly gets him into hot water. To spare the blushes of Dyer's latest dolly bird, 007 finds himself regretfully having to use lethal force against said electronic device. Thankfully, his handsome Sky salary means he can comfortably afford to pay the bill subsequently forwarded to him by Dyer's solicitor.

[Note to readers: after this top secret mission, Kieron Dyer was 'relocated' to West Ham. Maybe something to do with the Witness Protection Plan, who knows?]

For Your Eyes Rodney: After plans for a new digital football highlights service are lost at a motorway service station, BSkyB begin a feverish search for them. As Bond (Stelling, Jeff Stelling) joins the search, he suspects Rodney Marsh of involvement in the affair. Bond finds an ally in the beautiful Kirsty Gallagher, a 12-foot-tall ex-supermodel-turned-secret agent, who blames Marsh for the troubled history of the Tampa Bay Rowdies. The plot thickens when Marsh takes a shine to Bond's bird, leading to Bond's abandonment of his original mission in favour of a bid to assassinate Marsh at the earliest opportunity.

In Her Majesty's Secret Service Station: Sky Sports Boss 'M' (Rupert Murdoch) assigns 007 (Stelling, Jeff Stelling) with the task of formulating a plan to foil the ambitions of BBC One's *Football Latest* programme, hated rival of *Gillette Soccer Saturday*. 007 repairs to his habitual haunt, Winchester Services on the M3, and enjoys his favourite, a pint of extra-strong coffee and a scone with butter.

Like I say, the internet is a scary place. But, if you ever feel bored one Saturday afternoon, if you're desperately single, or if you want to know what it must have been like to have been a footballer from the 1970s, why not play the official *Soccer Saturday* Drinking Game? If you're brave enough, the rules are as follows:

The Official Soccer Saturday Drinking Game

Necessary equipment:

- Lager
- A bottle of Jägermeister
- A bottle of whisky
- Red Bull
- A sick bag

Current Rules:

1 **Every time a goal is scored:** one shot of beer must be drunk.

2 **Every sending-off:** one shot of Jägermeister (or substitute) must be downed.

3 **Half-time:** absolutely no alcoholic beverages may be imbibed during this period.

4 Whenever Chris Kamara is talking: you must be drinking continually.

5 Whenever Paul Merson uses stupid rhyming slang (i.e. 'He's hit the beans on toast!'): one shot of Jägermeister must be drunk.

6 In the second half, competitors can only refer to teams by their nicknames: failure to do so results in a three-beer-shot penalty.

7 Whenever Swindon Town appear on the videprinter: last person to shout out, 'Mackerel!' takes shot of Jägermeister.

8 Whenever Dundee appear on the videprinter: last person to shout out, 'Football' takes shot of Jägermeister.

9 Every time Phil Thompson says, 'Stevie Gerrard': three shots of beer must be drunk.

10 Every time Jeff makes an 'A. Trialist' joke: three shots of beer must be drunk.

11 Each time your team scores: two extra shots of beer must be drunk.

12 Every time Matty Taylor and 'goal of the season' are mentioned in the same sentence: drink one shot of Jägermeister.

13 Every time Jeff calls Kenny Deuchar 'The Good Doctor': one shot of whisky must be drunk. Note: Given that Deuchar now rubs shoulders with the likes of David Beckham in the MLS, this rule is now defunct.

14 Any hint of racism (social or otherwise) from any of the pundits: 'Quad bombs' (four cocktails made of Jägermeister and Red Bull) must be drunk by all competitors.

Further note: This is a hugely unlikely incident, though I do remember one Spurs game being watched by Charlie Nicholas. The elastic on someone's shorts had gone and a replacement pair were fetched by the backroom staff. 'Here's one for the girls,' laughed Charlie. 'His shorts are around his ankles!' Thommo looked over and quipped, 'Maybe it's one for the boys.' Without thinking, I said, 'Maybe, but not the boys I associate with.' Later, there was a complaint that I had made a homophobic remark, though that was never the intention.

15 Every time Hartlepool score a goal: three shots of beer.

Highly unlikely to get you drunk on an afternoon. More's the pity.

16 Every time a pundit shouts off-camera: two shots of beer must be knocked back.

Of course, this happens all the time, though it all adds to the drama of the show. The studio is meant to have a relaxed atmosphere.

People have said that the show thrives on bar-room conversation, but I'd like to think that it has a more intelligent angle than that. But basically it is five mates standing in the pub talking about football, having a bit of a laugh and then watching the game afterwards. And yes, there is plenty of shouting. In fact, the studio has everything you'd want from a pub apart from alcohol, though if the guys had their way, they would have that, too.

17 **Every time Matt Le Tissier is mentioned in connection with a takeaway:** drink one shot of Jägermeister.

18 **Whenever Chris Kamara says, 'It's unbelievable, Jeff:'** all drinks must be downed.

In the 2007/08 season, Kammy was reporting on Spurs' 6–4 win over Reading at White Hart Lane. It was a quite spectacular performance from both the teams, and Kammy, who commentated on the game like a hyperactive Take That fan. When the show was over, a stack of emails were placed on my desk begging me to stop Kammy from shouting 'Unbelievable!' Apparently, there was a gang of drinkers in Brighton who were absolutely shot away.

19 **Every time Jeff uses the phrase, 'They'll be dancing in the streets of Total Network Solutions tonight':** take one shot of Jägermeister. This also counts if the team is referred to by their new name, The New Saints.

20 **Every time Jeff says, 'It's Doom and Gloom at ...':** take one shot of Jägermeister.

THE JEFF STELLING DRINKING GAME

21 **Every time the team 'Keith' is referred to as just being one person:** another shot of Jägermeister to be drunk by all.

22 **Every time Brighton and Hove Albion, or Dagenham and Redbridge, are jokingly referred to as two different teams playing the same opposition:** take one shot of Jägermeister.

23 **Every time Arbroath striker Kevin Webster scores and Jeff jokes, 'Oh, Sally will be pleased':** one shot of Jägermeister.

24 **Every time anything bad happens to Craig Bellamy (injury, o.g., booked, arrested for assault, and so on):** two celebratory shots of the spirit of choice.

Note: Of course, I would never wish anything bad on Craig Bellamy. He is a fine, upstanding professional. Ahem. Feel free to pick your own villain of choice.

25 **Whenever Northampton Town appear on the videprinter:** last person to shout out, 'Cobblers!' has to neck a shot of Jägermeister.

26 **Whenever the Carlos Tevez affair/scandal is mentioned:** drink a shot of Jägermeister. This is now getting out-of-date, so maybe an updated version of the rules could feature the Gareth Barry/Liverpool affair instead? It's entirely up to you, dear drunkard.

JELLEYMAN'S THROWN A WOBBLY

Of course, given the current concerns over binge-drinking, and the never-to-be-forgotten pictures from Wayne Rooney's wedding, neither I nor anyone from Sky Sports (not even Paul Merson) would condone this irresponsible behaviour. Please drink sensibly – unless accompanied by an irresponsible ex-footballer from the 1970s, of course. Good luck!

What The Critics Said

Sky Sports' *Soccer Saturday*. A form of worship for some us, but if you're not converted, or have a life, then let me explain. It's all talk and no action in the *Soccer Saturday* studio. A bunch of fat footballers who spend six bum-numbing hours trying (and often failing) to describe matches with nothing more dramatic for viewers to watch than the shaving adverts that arrive every 20 minutes ...

[They feature] a panel of four ex-pros every week. Typically Matt Le Tissier, Phil Thompson, Alan McInally and Charlie Nicholas. Fence-sitting '110 per centers' to a man, all speaking a Yoda-ish, back-to-front footballers' English and each with their own verbal tics.

Phil Thompson, for instance, cannot complete a sentence without punctuating it with the words 'and everything'. A form of Tourette's that would drive a lesser man to beat him with a baseball bat.

ALLY ROSS, THE *SUN*

If Le Tissier is to make the chair his own, he will have to get used to jibes about his size, fitness and attachment to the south coast. 'It's a joke decision,' said Le Tissier of Steve Bennett's penalty award for Portsmouth. 'Something's got to be done about him.'

'Steve Bennett, Gordon Bennett,' Stelling commented, a sigh accompanying the stiletto. Brilliant.

ALAN FRASER, *DAILY MAIL*

Sportscaster, Jeff Stelling

Stelling is the presenter of Sky Sports' live football show, *Soccer Saturday*, and during his tenure his dapper style, lightning wit, corny one-liners and general over-excitement have earned him the title Broadcaster of the Year three times. Despite rumours of a big-money transfer, Stelling has remained loyal to the station, and that news should, as Jeff might say, delight football fans everywhere – from Kevin Nolan and his sisters to the supporters of Brighton and of Hove Albion.

NO. 51 IN 100 BEST THINGS 1998-2008, *GQ*

Who I Like This Week

The redoubtable Alastair Campbell doesn't need me climbing aboard his bandwagon, but I couldn't help noticing that he wrote a letter to the *Guardian* this week in which he all but called for Jeff Stelling, the presenter of Sky's *Soccer Saturday*, to be canonised. Apparently, Campbell was asked a whimsical question before the last general election in 2005: if the New Labour campaign were a person, who would he like it to be? He said, 'Jeff Stelling,' to the consternation of those who didn't know *Soccer Saturday* from a row of onions. For what it's worth, I'm with him all the way. Stelling is a genius. And a cheerful genius, which makes him an even rarer animal. *Soccer Saturday* has to be the most difficult programme of all to present, but he makes it look a doddle. I'd canonise him, give him a peerage, and make him Rear of the Year.

BRIAN VINER, THE INDEPENDENT

[*Soccer Saturday*] sidekicks have included Rodney Marsh – who once drank 23 bottles of champagne in one session with Malcolm Allison – and George Best, who once took Miss World back to her hotel room, threw £25,000 up in the air and was asked: 'Where did it all go wrong?' They were playmakers and playboys, legendary hell-raisers who wouldn't be tamed. Until they met Jeff Stelling.

DAILY MAIL

Jeff Stelling, a man of almost average height and equable temperament, is charged with holding [the show] together.

BILL BORROWS, THE INDEPENDENT

JELLEYMAN'S THROWN A WOBBLY

Sky's *Soccer Saturday*, said one of the backroom boys, is a bit like the proverbial swan: all calm on screen while everywhere out of shot, people paddle frantically to keep Britain's longest weekly programme afloat.

DAILY MAIL

Stelling is, I am convinced, a robot. A very realistic one, but mechanical nonetheless. There is no other way to explain his encyclopaedic knowledge of every Nationwide League player, shown in quickfire phrases like: 'And there's been a goal at Hull, where Bradley McSpeargarden has got his eighth of the season. A nice moment for a player who prefers butter to margarine.'

He weaves his way through the afternoon, a knowing smile here, a trumpet-like bellow of excitement there, and is (depending on how your team are doing) a friend, the bringer of bad news, or the man with a crumb of comfort in his outstretched palm.

STEVE MELLEN, *EAST ANGLIAN DAILY TIMES*

Soccer Saturday is a national institution. Of course, Broadmoor is also a national institution. And you could spot certain similarities between the two. I mean, who would have believed anyone would want to watch a bunch of retired footballers sitting behind desks staring at monitors, talking about games they could see but we couldn't? Madness.

CHARLIE CATCHPOLE, THE *SUN*

WHAT THE CRITICS SAID

'One Jeff Stelling, there's only one Jeff Stelling ...' If the anchorman of Sky Sports' *Soccer Saturday* afternoon football show actually played the game, such chants would be deafening. As it is, he merely talks a good game, but he does so with Ronaldo-like bursts of style and panache.

RADIO TIMES

If you've never come across *Soccer Saturday*, imagine a Samuel Beckett play in which a slick circus-master gets four retired clowns to describe a performance to punters stuck outside the Big Top. You will still be nowhere close to the absurdist drama that unfolds for six straight hours each Saturday on Sky Sports 1.

ESQUIRE

Soccer Saturday with Jeff Stelling on Sky Sports 1 is the best! Between 3pm and 5pm when the games can't be televised, they do this very inventive thing where they have reporters covering the matches without showing any of the play. It's just an incredibly creative TV show.

DAVID FROST, *RADIO TIMES*

Don't die, Jeff. Please don't die.*

THE *LONDON PAPER*

* READER'S NOTE: I can often be found murmuring these words to myself in the moments preceding the show. Or when Paul Walsh actually opens his wallet, which is very rare indeed.

71

7

The Sky Effect

Whenever I leave the leafy environs of my Winchester home and delve into the glamorous world of end-of-season presentations for under-14 football teams, pub quizzes and high-society cocktail parties, I'm often bombarded by a number of hard-hitting, socio-political questions. Of these, the most common tend to be: 1) Just how tall are you? 2) What was George Best really like? and 3) Do you have Georgie Thompson's mobile number? Normally, I'll field these enquiries with a blend of self-deprecating wit and expert analysis, often between slurps on a sharp Bellini cocktail (well, these end-of-season events can drag on without a drink or two) as a gaggle of interested onlookers draw towards me like Manchester United players to an ill-advised Christmas party.

Sometimes, however, I can come unstuck during these jovial events, though this generally happens when some bright spark asks a question that could potentially land me in hot water, and anyone requiring the answers to one, two and three above should refer to the Frequently Asked Questions At Cocktail Parties section, which can be found in the appendices of this very book.

THE SKY EFFECT

Often, a probing enquiry will revolve around whether I think Sky TV is the root of all evil and helmed by the megalomaniac spawn of Satan. Either that or whether Sky's presence is the cause of all manner of blights afflicting our once-beautiful game, namely spiralling player wages, ever-changing kick-off times and Cristiano Ronaldo's uber-camp beachwear.

As you can imagine, these are prickly subjects, especially as the aforementioned 'megalomaniac spawn of Satan' keeps me in fancy ties and pints of Hoegaarden throughout the year. I'm also very aware that shooting my mouth off could be viewed as an ungrateful bite at Mr Rupert Murdoch's feeding hand. But, with my Bellini set to one side for a brief moment, I'd like to point out that while satellite TV has been responsible for a number of heinous crimes – notably re-runs of *Two Pints of Lager and a Packet of Crisps* and the presence of Derek Acorah – I genuinely believe that Sky have contributed positively to football in a number of ways, some of them more obvious than others.

Don't believe me? Well, consider the Premier League's position as the greatest in the world, for starters. Sky has turned English football into a top box-office draw watched by millions of viewers across the globe. And while I know huge swathes of people will watch any old rubbish if it's put in front of them (see *Two Pints of Lager and a Packet of Crisps* and Derek Acorah for proof), our leagues have definitely improved during the Sky era: where once we followed the likes of Chris Kamara, Charlie Nicholas and Phil Thompson as our leading football stars, we now enjoy the likes of Wayne Rooney, Cesc Fabregas and Fernando Torres, all watched on *Soccer Saturday* by the likes of, er, Chris Kamara, Charlie Nicholas and Phil Thompson.

OK, I've digressed slightly, but the point I'm trying to make here is that without the influx of Sky money it's unlikely that

Manchester United would be able to keep Cristiano Ronaldo in diamond-encrusted Speedos, let alone attract him to rainy old England. And before you scream at me with accusations of disgusting player wages, image rights and agent demands, I think some of our game's superstars deserve every penny they get ... but only some of them. Like big-name actors or high-flying company executives, football's most talented exponents should be rewarded for their glittering abilities, but only the elite. It's the less-talented bench-warmers and sick notes that present the real drain on club finances. And it's always worth noting that football clubs aren't being forced by Sky to pay millions a year to mediocre and injury-prone, eight-goals-a-season strikers. They make that decision all on their own, usually with the help of agents.

It's the same debate with the foreign players – it's all about balance. Nobody could begrudge the world-class stars that have graced the Premiership – Eric Cantona, Gianfranco Zola, Jürgen Klinsmann and Thierry Henry among them. It's the guys that come in that you've never heard of before that are the problem; the ones (you know who they are – just about every club has two or three) that make absolutely no impact on the game whatsoever, while picking up a ludicrous wage in the process. Yes, Winston Bogarde, we are talking about you. These players also take away opportunities from English kids who might be just as skilful, which is always frustrating to see because every fan likes a local-lad-come-good.

I guess this first happened in Scotland when Rangers and Celtic were flooded with very ordinary overseas players, all of whom were earning good money. Now it's happening in England, and I honestly believe it deprives some English kids of a chance to make the Premier League grade. David Bentley is a case in point – he started out at Arsenal and couldn't get past a number of foreign players, and left first for Norwich, then for Blackburn Rovers and

Spurs. For a while he was regarded as a successor to David Beckham, and not just in the silly hairstyles department, either. Had he stayed at Arsenal, would he have had the chance to make such an impression? At the time of writing this David hasn't exactly been setting the world alight at Spurs, so maybe he's not the best example.

Thankfully, more and more clubs are now taking a wider interest in what takes place within their own backyard, and it's here that Sky money in part has helped the education of modern footballers: young players are now encouraged to learn other aspects of football – coaching, physiotherapy, agency work (booo!) – as an insurance plan in case the playing side doesn't work out as well as they'd previously hoped. Those that do make it to football superstardom are taught how to handle their money, they're given media training and a proper vocational education, as well as being taught how to invest their money wisely rather than blowing it all on fur coats and online poker.

This is an entirely new concept. In the past, young players would come in as an apprentice and clean someone's boots, sweep the terraces, and cower from the likes of Alan McInally, who were usually hungover (allegedly), and that was about it. To be fair, that sounds like my day-to-day routine in the *Soccer Saturday* studio. Nevertheless, this has changed for the better. I reckon Sky have encouraged those in a position of football power to realize that they have a responsibility to help and educate those people working in the game, especially the hopefuls that might not make it through the youth academies and reserve teams, rather than washing their hands of them should they be chucked to the scrapheap – or Hartlepool's reserves.

While I'm at it, the improvements in the game haven't just been about enhancing playing personnel either. Look at the money that's been pumped back into football and the improvements that have been made at stadiums up and down the country. Like it or not, you can sit in comfort at the Emirates Stadium or Old Trafford and stretch your legs. You can even fall asleep at the Emirates because it's so quiet during the less keenly-anticipated fixtures. But, oh how it's changed! I remember when I was a kid watching Hartlepool. Sure, you could go to the big games and get in cheap, but when I think back it was actually a very dangerous environment to be in. I remember the surges and swells of people that would take place when something exciting happened on the pitch (which admittedly was not a regular occurrence). You would get pushed down a dozen flights of stairs in a mad crush and it was a miracle that larger numbers of fans weren't seriously injured or worse, especially where children were concerned. If you were a kid, you went down the front so you could see, but of course, you didn't know what was going to come down behind you. It would have been very easy to get crushed. Sometimes, watching football was like going into a war zone.

OK, I know that I'm coming across as a real middle-class prawn-sandwich-eating fan here, but these things are important. Who wants to pay for the privilege of standing in the tipping rain with an aching back, while avoiding the cups of urine being thrown from the away end (when Millwall were in town), or Riesling (when Chelsea were in town)? You can also get something decent to eat these days, especially at Norwich City, where Delia Smith runs the show, and thanks to improving standards the days of the poison pie and pasty have long gone. Don't tell me this is not a good thing.

And lads, rejoice! You see more women at football these days, and for that we should all be grateful. I guess this is because the stadiums are women-friendly, not to mention the fact that the sport is a hell of a lot sexier than it ever used to be. I reckon that has a lot to do with the likes of Thierry Henry and David Beckham, but cool your pride lads, because more women at football is surely good news for men all round.

I guess it's easy to see how this change has taken place, for while husbands and boyfriends are sitting at home watching the game on Sky – and *Soccer Saturday*, of course – their partners are also watching. A lot of women are even falling in love with it. Sometimes I'd like to think that some of these fans are falling in love with me, but the mail for Charlie Nicholas tells me otherwise. Never mind, because members of the fairer sex are now going to games in bigger numbers than ever before. Thank god they haven't paid attention to any of those ads on the telly luring them to online bingo, eh lads?

Elsewhere, look at the investments that have been made in youth academies, local communities and the football infrastructure in general. In that respect I have no problem with promoting the Premier League because it's something I genuinely believe in, though I won't plug the Grand Slam Super Sunday 'phenomenon' which involves the top four clubs in the Premier League playing one another on the same day. Sure, I'll happily call it the 'Grand Slam Super Duper Sunday' or something equally 'humorous', but in general I think the name is overblown and only a handful of syllables away from the 'NFL Superbowl Half-time Show Featuring Jay-Z and the US Marine Marching Band with Bells On', or something equally crass.

Anyway, this brings me rather neatly to a commonly-held conspiracy theory among many football fans: namely that Sky encourages the Premier League to clump these fixtures between the top four together, thus creating a couple of must-see football afternoons throughout the season. I think it's pretty fair to assume that this is nonsense. As far as I know, everything is above-board, and when you consider that there are a number of possible combinations that could create a 'Pow Wow Super Duper Terrific Sunday With Bells On', then it's highly likely that these teams will be playing each other occasionally on the same weekend at some stage in the year. I don't think fans should be too suspicious. Having said that, it's a great day when you've got two fantastic matches back-to-back, and there can't be that many punters who would complain about it. After all, what's wrong with watching the country's best teams battling it out while drinking steadily for a few hours?

Right, now I'll get off my soapbox, because there are one or two things that we do in the modern game that I'm not entirely comfortable with myself. When it comes to delivering these Bellini-cocktail-fuelled monologues, I admit that I understand why fans get miffed at so many different football-related issues. For example, I just wish that the money enjoyed by the top flight was more evenly spread among the lower leagues, because that's where the disparity of wealth seems really unfair: the teams further down the football ladder don't have a chance and suffer accordingly.

I also shudder when I consider the unpredictable nature of the season's fixture list. Picture the scene: there you are, in August, presented with a wave of Saturday afternoon kick-offs, your year mapped out in front of you – holidays, visits to the in-laws, dirty weekends in Scarborough, a lost bank holiday with the lads. Weeks later, thanks to the TV schedule, European fixtures and police demands, those kick-offs have been changed to Monday, Tuesday, Wednesday and Thursday evenings, Saturday mornings and Sunday lunchtimes, at TV's behest.

THE SKY EFFECT

Of course, from a selfish point of view, I personally wish there were more games on a Saturday at three o'clock. The more games we can report on during *Soccer Saturday*, the better our show becomes, so I understand the frustration of football fans everywhere, because I'm a supporter myself. I know what it's like to have to hike up a motorway on a Monday or Tuesday night when you've got work the next day. It isn't ideal. Nor is a game on a Sunday, because for many people, Sunday is still very much a family day. On the other hand, Sunday is an ideal time to sit at home and watch football, so it's very much in the balance for a lot of people.

I guess I'm a traditionalist. I used to love nothing more than watching Hartlepool on a Saturday afternoon at three o'clock, though I can't remember the last time I got to do that, because of my day job. With that in mind, if all football were played on a Saturday afternoon, then I'd never get to watch a game for real. But if I'm at home, I'll do what any other fan does: I'll gather the kids up, put my arse on the sofa and have a burger with the match. It's lovely.

What isn't so lovely is the cost of watching football in this country. If you go to a game between the top teams in Italy or Spain, you can get into the stadium for a tenner. Here, I do fear that, at the top level, the average fan is being priced out of the sport. If you have a family and want to take them to a Premier League match, it's almost impossible, unless you're very wealthy. Some games may cost you as much as £50 for a ticket. If there are four of you going, you've spent £200 before you even consider the cost of travel, parking, programmes, food, drinks and the cursed trip to the club shop. It probably amounts to the cost of one of Paul Merson's gambling debts. I think the amount of money that is being made from TV deals, especially at the top level, should allow some clubs to reduce their prices, surely? After all, the ticket money through the turnstiles can't be that significant any more, not in comparison to the income from sponsorship, telly money and advertising, so why can't ticket prices be reduced?

But then football clubs don't think in the long term. Take Manchester City for example. When their sheikh owners arrived at the club in 2008, all the talk turned to spending hundreds of millions of pounds on a handful of players (all strikers, mind - that won't end in tears). Nice short-term fix. But why not ensure a legacy of fans by pumping a couple of million into the community, ensuring kids under the age of 16 go in for free? Alternatively, they could hand out a free club shirt for every fan with a ticket to various games. These gimmicks wouldn't take much effort from the club and it certainly wouldn't impact on the wealth of Manchester City's ludicrously rich owners. It would also mean that new fans coming to the game would go to City rather than United. Before you knew it, City would have a bigger fanbase, more ticket sales, club shop profits going through the roof ... Oh, forget it, you know they'll blow the money on some overrated striker from La Liga. In fairness to City they have an exceptional academy and some bright young local kids making the grade.

And another thing: why can't footballers be more approachable? The celebrity that Sky money has created has taken the players away from the fans. I remember, when I was a cub reporter (more of which we'll come to later), I could approach any footballer after the game. They would all walk out of the stadium's main car park to their car and you could talk to them or get an interview without a grumble or the threat of legal action. That doesn't happen anymore. Players from the likes of Chelsea, United, Spurs, Everton or Arsenal are cocooned away to such an extent that the fans can hardly get autographs. Certainly, they don't enjoy the contact that they once used to.

THE SKY EFFECT

But then, without sounding like an old man, those were the good old days. Probably we would have found things to celebrate and complain about in the modern game with or without Sky, and there's a lot to be said about rose-tinted spectacles after all. In fact, I'm sure ex-Arsenal skipper, Double-winner and former *Soccer Saturday* panellist Frank McLintock once told me that when Arsenal won the Double in 1971, he travelled to the celebrations on his bike. You couldn't see that arduous journey being undertaken by the likes of Pascal Chimbonda today. Well, not unless there were one or two Bellinis waiting at the end of it and a debate about Georgie Thompson to mull over.

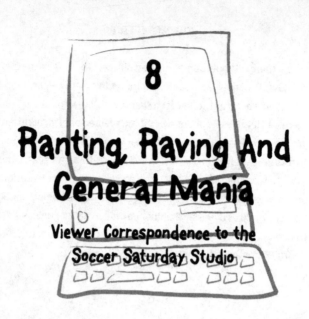

8
Ranting, Raving And General Mania

Viewer Correspondence to the
Soccer Saturday Studio

From: ANONYMOUS

To: YOURVIEW SKY SPORTS

Subject: SOCCER SATURDAY

Hi Jeff, we were at a charity event last night in Coventry and Chris Kamara was there ... He was singing onstage, and dancing ... He was unbelievable!

From: ALISON

To: YOURVIEW SKY SPORTS

Subject: SOCCER SATURDAY

Tony Cottee looking hot as usual 4 once don't mind my sons watching soccer Saturday! Alison, Colchester x

From: **ANONYMOUS**

To: **YOURVIEW SKY SPORTS**

Subject: **SOCCER SATURDAY**

Hi Jeff, love the shirt and tie ... very tidy! We don't know much about football but we do know we love Chris Kamara. Can he give us a wave - pleeeeeese!

From: **ANONYMOUS**

To: **YOURVIEW SKY SPORTS**

Subject: **SOCCER SATURDAY**

Jeff Stelling - God

Tony Cottee - God

Champagne Charlie - God

Big Al - God

Phil Thompson - Plum!!!

From: **TONY**

To: **YOURVIEW SKY SPORTS**

Subject: **SOCCER SATURDAY**

I wish that Jeff Stelling would stop picking on Thommo all the time.

Thommo might not have been able to play football like the rest of the panel, but he knew how to stop those who thought they could.

Tony from Boro

From: ANDY

To: YOURVIEW SKY SPORTS

Subject: SOCCER SATURDAY

We are playing Jeff Stelling's drinking game at the moment. Please can you tell him to stop going to Chris Kamara as we have to constantly drink while he is talking!! Also, please can you get Paul Merson to use more Cockney rhyming slang?! Oh and please use the James Brown statue!

Thank you!!

Andy Dawson (not the Hull guy!!)

From: MARK

To: YOURVIEW SKY SPORTS

Subject: SOCCER SATURDAY

Can I please highlight the ongoing campaign to have Jeff Stelling replace Peter Mandelson as Club President of Hartlepool United.

There are currently 250 members who want to see 'Mandy Out – Stelling In'. Jeff Stelling has done wonders for the promotion of Pools through his job on Sky Sports' Soccer Saturday coverage, with more and more 'second team poolies' springing up all over the country.

As the club is now in its centenary year, it would be great to see a proper fan take up the Club President role.

Mark Heslop – Bristol, Poolie-in-exile

From: JOHN
To: YOURVIEW SKY SPORTS
Subject: SOCCER SATURDAY

Jeff and gang

Just want to applaude you and your panel for the satisfaction ive had watching the scores come in and with charlies enthusiasm and thommo's unbiased reports on Liverpool (the wifes favourites) over the years Saturday would not just be the same without you all, ive recently bought my first butcher shop and now will have to work on Saturdays, it just will not be the same. Jeff you are a legend

Best regards

John from Morecombe

P.S. please ask your panel jeff if any of them fancy opening my shop, for a fee of course as its always sunny in Morecombe maybe you jeff will do it or all of you

From: ANONYMOUS
To: YOURVIEW SKY SPORTS
Subject: SOCCER SATURDAY

Matt Le Snoz got stick about his big nose at Upton Park one year. He answered it by curling a peach of a free kick in the top corner. We stopped jeering him and applauded instead. Great memory. Come on you Irons.

From: RUEY
To: YOURVIEW SKY SPORTS
Subject: SOCCER SATURDAY

Hi gang on soccer Saturday. Can u dress matt le tissier because he never looks tidy, rest of u look great, he ruins it 4 u all. Buy him a tie.

Thanx ruey x

From: GRAHAM
To: YOURVIEW SKY SPORTS
Subject: SOCCER SATURDAY

Perhaps if would help Mr Stelling and his team to listen to the wise words of the late Jimmy Sirrel, when discussing referees decisions. It went something like this. 'The score at the end of the game is a fact. The league table on Sunday morning is a fact. The rest is a matter of opinion.'

Regards Graham R J Dorsett

From: EDDIE
To: YOURVIEW SKY SPORTS
Subject: SOCCER SATURDAY

I love your coverage of the games on Saturday,

I also think that Charlie [Nicholas] is a real gentleman and handsome with it BUT can you perhaps have a sassenach sit along side him and tell us what wonderful commentaries he is making ... always makes it sound exciting but can't always understand ... he's a gem though.

Eddie Johnson

From: GAVIN
To: YOURVIEW SKY SPORTS
Subject: SOCCER SATURDAY

Can you tell me what happened to Charlie's hairdresser today?

Gavin Brownlie, Gants Hill, Essex

From: MARK
To: YOURVIEW SKY SPORTS
Subject: SOCCER SATURDAY

Who is the old guy with the ear ring? Does he think he's a teenager? Does he have a skateboard?

Mark

Sent from my iPhone – Apologies for typos

From: ANONYMOUS
To: YOURVIEW SKY SPORTS
Subject: SOCCER SATURDAY

Please tell stelling his Hartlepool are crap and stop creaming up to arsenal.

From: ANONYMOUS
To: YOURVIEW SKY SPORTS
Subject: SOCCER SATURDAY

Once again we listen 2 paul merson destroy the English language. An interpreter should be with Charlie Nicholas.

From: VIC

To: YOURVIEW SKY SPORTS

Subject: SOCCER SATURDAY

Up yours McInally we know you hate albion you smug villa nob you got no chance of top 4.

Vic

From: MARK

To: YOURVIEW SKY SPORTS

Subject: SOCCER SATURDAY

You're a true legend. Richard keys has nothing on you.

Mark from essex

From: ANONYMOUS

To: YOURVIEW SKY SPORTS

Subject: SOCCER SATURDAY

Geoff what a great show and what a great presenter. A colleague of mine met you on holiday this summer and she has a picture of you on her desk at work.

From: ANONYMOUS

To: YOURVIEW SKY SPORTS

Subject: SOCCER SATURDAY

Ha ha jeff stirling you lost on Tuesday 3 2 against leeds ha ha ha ha to you reply

From: **GAZ**

To: **YOURVIEW SKY SPORTS**

Subject: **SOCCER SATURDAY**

Forgive my impertinence jeff but could you tell me where Charlie buys his spruce suits from? I'd ask for your tailor's number but i don't want to look like an effeminate dolly mixture!!!

;-) gaz, stoke

9
Don't Touch That Remote Control!

There are plenty of things you could be doing instead of watching my mug on a Saturday afternoon from the comfort of your sofa. Have a think about it. Just how much more productive could you be if you were at Ikea/Sainsbury's/the in-laws/work/church? Wouldn't your soul feel purer? Of course not, because you would spend most of the time away from the telly checking your mobile phone for the latest scores, thus running the risk of offending your girlfriend/wife/extended family/boss or God. Seriously, sit indoors instead.

Alternatively you could flick away from *Soccer Saturday* and watch one of the other stations, or even listen to the radio, though I'll be honest: I've never taken an interest in the other TV channels during a Saturday afternoon. That's not because I'm disregarding what our rivals are up to, it's just that I never get the time to see what's going on at the Beeb, ITV or Setanta because I'm working. When *Football Focus* is starting up at midday, I'm in the studio doing my own thing. And I'd quite like it to stay that way, thank you very much. Give me the rubbish Sky tea and Charlie Nicholas's bad gags any day. I certainly wouldn't want to be watching Manish Bhasin and co. on BBC One. It would mean I was stuck at home rather than working in the studio.

Before I start receiving disgruntled letters from Manish's lawyers, I'm not knocking anyone here – I'm sure he's a lovely and expert presenter. The truth is, I wouldn't even want to be at home watching *Baywatch* and Pamela Anderson on a Saturday afternoon. I'm never more at home than when I'm sitting on the *Soccer Saturday* panel.

Still, I'd be lying if I said I didn't have a competitive streak when it comes to our opposition. Thankfully, nobody comes close in my opinion. I guess our closest rivals in terms of style arrived a couple of years ago when ITV emulated (a nicer word for 'copied', I think) us with *The Goal Rush*. And yes, I'll admit it: when their concept was first announced (think *Soccer Saturday*, but starting later in the afternoon), I was concerned, but only for a brief moment. Sky's executives were certainly worried because the show was pretty much identical to ours but it was positioned on terrestrial telly. This meant that ITV had the potential to secure a massive audience. We needn't have bothered with the sleepless nights, though. If I recall, *The Goal Rush*'s reviews were hardly sparkling. In fact, former England player and *Goal Rush* presenter Barry Venison came up to me one day when I was watching a mid-week game at Southampton. I said to him, 'How's *The Goal Rush* going, Barry?' He sighed. 'It's going crap, Jeff.'

I took that as a very good sign. Yet, I know ITV were frustrated with *The Goal Rush*'s lack of success. They couldn't work out why it wasn't drawing the same viewing figures as *Soccer Saturday*. I think the main reason they couldn't pip us was simply because we were the first ones to come up with this concept – we had built a level of familiarity and trust with the viewer. That put us in pole position in the ratings war, which ultimately was why *The Goal Rush* didn't last: they were second-best.

In ITV's defence, they were hamstrung by the structure of the station. Working on a satellite channel gives you an advantage – you're able to treat the product like a football magazine show much more seriously in terms of time than terrestrial TV. *Soccer Saturday* started at midday and went on until six o'clock in the evening. Any normal station could never do that because of the demands on their schedule – paying advertisers, the lifeblood of stations like ITV, wouldn't be interested in buying airtime in a six-hour-long programme. They had to shorten the format, but when it came to picking up viewers for *The Goal Rush*, ITV's number-one problem was that they wouldn't come on until four o'clock, by which time we were up and running and well into our stride.

I used to see former head of ITV and one-time head of the FA, Brian Barwick, quite a lot during those days. He would always say, 'Christ, Jeff, it's so depressing. I go to football grounds and all I see is your bloody programme on the TV screens in the ground. It's never ours.' He reckoned he would go shopping on a Saturday afternoon and would see my face looking out at him from all the tellies in Dixons and Currys. It was never *The Goal Rush*.

The Beeb were the same. I don't think they really gave it a real go. I hear that their *Final Score* round-up really only gets started in the second half and they don't seem to generate the same sort of excitement as *Soccer Saturday*. A well-known English player who still works for them (so I won't name him) once told me that working on the likes of *Football Focus* and *Final Score* was 'boring'. Ouch.

A number of backroom staff at the BBC even refer to us as 'that comedy programme'. Well, that's fine – I'll take that as a compliment. Maybe some of their shows need a bit more 'comedy' injected into them. Yes, we mess around on the show, but we're informative and passionate too. Humour and passion reflect the personality of football. You go to a football match and what's the first thing you hear? Probably people in the seats around you, taking the piss and having a laugh. That runs right through the game, from the terraces to the fanzines, to the forerunners of football magazine shows like *Saint & Greavsie* and then on to us. You can't have football without humour.

What I do know is that, when it comes to guests, we like to take a few risks. I certainly couldn't imagine the BBC employing somebody like Paul Merson. To me he's appealing and he's funny and he's human, but I couldn't picture him on the *Football Focus* sofa alongside Manish, Garth Crooks and Alan Shearer. Likewise, Chris Kamara. Or Rodney Marsh. The Beeb would never employ pundits in that style, because they're probably viewed as being a little bit dangerous.

That's not to say we'll employ any old Tom, Dick or Harry with a repertoire of gags and anecdotes – our pundits need to be names. They need to have been prestigious players who competed at the top level. That's a necessary requirement if you're going to sit there and criticize modern-day, professional footballers on the show. The likes of Thommo and Merse can say, 'I've been there, done it, here are the medals.' That validates their opinions. Sadly, the same can't be said of Matt Le Tissier, but never mind.

Still, for any future panellists reading this: you need humour on our show. You need to be able to bounce off people in a debate. You certainly shouldn't be too long-winded or too wordy when it comes to talking about the game. I can think of one or two people on the other stations who fall into that category. The other 'must' for contemporary pundits is that they should be willing to criticize people who might have been their mates at one stage, and that isn't always easy. You can praise them as well, but it has to be an honest assessment. Some people who have recently come out of the game are just a bit afraid of upsetting people for that very reason. That certainly doesn't apply to Merse, Le Tiss or Charlie Nicholas.

That uncompromising attitude puts us one step ahead of everyone else. Nobody can sit on the fence during our show. But my worry is that it's becoming bloody hard to find good pundits these days. A lot of this stems from the money in the game. In the days of Frank McLintock, Rodney Marsh and George Best, players didn't experience the financial rewards that the stars of today enjoy. They had to find alternative employment when they retired from playing. Footballers leaving the game today won't need that financial security, so anyone wanting to move into TV punditry must really want to do it for enjoyment, rather than the financial reward (because, let me tell you, the pay isn't that great).

Matt Le Tissier is the perfect example. Le Tiss doesn't come onto the show for the paycheque. He does it because he loves doing it. I think the same applies to Lee Dixon and Alan Shearer on *Football Focus* – unless something disastrous has happened to their bank accounts, they surely can't need to get up on a Saturday morning to pay the mortgage. They must be doing it for the love of the game.

Despite these prestigious additions to the *Soccer Saturday* panel, the pool of potential pundits is shrinking. So many of the Premier League's stars are foreign and it's hard for them to fit in and understand the English humour, which writes off a large chunk of potential panellists. I remember presenting the Chelsea end of season awards in 2007/08. At the end of the show, Joe Cole came up to me afterwards and said, 'Thanks for that, Jeff. All the English boys laughed their socks off. But Michael Ballack just didn't get it.' I guess, at times, it's difficult for our humour to translate.

Despite my unswerving love for all things *Soccer Saturday*, I must admit that my head was turned – for a fleeting moment – when I was offered the job of anchoring ITV's coverage of the 2006 World Cup. At first, I was tempted to jump ship, but only because England were tipped for great things, believe it or not. To present their road to World Cup glory would have been a fantastic opportunity. In hindsight I needn't have fretted. Sven-Göran Eriksson scuppered any dreams of us picking up the trophy with some confusing tactics and personnel selections.

And yes, I'll be honest, the cash on offer was fantastic. The opportunity came from a guy called Mark Sharman who used to work with me at Sky. Out of the blue one day he called me and made me a fantastic offer to work for ITV. My mind boggled. They wanted me to front their World Cup coverage and all their football ... and pay me handsomely. It sounded fantastic, so I invited him over for a pint at my local pub and we talked through the idea. I was very excited.

Everything about it appealed to me. I didn't have any massive desire to leave Sky, but it seemed too good an opportunity to pass up. Mark and I are friends and I agreed to the deal. We even shook hands on it. I went home that night absolutely intent on going to ITV. In the morning, I left for work, set on handing in my resignation, but the date was somewhat significant: it was the day of the London Tube bombings – 7 July 2005. Of course, everybody was in shock. I had managed to get into the office before it had happened and, one by one, various members of staff began to trickle in. I had to tell somebody, because I didn't want the rumours to start flying around once ITV executives learned that they'd managed to get their man. Nervously, I went in to see head honcho, Vic Wakeling. I told him, 'ITV have made an offer that you couldn't possibly match.'

Naturally, this got his gander up. He looked at me and said, 'Jeff, after the World Cup, what then?' He asked if they had enough sport to keep me happy throughout the season. Could I cope with presenting a handful of internationals and some Champions League games? And would I be satisfied with life after *Soccer Saturday*? To convince me further, he more than matched the offer made by ITV. And so I stayed.

Now I know that this shifting loyalty makes me the Cristiano Ronaldo of sports broadcasting (though don't think for a minute that you'd ever see me in the skimpy shorts he wears during his summer holidays). But I think in my heart I didn't really want to leave Sky, so staying was easy. I felt bad because I had shaken hands with Mark Sharman. He was annoyed, and understandably so. He rang me in the car that afternoon to see if I would change my mind, and later again that night. But my head was set and I stayed at Sky.

In hindsight, I wouldn't have got the satisfaction at ITV that I draw from presenting *Soccer Saturday*. There's no better day than a Saturday for me – when I go into work I absolutely enjoy every second of it. I don't enjoy presenting the live games nearly as much as I love presenting the show on Saturday – it's not nearly as much fun. I realized I would be sacrificing that for an easier life, which is fine, but it would have been boring. Live matches are more formulaic – here's the intro; here are the guests; here are the managers and the teams. It's boring! On *Soccer Saturday*, you never really know what's going to happen next. And that's what keeps it leaps and bounds ahead of everyone else on the telly.

10

A SELECTION of SOCCER SATURDAY'S GREATEST GAFFES, BLOOPERS and ONE-LINERS

JEFF STELLING : 'Lee Bowyer has returned to West Ham, his old stamping ground.'

JEFF STELLING : 'Southampton are losing £39,000 a week.'
PAUL MERSON: 'I know how they feel.'

MATT LE TISSIER: 'He's taken him from behind. Er ... er ... he's taken his legs from behind.'

DAVE BASSETT: 'He goes down easier than my daughter.'

JELLEYMAN'S THROWN A WOBBLY

PAUL JEWELL: 'He's gone down with a twisted sock.'

JEFF STELLING: 'Oh, Liverpool have gone, oh, so close, haven't they Alan?'
ALAN SMITH: [Confused look. Talking to *Soccer Saturday* producer Karen Wilmington] 'Oh no, I've lost you there, Karen.'
JEFF STELLING: 'I'm quite embarrassed at him using my pet name.'

RESULTS READER: 'York City's game with Dagenham & Redbridge is running about an hour late because of some problems with the away team's coach. That's the multi-wheeled variety, not the two-legged.'

JEFF STELLING: 'We're all heading to Burtons in Bristol. The reason? Gary Johnson, the Bristol City manager, vowed he would bare his backside in Burtons' window when Liam Fontaine scored a goal. Well, there it is, Gary: 27 minutes gone. Looking forward to seeing you turn the other cheek, so to speak.'

CHRIS KAMARA: 'Their football, Arsenal, is on another level, but Spurs are fighting like beavers ... defending for their lives. It's a terrific game. 1-0.'
JEFF STELLING: 'Did I hear that correctly? Fighting like beavers [laughs].'

Five minutes later ...

CHRIS KAMARA: 'They're carving 'em up as easy as ... as easy as anything Jeff.'
JEFF STELLING: 'They're carving them up as easy as ... as easy as ... beavers was the word you were looking for, Chris.'

FRANK McLINTOCK: 'I remember the great teams of the past and how much nonce they had ...'
NIGEL SPACKMAN: 'Er, don't you mean nous?'

JEFF STELLING: 'Alan McInally, I hear you were delayed to the gantry [the area from which our match reporters work] by autograph-hunters. How many members of your family are there today?'

JEFF STELLING: 'Are you a fan of Showaddywaddy, Rodney?'
RODNEY MARSH: 'Who does he play for?'

PART 2

INTRODUCING THE REAL CRAZY GANG:

THE SOCCER SATURDAY PANEL

11
Welcome To The Muppet Show

Bedlam, the dictionary definition: extreme confusion and disorder. A very apt description of our *Soccer Saturday* panel today.

Love 'em, or hate 'em, the *Soccer Saturday* panel are the true stars of the show. And if you don't believe me, try imagining an afternoon without the likes of Paul Merson, Matt Le Tissier, Charlie Nicholas and Phil Thompson looking, somewhat wild-eyed and wilder-haired, from your telly box. Sure, hearing disorders up and down the country would diminish overnight without them – not to mention incidents of shattered TV screens and kicked cats – but without the panel, there would be no insight, no drama and no studio backchat. There would be no oohing and aahing, no screaming and shouting, no singing and dancing, no to-ing and fro-ing, and definitely no ranting and raving. There would be no gaffes, blunders, shouts, yelps, screams, sighs, moans, gripes, grudges, laughs, tears, giggles, texting, gambling, scoffing or wind-breaking. In fact, a good way to imagine *Soccer Saturday* without the panel would be to imagine *The Muppet Show* without Waldorf and Statler, Fozzie Bear and Miss Piggy – I'll leave you to make up your mind as to who would play whom at Sky Sports.

There's been quite a legacy of superstardom within the Sky studio since the inception of *Soccer Saturday* in 1997/98. Since those early days, the desk has been graced by the likes of George Best, Frank McLintock, Paul Walsh, Paul Merson, David Ginola, Dave Bassett, Kenny Sansom, Alan Mullery, Alan Smith, Alan McInally, Charlie Nicholas, Iain Dowie, Matt Le Tissier, Mark McGhee, Gary Mabbutt, Gordon McQueen, Lou Macari, Rodney Marsh, John Salako, Clive Allen, Phil Thompson and Neil Warnock. Which would probably make for quite a good veterans XI. Well, maybe without Neil Warnock.

It's this cast of characters that drive the show's playful spirit – I think *Soccer Saturday* was the first show since *Saint & Greavsie* to tap into the humour of football on a Saturday afternoon. Obviously, *Soccer AM* started that atmosphere in the mornings, though that was strictly terrace humour. Elsewhere *Fantasy Football League* worked very well during the international tournaments with comedians David Baddiel and Frank Skinner. But the *Soccer Saturday* experts gave viewers that mix of insightful analysis (we hope) and comedy throughout an afternoon of live football. It was perfect afternoon TV, though maybe not as easy on the eye as *The OC*, or as exciting as re-runs of *Airwolf*, but we quickly realized that a group of ex-pros could deliver intelligent comment and entertainment over six hours without boring the viewer.

Whether it was by luck or by judgement, the producers got together a group of people who could not do a serious show if they tried. For example, former panellist Rodney Marsh was unable to sit quietly in a room for six minutes, let alone six hours, without messing around, or insulting large sections of the nation for that matter.

Because of individuals like Rodney, Frank McLintock and George Best, the show quickly became a humorous and contentious vehicle for the day's football results. Since then, we've looked for panellists who can carry both a fantastic chemistry of expert opinion and a great sense of humour.

We could have gone a different route, but while it's all very well getting big-name stars to come into the studio and describe the games superbly, if they're as dull as ditchwater then we don't really want them to be involved – they don't bring anything to the party. In general, the people we've brought into the team have possessed that spark, that comedy. Paul Merson and Phil Thompson, for example, both have a fantastic sense of humour, as do Charlie Nicholas, Alan McInally and Matt Le Tissier. We've also used out-of-work managers on the panel that have carried that attitude, too: Mark McGhee, Steve Bruce and Paul Jewell among them.

A great addition was Peter Reid, who had previously worked on the Beeb's *Football Focus*. Apparently, his sense of humour hadn't sat well with their producers and it was thought that Reidy didn't carry enough gravitas or sobriety, which if you've ever been drinking with him comes as no great surprise (more of which we'll come to later). The Beeb's problem? There was always a mischievous grin on Reidy's face whenever he was on the sofa, which isn't that much of a shock given he was sharing studio space with Garth Crooks. Their issue was that you never really knew what he was thinking. Still, he fitted in well at Sky with his impish humour, so their loss was our gain.

Of course, working with characters in the vein of Rodney Marsh, Paul Merson and George Best also brought its own set of challenges and complications. A cracking example of how things can

go wrong was in the early days of the show. The then-three panellists were sitting on pedestals at one end of the studio. After the
initial hour of predictions and punditry we would cut to a commercial break before the panel reported on their designated
matches.

On this one particular occasion, Frank McLintock decided to pop
off to the loo and took rather longer than expected. So long, in fact,
that a goal was scored in his game between Aston Villa and
Crystal Palace before he'd managed to return to his seat. I'd been
told the news in his absence and was stuttering and stumbling
because I knew that Frank wasn't in his chair. A producer was
screaming in my ear to cut to Frank, but I knew full well he wasn't
on set. Worse, when Frank finally returned I could see that he
hadn't got a clue what was going on.

As he sat down, quite cruelly, I cut to him almost immediately
for some info on the goal: 'And let's find out about that goal in the
Villa–Palace game from Frank McLintock.'

Frank looked at me open-mouthed. He couldn't believe what
had happened. Thankfully, and this was from an unlikely hero,
George Best saved the day with some quick and sober thinking.
As Frank began to stumble through his bluffed analysis, George
began scribbling down the goal details.

Frank stumbled through. 'Well, there has been a goal, Jeff, and
it's been the worst possible start for … the worst possible start
for …'

George wrote down the word 'Palace' in big letters.

'… Palace. And it's been a goal from … a goal from …'

George wrote down the scorer, though there was absolutely no
description of the goal or its scorer whatsoever. Somehow, Frank
managed to blunder his way through it all. It could have been a
header, a 30-yard wonder-strike or a fluke goal that had bounced

106

in off the ref's arse. You wouldn't have known, because Frank had not seen it at all. It was a tricky moment.

Of course, there's always a temptation to stitch up various members of the panel, especially if you can see they're misbehaving. Matt Le Tissier often bears the brunt of the tricks because he's forever stuffing his face. I'll always try to take a look at what he's eating and throw in a line about the food on his desk, which is usually quite a lot – there are always sandwiches and chocolate and biscuits flying around the studio. And if you know somebody's got a mouthful of food and they're waving their arms around for you not to cut to them, it's impossible to resist dropping them in it. I once remember Charlie Nicholas nearly choking on a satsuma as I threw the cameras over to his game. Apparently a goal had been scored, but as he gagged and his eyes bulged, he had to admit that he couldn't talk because he was spluttering so badly.

Also, there are times when the panel forget they're in a television studio. As I've mentioned before, more often than not the four of them will argue over a bet or study their accumulators noisily as I read through the half-time scores. There have even been times when I've had to tell various members to shut up, and it's most definitely against the rules to have a phone in the studio, but Matt Le Tissier is always playing around with his mobile throughout the programme. He's forever texting people. Sometimes I wonder whether he has Pizza Hut on speed-dial.

At first there was always a pecking order on the desk. If you were sat next to me, you were viewed as a senior figure. Rodney Marsh used to sit in that seat and nobody else. Frank McLintock was always positioned next to Rodney as a simple matter of seniority. The boys would often be taken aback if somebody unfamiliar with the playground rules sat in their seat when they arrived. At times, there was a real sense of territorialism.

Certainly, Rodney was the star of the show for a while, even though he was a panellist rather than the anchorman. It was every bit as much his programme as it was mine. One year we even had a Christmas special that was called *Jeff, Rodney and Friends*. Nobody else got a mention. Because of that, Rodney was very protective of his position on the panel, even though a lot of the time we thought it would be better to have the new faces alongside me so I could give them some guidance as they watched their first game.

The desk also proved a famous myth about newsreaders and TV presenters: the top half is often sartorially elegant; the bottom half is a fashion disaster. It's exactly like that on *Soccer Saturday*. Most of the boys are wearing jeans below their suit jackets and shirts. Rodney used to wear a smart(ish) jacket and tie, but from the waist-down he was kitted out in Bermuda shorts and a pair of flip-flops. If he was wearing trousers, he'd tell you (usually as you gulped down the first coffee of the afternoon) that he was performing 'commando-style'* that day. It was a really awful thought.

Not that I can criticize. Originally, I used to wear the Richard Keys-style, multicoloured array of jackets in various hues of red, mustard, green and blue. On occasions, I resembled a backing singer from the 70s group Showaddywaddy. As a presenter, Richard used to do it to make him stand out and give his show, *Super Sunday*, a distinctive face. Unwisely, I tried to copy him, thinking, 'If it's good enough for him, it's good enough for me,' even though I did resemble a fashion disaster from *What Not To Wear*.

*For the more sophisticated/hygienic readers, to go 'commando' is to eschew the wearing of underpants.

Eventually it was hinted at that the gaudy days were behind Sky. Executives suggested we should be going for a more sober look. Sky Sports reporters started wearing shirts and blazers with the company logo emblazoned on them, and for a while there was a move afoot for us to follow suit (excuse the pun), though that was brushed aside pretty quickly. Can you imagine Charlie Nicholas in an official suit and tie? I don't think so. Or Matt Le Tissier for that matter? But then it's worth remembering that Matt Le Tissier has never worn a tie in the studio, not that he hasn't been nagged.

A few years ago there was a move to smarten up his image when Vic Wakeling and Karen Wilmington, producer of *Soccer Saturday*, went so far as to go to Richmond one afternoon to buy him some suits and ties. It didn't work and, the following weekend, Matt had 'forgotten' to bring any of them along. He was so scruffy at times, we used to call him Worzel Gummidge. In hindsight, maybe we were being unfair. At least he wasn't working 'commando-style'.

12

Hotel Babylon

Like most Premier League superstars, the *Soccer Saturday* panel tend to do most of their 'team bonding' on a Friday in a swanky London hotel where we gather for an evening of drinks before the big day. Unlike most Premier League superstars, however, our bonding process does not involve marauding WAGs-in-waiting or drunken punch-ups. To my knowledge, nobody has battered a fellow panellist with a golf club for not taking part in a karaoke session.

Of course, I won't divulge the name of our regular meeting place for fear of attracting groupies and snooping tabloid journalists. What I will say is that, over the years, the hotel has become a ritual: at 10 o'clock, the boys – Phil Thompson, Charlie Nicholas, Matt Le Tissier (occasionally), Alan McInally and Chris Kamara, if he's commentating on a London game the following day – will usually get together at the bar to discuss four main topics of conversation: beer, gambling, girls and football. Usually in that order. By the time we've got to football, we'll be chewing over the events of the week and a few drinks will have been sunk, so everybody is into the full swing of things.

This is a massive help for the show, because you can really get a feel for what the panellists' ideas are on different issues – it's always important to know what they might say on a managerial appointment or controversial decision, if asked. You also get an idea for which players might be moving, and to where, during the transfer window. The boys have a lot of contacts within the game and often hear various whispers, but they've also got an ear to the ground when it comes to most football rumours.

We're lucky enough to meet in a hotel that most clubs tend to use if they're playing either Fulham or Chelsea. That's also useful because we frequently see managers, coaches and backroom staff, and occasionally chairmen, for a drink, and the conversations can sometimes give us a real insight into what might be going on at a club. You can occasionally find out who's playing the next day and who's not; who is struggling with injuries, and which emerging stars are rising to prominence in the reserves. But it's also useful to build up a rapport with the managers. It's much easier to talk to the likes of David Moyes when you're sitting with a beer, rather than talking to them in a press conference or shoving a microphone in their face.

We've met dozens of managers along the way. Manchester United sometimes stay in the hotel, though Sir Alex Ferguson tends not to come down to the bar. West Ham often check in, too, even though they're only moving across London to play Chelsea. We've had drinks with Alan Curbishley, Alan Pardew and Mervyn Day. When Alan Pardew came in for a drink, he'd been getting a hard time, not only from the West Ham fans but from the press and the *Soccer Saturday* panel, too. When he walked into the bar and saw us, I was a little concerned that he might have been offended by some of the stick we'd given him. I needn't have worried. To be honest, he was an absolute charmer and I was really impressed with him. I said that I was sorry that we'd given him a bit of grief, and he said, 'Hey, that's fine, it's the job. I understand that.'

We had a drink together and it was a great night, but he got his own back for the criticism a couple of weeks later when we were doing the show. A live link was set up with Alan at Upton Park. During the interview he asked me how I was feeling. I said, 'What do you mean?' Alan laughed. 'Well I know what you guys get up to in the bar on a Friday night,' he said cheekily. Touché, I guess.

But what with all the work that goes into the show, I view our Friday nights in the same way a Premier League footballer would view his pre-match warm up: as essential preparation for 90 minutes of sheer hell. Nevertheless, despite the relative sobriety among the *Soccer Saturday* team (we are professionals, after all) there have been enough controversial incidents at the hotel bar to get the headline-writers drooling ...

Peter Reid 'Sinks' Premier League Manager!

Former England midfielder and Sunderland gaffer Peter Reid was once a regular panellist on *Soccer Saturday*. To be honest, I'm glad he's not so regular these days, because Reidy would drink absolutely anything, and in large quantities. He was an animal. His idea of an early night was to go to bed when the sun came up, and he even told me that he'd once drunk vodka and Listerine from a shoe – he was pissed as a fart, but his breath smelled fantastic afterwards.

One night, I remember Reidy having a rather large session with a Premier League manager who was staying at the hotel. For legal reasons, it's best if I don't name him, though what I can say it that the pair of them were propping up the bar until four thirty in the morning. That particular Premier League team were then walloped six-nil the next day. I felt that if I were a fan of that side and knew what had happened in the hotel that night, I would have been pretty miffed.

Reidy has a reputation as a drinker throughout the game (and beyond, most probably), but as long as he can cope with his job on the show, then there's absolutely no problem with him staying up into the early hours of a Saturday morning. Still, you go into a session with Reidy at your peril for two reasons: the first is that you're likely to end up under the table with laughter (he often tells us that he drinks brake fluid, but only because he can stop at any time); secondly, I swear he has hollow legs. There have been many times (usually on a hungover morning) when I've wished that somebody would give him a job back in football, because he's such a good manager.

Soccer Saturday Drinks Bar Dry!

And so to the panellists' drink orders:

Charlie Nicholas: Red wine, white wine, gin and tonic - but not in the same glass. It would be fair to say that his playboy reputation from the 1980s has diminished. Certainly, the tag of 'Champagne Charlie' doesn't sit right, mainly because he's not a champagne drinker in fairness. We leave that to former Aston Villa, Bayern Munich and Celtic striker and panellist Alan McInally. But McInally won't just drink any champagne. Oh no, he's a pink champagne man. Please stifle your giggles, because it's got to be a decent bottle as well, none of your tat. The Big Man is a bon viveur - he won't travel cattle-class on a plane, even if he's paying for the ticket himself. Which he rarely does.

Phil Thompson: white wine (anything with a good nose), or Budweiser, but only because the label comes in Liverpool colours.

Jeff Stelling: I like a diet Hoegaarden - a pint of Hoegaarden with a slice of lemon in it - because I'm an athlete. I normally have a pretty big workout in the gym beforehand. Well, big by my standards: an hour on the treadmill, a few weights, and 15 minutes in the steam room. By the time I've got to the bar, I've worked up a thirst. It's this strict regime that has made me the sex symbol I am today, not only among the ladies but some of the men as well.

In April 2008, radio DJ Christian O'Connell admitted to having a crush, or 'bromance', on me in his column in *GQ* magazine. 'Two words to strike fear in most modern men,' he wrote. 'Man crushes. A quick look at the excellent website Urban Dictionary sheds some light onto the condition: "Man crush: a man having extreme admiration for another man, as though he wants to be him. Man crush is a very strong feeling that one straight man has for another, bordering on the romantic but not the sexual. It's love all right but not the love that makes you want to get into his pants. It can be stronger than the love between a man and a woman. Ben Affleck has had a man crush on Matt Damon for a long time ..."

'My own man crush, which I've had for years now, is on Jeff Stelling from Sky Sports' *Soccer Saturday*. Every Saturday afternoon I find myself giggling like a teenage schoolgirl over Jeff's masterful handling of the football results. I constantly want to be with him. I want to hang out with him. I want to be the Wise to his Morecambe. I know that if I was as good as him I'd have more listeners to my radio show and thrash Chris Moyles and Terry Wogan.

'A recurring fantasy of mine involves Jeff and me holding court in an old-school pub. He's wearing a V-necked sweater with his hairy chest showing, immaculate Farah slacks and a pair of lovely loafers. He's also smoking a Hamlet cigarillo (I don't know why, but it adds to the mystique). Everyone's laughing at our jokes, and are jealous of our matey banter. Drinks are offered to us left, right and centre from hangers-on and wellwishers. But suddenly, Jeff turns to me and with a deadly serious look on his face he purrs:

> **Christian, you just might be the best friend I've ever had. Well, apart from Chris Kamara that is, but sometimes I find the way he laughs annoying. Let's say we blow this joint. Let's pop down to the shed. I'm going to teach you how to bang stuff in with a hammer.**

It's pretty racy stuff and I'm beginning to wonder if Mr O'Connell has an unhealthy obsession with me (I fear he isn't be first and won't be the last), because he later wrote a *Guardian* column that argued: 'Jeff Stelling wouldn't look amiss in a Brut advert, splashing it over his rugged face, then turning to camera and growling, "Grrr, I'm Jeff Stelling. Get your knickers off." It would double his wages.'

Now I know how David Beckham feels.

You can laugh, but we do get people in the bar wanting to have photographs with us, especially those of the fairer sex. True, they do usually want their picture with Charlie and Kammy, rather than the slightly-below-average-height anchorman, but I once remember a group of girls in the bar coming over for photos and being quite curious as to what I actually did for a living. We got chatting and the boys began explaining who they were, while outlining the highlights of their glittering careers. The bloody show-offs.

Phil Thompson – ex-Liverpool and England captain. Charlie Nicholas – ex-Arsenal bad boy and Scotland striker. Alan McInally – ex-Celtic, Aston Villa and Bayern München (he always refers to the München part).

Then they turned to me. Not wanting to be left out I explained that I was 'Chopper Stelling, a Tottenham and England right-back for many years.' More unbelievable than the lie that tumbled from my gob was the fact that they actually fell for it. The boys played along brilliantly, so if you ever hear them referring to me on the show as 'Chopper Stelling', you'll know what they're talking about.

Chris Kamara: A beer man. It reflects what he was like as a footballer – straight-laced and no frills.

Matt Le Tissier: Mr Malibu and Coke, though he will occasionally have an alcopop, probably as a dessert. Rumours once swept the *Soccer Saturday* office that Le Tiss was a long-suffering Coke addict – not in the Mark Bosnich sense I hasten to add, but because of his fondness for a particular brand of fizzy drink. At one awards dinner, 12 cans of pop arrived at his table, all of which were for Matt. I remember going to a gourmet dinner at Southampton with him. It was fantastic – every course was accompanied by a suitably-fine wine, but Matt had an ice bucket with six bottles of alcopops, one for each course. On the occasions he does join us for a night out, it's always very difficult. Well, how do you keep a straight face when ordering a Malibu and Coke for a man of his size? That's my excuse for not getting him one, anyway.

Steve Bruce Confesses Premier League Woes!

At the beginning of the 2007/08 season, Birmingham City were due to play Fulham at Craven Cottage, and the team were staying in our hotel. Steve was sitting at the bar on his own and looked a bit morose. When he saw us he came over to say hello and I asked him how things were.

'Oh, we're in big trouble,' he said. 'We could go down this season, it's that bad.'

I couldn't believe it; the season had only just started and this was pessimistic by anyone's standards. I said, 'Come on Steve, surely it can't be that bad.' All the boys had gathered round at this point. Immediately he began telling us all the reasons why he thought Birmingham weren't ready for the start of the campaign. He felt the club hadn't worked on his ideas in the transfer market and he couldn't buy the players he wanted to strengthen the squad. I think Steve felt that the board's ambitions didn't match his own. He was convinced the team were going to be in trouble.

Anyway, the next day Birmingham went to Fulham and played out a one-all draw, which was a pretty good result. During the show that day I mentioned that Steve had seemed a bit despondent the previous evening, but given the result I figured he had been needlessly concerned. I was wrong. At the end of the campaign, Steve's worries had become all too real and Birmingham were relegated.

David Moyes In Nice Guy Shocker!

Now, I have so far avoided making judgements on the personalities of footballers and managers, but sometimes, just sometimes, you catch an insight into a personality simply by examining their demeanour during 90 minutes of football. For example, you're unlikely to want to ruffle Sir Alex Ferguson's hair as he sits seething on the Manchester United bench, though you'd probably be able to yank on Dimitar Berbatov's Alice band without too much trepidation. But when it comes to Everton gaffer David Moyes, I am absolutely terrified.

Study Moyes on the touchline and what do you see? A blur of haymakers and waved fists, most probably: the furious altercations with fourth officials; the kicked water bottles; and those piercing, Jack-Nicholson-from-*The-Shining*-eyes that would probably reduce Duncan Ferguson to a blubbering wreck. So, when I saw Moyes arriving in the hotel bar, accompanied by his backroom staff, which included former England keeper Chris Woods, I didn't know whether to run or reach for the nearest crucifix (not that I'm likely to find one in a hotel bar). He waved out and I waved back, whimpering nervously as he approached me with an extended hand. I really didn't know what I was letting myself in for.

'Fancy joining us for a drink?' he said. I nodded, grabbed my drink and hoped for the best. Moyes clearly doesn't suffer fools gladly. I didn't want to come across as a fool, especially as I'd already had a diet Hoegaarden or two. Thankfully, the Everton gaffer proved that you shouldn't judge a book by its gory, bloodstained cover. We talked about a number of players that Everton had looked at during the recent transfer window, including striker David Nugent, who was at Moyes's former club, Preston North End. We talked about Nugent's Premier League credentials. Moyes reckoned he was good enough to do a job in the top flight. He pointed to Woods, and his assistant Alan Irvine. 'But this lot think I'm wrong,' he sighed.

It was an interesting insight into the managerial mechanics of the Everton set-up. I'm not saying that the club's way of signing players depended on the opinions of all three coaches, but there was clearly a democracy in place where everyone could have their say before David Moyes made the final decision. It turned out to be a great night, and as a stranger it was fascinating to be involved in a conversation like that. My opinion on Moyes had changed, too. He wasn't the arm-waving manager we had all seen on the telly. He was friendly, warm and good company. A pussycat in fact (but don't tell him I said that).

Gareth Southgate: He's Mr Wonderful!

Gareth Southgate was in the hotel one night and he'd recently been made Middlesbrough manager. We were unsure whether he was the right man for the job and at the beginning of the 2006/07 season we'd asked a lot of questions about his ability. Was he too inexperienced? Was he too nice? Was he too naïve? Was he buying the right type of players? We'd thrown all these questions into the debate on the telly for a couple of weeks, and when Boro came to stay, Gareth was at the bar.

I thought, 'Oh god, will he be upset with us? Is there going to be a showdown?' But we had a couple of drinks together and he struck me as being a very nice guy. I'd be lying if I said it didn't temper my criticism of him afterwards. I thought, 'He's a good, decent man, maybe we've been a bit tough on him.' My belief is that it's our job to criticize when managers and players are performing badly, but I'm quite keen that we don't stick the knife into people unnecessarily.

Soccer Saturday Smackdown!
Champagne Charlie Versus Mick McCarthy

So far there hasn't been a bar-room brawl involving the *Soccer Saturday* crew, but there have been near-misses, most notably when Charlie Nicholas and Mick McCarthy had a heated row one evening. Now before the mud starts to fly, I'd like to point out that I get on great with Mick, I always have done. He's a straight-talking guy, and he's very humorous with it

At this time, Mick was at Sunderland and the team came to the hotel during the 2005/06 season. When I arrived, there was a big group of the backroom staff in one corner of the bar. Chris Kamara was already there and they asked me to join them. Charlie came in and joined us as well, which was when the fireworks started to explode.

I wasn't sure whether there had been any history between Mick and Charlie or not, but Charlie, between you, me and the female population, fancies himself as a snappy dresser in his jeans, T-shirts and fancy waistcoats. I think he could do without the diamond ear-ring (as TV critic Ally Ross always points out in the *Sun*), but I'm digressing. That night, Charlie was wearing a shirt that a) I could tell was bloody expensive, and b) was really rather stylish.

'Bloody hell, Charlie,' Mick roared in that distinct Yorkshire accent. 'What are you wearing?'

Our hearts sank. The one thing we've learned over the years is never to interrupt one of the Scottish panellists if they're ordering drinks – they never go to the bar more than once in an evening.

'If I ever want advice on how to dress,' seethed Charlie, 'then you'd be the last person I'd ask.'

Mick was not best pleased at being criticized in front of his back-room staff. He fired another remark; Charlie snapped.

'You know what, Mick?' he yelled. 'Roy Keane was right about you.'

Bang! This was a reference to the former Ireland captain's dig at Mick while he was in charge of the Republic team during the 2002 World Cup. Keane had publicly criticized Mick's training methods and the facilities at their disposal. Charlie's comment was designed to light the fuse.

I thought, 'Oh my god.' The situation had turned from being rel-atively good-humoured (with a slight edge) to a pretty naughty and volatile vibe. If you want to imagine what it was really like, recall a loud faux pas from a 'druncle' at a family gathering. Remember the awkward silence afterwards, where the only noises clipping an uncomfortable silence are the clinking of cheap cutlery? Magnify that by a thousand and throw in some pretty big football egos and you're halfway there. It was awful.

I didn't know what to do, nor did Kammy, who sat there desperately trying to change the subject, though I don't even think a burst of song would have saved the situation. Thankfully, some light relief arrived when Phil Thompson walked into the bar, though this lasted all of five seconds. Thommo, unaware of the situation, sat down and asked innocently, 'Is Bob Murray, the chairman, here?'

Mick was in the process of doing a new deal at Sunderland. Thommo, in his mind, was saying hello with a perfectly innocent question and wasn't to know of the powder-keg atmosphere. Mick snapped back, 'Are you after my job already?'

Phil was gobsmacked, but it was just a storm in a teacup. A truce of silence was established soon after, and I remember parting company with Mick on good terms and shaking hands, so it was all fine. But for a while, it was an awfully uncomfortable situation that could have exploded into something far, far worse. Typically, nobody backed down or apologized (because that's the way the *Soccer Saturday* crew roll). But thankfully, nobody got their jaw broken either.

Thommo Slams Bolton Playmaker! [Do Bolton Really Have 'Playmakers'?]

There's nothing like stitching up one of the panel, especially Thommo. I remember, for a while, midfielder Kevin Nolan was being talked about as a potential England player. He'd been overlooked by Sven-Göran Eriksson, despite some impressive performances at Bolton, and I argued that his exclusion was down to the fact that he played for a rather unfashionable club. The debate rumbled on over a few drinks in the bar, and Thommo had some pretty forthright views on the matter.

'Look at some of the players that have got a cap under Sven,' I said. 'Michael Ricketts, Chris Powell, Paul Konchesky, Scott Parker … everyone is getting a cap except Kevin Nolan.'

Thommo piped up that he thought Kevin Nolan was crap. 'We have Stevie Gerrard, Frank Lampard, David Beckham in the England midfield,' he said. 'How's he going to get into the team? He's nowhere near good enough.'

It was obvious that I was very pro-Kevin Nolan, it has to be said, but Thommo wouldn't budge. When the topic was brought up on the programme the next day, I turned to Thommo first.

'So Thommo, do you think Kevin Nolan should get a chance with the England squad?'

He stalled. 'Well, England's midfield is as strong as it has been for a long time,' he said. 'It'll be hard for him to force his way past the likes of Gerrard and Lampard.'

I then asked him whether he thought it could be down to the fact that Nolan played for Bolton (at the time of writing he's at Newcastle), rather than a fashionable team like Liverpool or Arsenal.

'Well, possibly,' he said.

I couldn't believe he was being so diplomatic.

'Well, that's strange, Thommo,' I said. 'Because when I asked you this last night, you told me it was because you thought he was useless.'

Anyway, Thommo was flustered. He went as red as the Liverpool home kit. He tried to backtrack, but none of the boys would let him off the hook. He was cornered. He even turned to the camera at one point and said, 'Kevin, I didn't say it.' It was his way of getting out of it, but of course he did say it, Kevin. He said you were crap. (But he was only kidding ... I think!)

13

Gorgeous George

FACTFILE: GEORGE BEST

BORN: 22 May 1946

DIED: 25 November 2005

CLUBS: Manchester United (1963-74), Dunstable Town (1974, loan), Stockport County (1975), Cork Celtic (1975-6), Los Angeles Aztecs (1976), Fulham (1976-7), Los Angeles Aztecs (1977-8), Fort Lauderdale Strikers (1978-9), Hibernian (1979-80), San Jose Earthquakes (1980-1), Bournemouth (1983)

HONOURS: (Manchester United) League Championship 1965, 1967; European Cup 1968

INTERNATIONAL CAPS: (Northern Ireland) 37

I'll never forget the first time I met George Best. I was playing in a charity game somewhere in Kent quite a few years back. He was in pretty good shape, and 'Chopper Stelling' certainly wasn't. I was also somewhat overawed by the fact that, for an afternoon, I was having to mark one of the greatest names ever in world football. I use the word 'mark' loosely, of course. For the best part of 90 minutes, I didn't see much of George or the ball because I couldn't get close to him. In fact, during our first clash he nutmegged me. Worse, as he nutmegged me, I turned around to face him and he popped the ball through my legs again just as I was going back the other way. It was a moment of sheer brilliance. Everyone on the park was in tears of laughter, including me. He must have been 40, but he still had that crowd-pleasing ability.

As anyone over a certain age will tell you, George was the greatest player to grace the *Soccer Saturday* studios. He was in a class of his own as a player, and who couldn't admire his talent? Those great goals, mazy runs and fearless flashes of showmanship are something that will live long in the memory of any football fan. He was a star and the viewers loved him. I lost count of the number of letters I received that would start, 'Dear Jeff, I love the show, I think you're great and I think the pundits are great. Can I have George Best's autograph please?'

I understood it, though, because George was a superstar, and every Saturday there would be a mountain of old letters and shirts and pictures on his desk. He would sign every single one, chatting away as he sat there patiently, scribbling his name again and again without a complaint or a whinge.

At first, it was quite a coup to get him on the show – he was one of the original panellists and everyone knew his importance. I even recall Vic Wakeling saying, 'No matter what happens, George Best has a job for life here.' It didn't matter what sort of mischief he got up to (and sometimes George could be pretty naughty): if he didn't turn up, as he sometimes wouldn't, it wasn't a disciplinary problem because he was George Best. We couldn't replace him because we knew he was a one-off.

As we all understood, George had his personal problems. He battled with the booze for years and sometimes this took its toll on the show. For example, you could never tell when he was going to turn up and when he wasn't. I remember that it was hard for him to commit in the programme's early years. We'd try everything to make sure that he arrived in the studio on time, and we would even send a taxi to collect him. Alex, his wife, would put him in the car and say, 'Just take him to Sky,' but then 20 minutes before the show, he still hadn't arrived. We'd then contact the cab firm only for the driver to say, 'I can see him right now, he's sat 15 yards from me, but he's in the Phene Arms and he says he'll be out in a minute.' Unsurprisingly, George wouldn't show after that.

It was because of these occasional lapses that we became probably the only football programme in broadcasting history with a sub's bench. We'd have local guys on standby like Nigel Spackman or Alan Mullery. They would come in just in case George decided he wasn't going to turn up. This was vital – there were too many times when Bestie had dropped out at the last minute and we had to work with a panel of three when we really needed four.

In a way, all of this was part of George's character. He was a maverick on the pitch and he was a maverick off it, especially when he worked for us, but at times it became problematic. There was one moment when he invited me to a big charity dinner at Manchester United for the Liver Trust. This was a cause that had been very close to his heart, quite literally, given that he had required a liver transplant. He'd supported it for a long time and had convinced all the Manchester United European Cup-winning team of 1968 to attend this event, including Sir Bobby Charlton and Denis Law, not to mention some of the old Man City boys like Mike Summerbee and Franny Lee. George's liver transplant surgeon was even there, so it was quite a roll-call of guests.

It promised to be a brilliant night, too. The tickets had cost something like £160 a head. George had raised a hell of a lot of money. I was very honoured when he asked me to host this fantastic charity night at Old Trafford. I told him I would love to do it and I travelled up to Manchester, but at around three o'clock on the afternoon of the event, his agent called me.

'Jeff,' he said. 'What's the worst thing you could think of that could happen tonight?'

Well, I told him that would be the awful possibility that George wouldn't turn up. There was an awkward silence on the other end of the phone.

'Well, you're right, he's not coming.'

It was terribly embarrassing. My first job that evening was to announce to an array of football legends that the man who had organized this lavish event in his name – and had invited them there in the first place – wasn't showing up. I did what I could.

'Sadly,' I said, 'George is unwell and won't be with us tonight.'

But of course, George wasn't unwell. He was just a little 'under the weather', as they say. In fact, he was under the weather in a bar in Ireland. His agent told me that Alex was trying to get him on a flight to Manchester, but I told him not to bother. If George had been drinking, then there was no point in him being there. The last thing you wanted was for a sozzled George Best to turn up at a fund-raising event for a liver charity. Of course, he was desperately apologetic about it afterwards, and the night went well, but this was the sort of behaviour that you sometimes had to expect from George.

This wasn't the first or last time George would let me down. On one infamous occasion, he had been to a function in Manchester the night before *Soccer Saturday*. Somehow, against all expectations, he arrived in the studios at an unusually early time – half past eight in the morning in fact, which was unheard of for him. We couldn't believe it. He came in and we had breakfast together, drank some coffee and enjoyed a bit of a chat to while away an hour or two. I figured we had him for the day.

The one thing I remember was that it was a really nice morning because we were unrushed – I always loved talking to George on days like that. He was a great conversationalist. All he wanted to chat about were his dogs, because he was a real dog-lover. Either that or we were discussing his bets for the day. As we all knew, George was a gambler, but despite what people might have thought about him, he was a small-scale chancer at best – he really only ever put a fiver a time on horses. He always told me that he had an amazing habit of winning a 50–1 race, but when he'd show me his betting slip, it would say '£250' because he'd only put a fiver on.

That was how he backed horses too, which was funny because there were a couple of so-called big exposés in the national press where George had been described as a 'gambling addict'. This was utter nonsense. He would only flutter a couple of quid at a time and I remember he would get so frustrated, because he would go into a betting shop only for a reporter to come in and scrabble around on the floor to find his used betting slips as he left.

But that morning, George was in fine spirits and after breakfast we all went down to make-up. Once I'd finished having my 'guy-liner' and slap applied I got myself into position for the show at five to twelve. I looked around and realized that George wasn't next to me, even though the rest of the panel were in place. I said to the producer, 'Where's George? Isn't he out of make-up yet?'

JELLEYMAN'S THROWN A WOBBLY

There was an ominous shrug of the shoulders. Nobody seemed to know where he was. He'd disappeared. We started the programme without him and began a manhunt behind the scenes. Later it turned out that when he had finished in the make-up department, George had left the building. Instead of turning left and walking towards the studio and his seat, George had turned right out of the Sky offices and walked across the road to the local rugby club. He then spent the afternoon watching the show with a few drinks. In fairness, when we came out at the end of the programme and walked to the bar, he was there waiting for us with a cheeky grin on his face. He'd even bought a round for the boys. The truth is, we had a right laugh about it, even though he had let us down. Like I say, he could be unreliable at times, but his charisma carried him through.

George's superstar presence was great for us. What he brought to the show was a huge level of credibility, mainly because of who he was. As a pundit he wasn't a shouter – he was quiet, he was gentle and he was thoughtful. That gave him an understated authority and he was a nice counterpoint to Rodney Marsh, who was loud, funny and abrasive. George and Rodney were good friends and they brought a good balance to the panel.

But despite all that, George wasn't afraid to speak his mind – as in 1999, when the then-England manager, Glenn Hoddle, argued in an interview with *The Times* that disabled people were paying for sins lived out in a previous life. It was a hugely controversial statement that would ultimately cost him his job. The scandal had broken on the Saturday morning and I decided to make it the lead story in the show because it was such an explosive subject, but for whatever reason, everyone seemed really quiet on the matter when I raised it on air. I was cajoling the panel, hoping someone would say something lively. Rodney and fellow panellist Frank McLintock were unusually non-committal, so as a last resort I turned to George. I assumed he would follow the party line by claiming it was a storm in a teacup. This time, though, I was wrong.

'So George,' I said, 'do you think it will all blow over?'

He shook his head. 'No,' he said. 'I think he should be sacked.'

I couldn't believe it. I thought, 'What?!'

Before I could respond, George made it clear that he hadn't finished. 'I really think he should be sacked,' he said. 'It's an outrageous thing to say.'

Suddenly the show had a powerful start. George certainly didn't have anything against Glenn Hoddle personally, and if you look at Glenn's record as England manager he was fantastic and we were very supportive of him. But George genuinely felt that Glenn had insulted a group in society and decided to speak his mind. His comments were quoted in a lot of papers the next day, and from that moment onwards, a snowball effect began to build. It very quickly resulted in a sacking. The England manager's comments were condemned everywhere and he was booted out of the FA. It was sad, because I know Glenn and I like him. I thought he was a good England manager, but that was George's impact.

Bestie loved Manchester United as well – the club really was his life. I was looking back at some old tapes recently and I found one where we'd sent George to interview Sir Alex Ferguson at Old Trafford. On paper, this was just a great meeting of minds, but it was George's first attempt at an interview, and you got the impression that Fergie knew it. There was a slightly nervy atmosphere surrounding the whole occasion. Still, it was a wonderful football moment: here were two United legends coming together – the great disciplinarian manager and the blessed football maverick. It couldn't fail to entertain.

Their mutual respect was there for all to see. At one point, Sir Alex said to him, 'We've learned a lot from you at Manchester United, George. When you were at the club nobody had ever experienced the exposure and superstar status and media attention that you received. Nobody knew how to react to it. Certainly nobody knew how to handle it. There wasn't anybody at the club who knew about media coverage in those days. Sir Matt [Busby] was caught totally unawares. We learned lessons from that, and with the kids we have at the club now, we make sure that we don't leave them open to the sort of coverage that you suffered.'

Bestie laughed. 'So I'm responsible for winning all those trophies then?' he said. I don't think he was joking, either.

It was a massive blow when he died in 2005. The thing about George passing away was that he had been ill, on and off, for so long. During his last year with us, he'd lost a lot of weight. At times he would come into the studio looking gaunt and yellow. Despite having a liver transplant, he continued to drink heavily. At times it was hard to recognize him.

Eventually, the drugs he was taking to prevent his body from rejecting the new liver infected his kidney. George was hospitalized. Still, there was a feeling that he was indestructible – he was George Best after all. Prior to his final illness, there were times when he would come into *Soccer Saturday* looking desperately unwell. A week or two later he would be fine, so we figured the same could happen again. I guess we always believed that George was a superhero. It wasn't until the last few days of his life that it dawned on me that maybe his time might be up. Even then I wasn't convinced. Despite the fact that so many people were saying that it looked really bad for him, that he might not have long left, I still thought we'd see him back on the show.

Despite our faith in George's stubborn nature, in the last couple of days it became apparent that the end of the road was near. It was agonizing to hear about his condition. There were TV crews camped outside the hospital. People wanted interviews from us. And when he finally went it was a big blow. Ultimately he picked up a lung infection and a multiple organ failure killed him. He was 59 years old – too young to die, really – and the week that he went I'll be honest, like any other TV programme, we had an obituary planned. It was a horrible moment.

That first show without him was the hardest we have ever done on *Soccer Saturday*, bar none. George had been part of the team for 10 years. Some of the panel knew him a lot longer than that: Rodney and George, for example, had been friends for years – they played at Fulham together, they played in the NASL in America, too. I think Rodney went to see him the night before he died, and so he took his death very hard.

But we've always tried to celebrate his life on the show, which was great because there was so much to be thankful for. I remember asking him once, 'George, can you tell me what happened on this very day in 1981?'

He looked at me as if I was mad. 'You're kidding,' he laughed. 'I can't even remember what happened last night.'

On another afternoon in 2004, we linked up live with Norwich City chairman Delia Smith on the Carrow Road touchline. The Canaries had just been promoted, Delia had clearly enjoyed a liquid lunch by way of a celebration, and by all accounts she'd taken out the entire Norwich staff, too. Despite all this, at ten to three she was back in the stadium for the kick-off and a *Soccer Saturday* interview (not something to be taken lightly). Unfortunately for

Delia, she was unable to hear the link between her headset and the *Soccer Saturday* studio. The noise in the stadium was unbelievable. A mild panic swept across the panel as a slightly 'refreshed' Delia began to proclaim her love for the show.

'Jeff, I love you,' she slurred. 'And Rodney, I love you, and George, I really love you.'

George in his quiet way deadpanned, 'I think she's been at the cooking sherry.' The studio broke into fits of laughter. The following Monday, Martin Kelner of *The Guardian* wrote, 'That's the thing about *Soccer Saturday*: you always get an expert opinion.'

When it comes to his playing career, though, everybody remembers the same things about George – the great European nights, the six goals against Northampton, El Beatle. But the one thing I recall about him wasn't his brilliant ability, or that he tormented fullbacks for fun – it was his bravery. The harder the tough men tried to act against him, the more they tried to kick him, the better George would play. A defender would whack him, but he enjoyed going back for more. Bestie appeared unbreakable. That's something we don't have in the game these days. Players today go down so easily, but George was tough, tough, tough. He could give it out a bit as well, and at times he would show a nasty side. Nevertheless, his wonderful balance and poise, not to mention the speed with which he ran at people, were just awe-inspiring.

Off the pitch, George was the first footballer that made front-page news as well as being a back-page superstar. He was a headline machine from the moment he made it into the United first team to the day he died, but it wasn't a whirlwind working with him, because, socially, we didn't go out a lot. On the occasions that we did, it was chaos. If we were having a drink or a meal together, everybody wanted autographs and photographs with George, but he was incredibly patient with all the fans.

One evening, a group of us went out and George joined us with Alex. She hadn't been his wife for very long, and they were clearly close, but girl after girl after girl came over, each one asking for a picture with George. It would have been understandable if either of them had lost their temper. Instead, they both kept very calm and handled the situation with good manners. They must have endured that attention all the time, which would have made their life so difficult.

George deserved to be loved, though, mainly for what he did in the game and also for the way he treated other people. I think, in fairness, Sky supported him in his last few years of life. They certainly gave him a focus. They also gave him more leeway than anybody else could have expected on the panel, but that was because he was the one and only George Best. And he was bloody sensational at it.

14

Bigmouth Strikes Again:

The People Versus Rodney Marsh

FACTFILE: RODNEY MARSH

BORN: 11 October 1944

CLUBS: Fulham (1962-6),
Queens Park Rangers
(1966-72), Manchester City
(1972-5), Tampa Bay Rowdies
(1976), Cork Hibernians (1976), Fulham
(1976-7), Tampa Bay Rowdies (1977-9)

HONOURS: (QPR) Third Division Championship
1967; League Cup 1967

INTERNATIONAL CAPS: (England) 9

'Ladies and gentlemen of the court, please rise. You are gathered here today to pass sentence on the misdemeanours of former *Soccer Saturday* panellist and showy England midfielder Rodney Marsh. Judge Jeff presiding.'

It's true, a lot of people didn't like Rodney Marsh when he was a *Soccer Saturday* panellist. During his time on the show, he secured a reputation for being provocative, prickly, brash and opinionated, and that was just among the members of his immediate family! In the wider world, some viewers regarded him as self-righteous; someone not to be taken seriously; a motormouth. Infamously, he proved his critics right when that freewheeling gob caused his sacking in 2005. Rodney had made an inappropriate comment about the Asian tsumani on live television. There was no way back for him after that.

Despite the blunders, he had a vast legion of fans – myself included. I was of the opinion that Rodney was a vital member of the team, mainly because he was articulate, intelligent and opinionated. To that end ladies and gentlemen, it's time to hear the charges levelled against *Soccer Saturday*'s most controversial pundit to date. As you'll see, there are quite a few ...

The people Of Bradford Versus Rodney Marsh

In the summer of 1999, Rodney somehow managed to offend the entire city of Bradford with his mouthy antics. Bradford City were newly-promoted and their fans were looking forward to a season in the top flight; Rodney was convinced they wouldn't beat the drop and was more than happy to say so.

'Bradford City are a Nationwide side out of their depth,' he said. 'They are a very poor team; they have no right to be in the Premiership.' Bradford fans were rightly infuriated by this judgement, but as the season went on, Rodney, being Rodney, stuck to his guns. We all knew that in situations like this, Rodney would be more controversial than ever. Like a school bully, he was less inclined to let an issue go if he knew his comments were hitting a nerve. Clearly, his comments were hitting hard and fast, as Bradford's local paper, the *Telegraph & Argus*, were only too happy to report:

❛ Sky Sports pundit Rodney Marsh has stepped up his "war" on Bradford City with a renewed attack on the TV company's website. And Marsh, who has infuriated City fans with his constant putdowns of the club, is prepared to confront his own critics head-on.

Tomorrow night, in what promises to be a lively debate, Marsh will lock horns with chairman Geoffrey Richmond in an hour-long radio phone-in. The head-to-head, with fans invited to call in, is on *Classic Gold* at 7pm. In Marsh's new attack on the website he says it will take more than a challenge from the City boss to make him change his mind.

He said: "Bradford had a great result against Leicester on Saturday and I applaud the Bradford supporters for having a go at me and singing, 'Are you watching, Rodney Marsh?' because I can take it as well as give it. I just hope that on their last day of the season, the Bradford fans will sing 'Are you watching, Rodney Marsh?' as they plummet back into the Nationwide.'

Last weekend, former QPR hero Marsh stepped up his onslaught against the Bantams when he said City had no right to be in the Premiership. [Bradford manager Paul] Jewell hit back in the *T&A:* "I am disappointed with myself at getting annoyed with him because he is someone who just chases a cheap laugh.

"If it was someone with any credence making these comments such as Andy Gray or Graeme Souness, who both know what it is like to run a football club, then it would be different."

Marsh replied: 'I applaud Paul Jewell's astuteness and his observations, which I believe are accurate. I would like to point out that any comments I make on Sky Sports are from my point of view as a former player at the highest level and not from a manager's perspective.

'If Paul Jewell dismisses my analysis based upon the fact that I've never managed a football club in Britain, does that mean that the only people allowed to have an opinion are those that have ever managed a football club?"

Marsh angered Jewell on the opening day of the season by saying there were three leagues within the Premiership with City occupying a fourth on their own.

Marsh had said: 'I think Bradford are the worst team ever to play in the Premiership. They are like a cat with a long tail in a room full of rocking chairs. Everywhere they turn they'll get turned over.

'They've got a poor, small stadium. Bradford will get stuffed at some point.'

Jewell today refused to become embroiled still further in the war of words, declining to comment on Marsh's latest outburst. **)**

The people of Bradford were up in arms. Rodney didn't care. It even got to the stage where he promised, 'Look, if Bradford City can stay up in this division, I'll shave my head.' Well, this was brilliant. Suddenly there was a challenge and, somehow, Bradford managed to win against Arsenal. They picked up a couple of good results, and before we knew it, they moved closer to saving their place in the top flight.

With every win the crowd would be singing 'Are you watching, Rodney Marsh?' louder than before. Rodney couldn't care less. He would wind them up even more. I remember when he went up there for his live interview with the City chairman, Geoffrey Richmond, he even said, 'Look, if people want to speak to me, or write to me, or send me an email on the internet ... Hang on, do you get the internet up here?' That was Rodney all over. He had no care for his personal safety at all.

Anyway, on the last day of the season, Bradford secured survival when they defeated Liverpool one-nil. That was Rodney's lot, but fair play to him, he stuck to his guns. On the first day of the following season he went onto the pitch to get his head shaved. Such was the excitement that the local press worked themselves into a frenzy yet again, the *Telegraph & Argus* reporting in its issue of Friday 7 July 2000:

TV pundit Rodney Marsh has a prickly message for Bradford City fans – you might have survived last season, but you've no chance next time. The controversial Sky TV analyst, who upset Bantams fans last season with his forecasts of doom for the team, says City will definitely be relegated from the Premiership at the end of next season. Marsh is already facing a scalping at Valley Parade before the Leicester City game on August 26 after the Bantams proved him wrong by staying up.

He will have his head shaved live on Sky Sports' *Soccer Saturday* programme on the Valley Parade pitch with money being raised for Bradford Royal Infirmary's burns unit. Marsh is hoping that a sum of around £50,000 can be raised from the event.

Now he is urging City fans to challenge him face-to-face over his predictions when he attends a sports dinner in Bradford next month along with former City boss Chris Kamara.

"It's like watching a bad American B-movie with someone in the electric chair," Marsh told the *Telegraph & Argus*. "Then the governor comes along and gives him a stay of execution. Well, City got their stay of execution last year. But this will be the season they go down."

Despite his gloomy prediction, the pundit is full of praise for City's achievement in staying up last season. "It was fantastic and I was delighted," he said. 'Paul Jewell and the players did a great job. And I think Geoffrey Richmond is a great chairman. But in my opinion they won't have the quality this year. They'll go down with Ipswich and Derby.

"I'm not being personal. It's just my professional opinion." 9

Before his public humiliation, what we knew and what Rodney didn't know was that the hairdresser who was shaving his head wasn't going to hold back. Marshy thought he was going to be cropped to a number two in length, a reasonable look for a man of his advancing years – it's short but not bald. What we knew was that he was getting a number one. For an idea of what that looks like, think ex-referee Pierluigi Collina. We anticipated it had the potential to be one of the greatest moments in the show's history.

As he prepared for his very public punishment, I began to tease him. 'Bad news, Rodney,' I said during a live studio link. 'Your usual Bond Street hairdresser has missed his train from London. Instead you'll be groomed by Savage Sam from Bradford.'

The fans were in the ground in force. They were loving every minute of it. There were even banners reading 'Rodney Marsh: Plonker!' as the hairdresser took his clippers to Rodney's bonce.

We were watching from the studio and it was quite a sight. There were tears running down our faces because we knew what was coming and he didn't. As the hair began falling around his ears, I think the full horror of what was happening to him began to sink in.

Rodney went to stroke the top of his head. When he realized how close the shave had been he went a funny colour. 'Christ, this is a bit short, isn't it?' he said nervously. The crowd were roaring by now. So were we. For once, justice had been served.

VERDICT: Guilty; sentence completed.

Ivan Campo Versus Rodney Marsh

Rodney had a run-in with Bolton Wanderers when he claimed that their international defender Ivan Campo looked like a Sunday-morning pub player. This was a bit extreme. I guess he resembled a Sunday-morning pub player in his appearance – with his cauliflower hair and stubble, he wasn't the smartest – but Rodney was actually referring to his playing style. This was totally off the mark. Campo has secured a fantastic reputation as a player, especially during his time at Real Madrid. You don't win all those medals by being a pub player, otherwise the Stelling trophy cabinet would be close to breaking point.

VERDICT: Guilty.

David Ginola Versus Rodney Marsh

Think of David Ginola and what do you see? Those swashbuckling runs down the left flank for Newcastle and Spurs. The glitzy goals. The shampoo ads. The swooning ladies. And Rodney didn't like it one bit.

On one weekend, we had Rodney, Matt Le Tissier, Charlie Nicholas and David Ginola all on the same panel, which must have been one of the most skilful punditry teams in the history of the game. David came into Sky and was Gallic charm personified. He went down to make-up, kissed all the girls, and introduced himself as 'Da-veed'. Some of the staff, with the best will in the world, are on the wrong side of 50. Nevertheless, he treated everyone with the same level of grace and charm, and of course all the girls' tongues were hanging out. Some of the blokes, too, I'd imagine.

Not Rodney's. During the course of the afternoon, he disagreed with Da-veed over most things. It got to a stage where, even though they were sitting next to each other on the panel, they were almost back-to-back in their chairs. The atmosphere was awful, not that it bothered Rodney. He thrived on it. When we began to discuss Manchester United's home form, Rodney turned to Da-veed and said, 'I don't know. What do you think about this one, Dave?'

Ginola just looked at him and said, 'Dave? My name is Da-veed, not Dave.'

This was exactly the reaction Marshy wanted. From then on, he would not let it go. 'You're getting a bit shirty there, Dave,' he sniped. I remember as we left the studio that night, I was walking through the car park with Da-veed and I asked him whether he enjoyed being on the show. He gave that Gallic shrug and sighed.

'I deed very much, Jeff. But that Rod-nee. Ee is not a very nice man, is ee?'

Certainly Rodney could go too far at times. I remember we had a live interview with the then-Sheffield Wednesday manager, Chris Turner. Now Chris is a lovely bloke and an interesting guy as well. I suppose he has a slightly monotone voice, but when I was interviewing him, Rodney sat next to me tapping his pen and yawning as loudly as he could. I'm sure Chris could hear him. And when the interview finished, Rodney said, 'God, how interesting was he?'

I was livid. I said, 'A lot more interesting than you usually are.'

I felt I had to put him down at points like that, otherwise he would have considered it the norm and tried to push it even further next time around.

VERDICT: Guilty.

Jeff Stelling Versus Rodney Marsh

For reasons unknown, people seemed to think that Rodney and I didn't get on. That may have been down to our prickly relationship on-screen, but in reality, no matter how often we argued in the studio, which was often, we were great friends away from the cameras. The bickering and debating was all part of the show. Often it made for great telly, especially when discussing the not so exciting facets of the Premier League. You can't beat a good row, can you?

You had to be sharp with Rodney, because Rodney was a very sharp guy. In many ways, he was the star of the programme. Whenever people referred to the presenters on the show they would always talk about Jeff and Rodney, or Rodney and Jeff. He was definitely the top draw on the programme and he loved it. There was nothing wrong with that, but it meant you had to be on your mettle with him all the time because he was desperate to make a scene whenever he could.

By the end we had an almost-telepathic understanding between us. I knew if I asked Rodney a certain type of question, I would get a certain type of answer. He knew the response I generally expected to get and he would deliver it, without fail. Think of it as an old strike partnership in the same vein as Alan Shearer and Teddy Sheringham, or Gary Lineker and Peter Beardsley of England. With me being Gary Lineker, of course. We were on the same wavelength 99 per cent of the time.

I remember he was watching one game, and I asked him, 'What's happening at Anfield, Rodney?'

He looked across at me blankly and said, 'Nothing.'

'What, nothing? Nothing at all?'

'No, Jeff, nothing at all.'

'Well, come on Rodney, who's the better team?'

'Neither of them are, Jeff.'

'Somebody must be?'

'No, Jeff, they're both rubbish.'

This would happen in a quickfire way and it would work really well. But he could be prickly, and difficult, and spiky, and awkward and opinionated as well, but he could also be really funny. He would come into the studio in varying moods. I remember asking him a question about the England manager's job and he looked across the desk and said, 'Why are you asking me?'

I couldn't believe it. I said, 'Because you are paid to give an opinion, Rodney.'

Then he had the cheek to say, 'Why don't you ask one of the others?'

I insisted on asking him and he responded by saying, 'Oh, I don't know, what do you think, Frank [McLintock]?'

That was his way of getting out of it because he didn't want to get involved in the debate. On other occasions he would jump into somebody else's response because he wanted to get involved. But that was the way he was. He was a maverick, and some people thought of him as a comedian or a clown. But he was spot on in his opinions more often than not, even though at the time he seemed to be talking rubbish. For example, we laughed at him when he said, about six or seven years ago, 'Jeff, I'm telling you now, in five years time, there will be players in the Premier League earning over £100,000 a week.' We thought he was mad. Sadly, he was absolutely on the money. Quite literally.

Then, of course, he would come up with ludicrous Native American sayings and present them on air, usually as nuggets of football wisdom. I'm sure they were phrases he'd picked up from the inside of a fortune cookie, but among the highlights were:

'The longest journey starts with a small step.'

Translation: (Sounding a lot like an ancient Chinese proverb!) If you're going to win the Champions League, you'll have to beat the rubbish Icelandic no-hopers in the opening round.

'Even the blind squirrel can sometimes find the nut.'

Translation: Sometimes rubbish teams like Bradford City can get a result against great teams like Arsenal.

He could also be quite provocative. You knew something controversial was coming out of his gob when he started a sentence with the words, 'In my opinion, and this is only my opinion, Jeff ...' which would then be followed by, 'I would rather stare at the sun than watch Titus Bramble play,' or, 'I'd rather have broken glass jabbed into my eyes than watch Middlesbrough.' As you can see, it was all rather charmless, but it made for great TV.

Rodney was also one of the first panellists to start the whole shouting phenomenon during match reports, but he would use that to wind you up, too. During the show he would shout loudly. Naturally I'd assume that there had been some dramatic turn of events at Anfield or St James' Park, and would yell excitedly, 'What's happened at Newcastle, Rodney?'

'Half-time, Jeff.'

It was brilliant entertainment.

He would also rub the other panellists up a treat. During one debate he said to Phil Thompson: 'Thommo, you've made a really good point there ... for a change.' Thommo did not like it one bit. But he wasn't the only one who suffered. Rodney was constantly making barbed comments at other people in the studio, but it really livened up the show. It was his maverick side coming out and he felt he had to build that image to a degree.

Thinking about it, he was exactly the same as a player: when he was on the field for QPR, Manchester City and Fulham, he was different. He was different class, too, but it's best not to mention that to him in case his ego spirals even further out of control. Still, Rodney was brash and flash on the pitch. He was flash and brash as a panellist, too, and it worked really well. I remember thinking he was a fantastic signing when he first joined. It was such a shame that he left under such a cloud in 2005.

VERDICT: Not guilty.

The World (And Mother Nature) Versus Rodney Marsh

Rodney was sacked by Sky under controversial circumstances. He had gone onto Sky's late-night phone-in show, *You're On Sky Sports*, and was asked a question about Newcastle United. There were rumours that David Beckham might be on his way to St James' Park. Rodney was having none of it.

'Becks won't be going to Newcastle after what the Toon Army did in Asia,' he said.

Of course, this was a reference to the tsunami disaster that had killed so many people months previously and it was indefensible. I didn't see it at the time, but I heard about it the next day. Sky issued an apology and Rodney was dismissed. Typically Rodney's comments made national news, as this report from the BBC demonstrates:

Football pundit Rodney Marsh has been fired by Sky Sports for making a joke on air about the tsunami disaster.

The ex-Manchester City striker, 60, joked David Beckham had turned down a move to Newcastle United because of trouble with the 'Toon Army in Asia'.

A Sky Sports spokesman said: "These remarks should never have been made and Sky would like to offer its apologies to those who were offended."

Marsh said: "I am hugely disappointed in myself for letting them down."

"Toon Army" is a term used by Newcastle's fans to describe themselves.

Marsh made the comments during a live phone-in programme, *You're on Sky Sports*, on Monday. A spokesman for the channel described the joke as "offensive and inexcusable".

"An apology was made within the programme and Rodney's comments were edited and removed from later transmissions," he said.

Marsh, who also played for Fulham and is known for his outspoken views on football, insisted he did not intend to offend viewers.

"I apologize unreservedly for any offence I caused by my thoughtless and inappropriate comment I made last night," he said.

"My intention was to make a light-hearted football joke."

The daftest thing was, Rodney told me afterwards that he'd thought of the gag in the commercial break. He then sat there thinking, 'Shall I use this or not?' Later, he decided to go with it. He then told me that it was the worst decision he'd ever made in his life. I said to him, 'Rodney, even if it was the best gag in the world, if you had the slightest sliver of doubt about it, you shouldn't have used it.'

Of course, he did, and it rightly caused uproar. Thousands of people had lost their lives. Others had lost loved ones in the tsunami. It really wasn't something you could make light of in any shape or form and Rodney was taken out of his job immediately. Clearly, it was just an error of judgement, and in live TV, presenters will always make errors of judgement, but this one was more costly than most.

I must admit to immediately thinking, 'How are we going to get by without Rodney?' – because he was such a big part of the show. I also thought that it would just blow over and he would be back in a couple of months. But of course he wasn't. There was even a debate about it on talkSPORT radio. Mike Parry was talking about whether 'Jeff Stelling had anything to do with Rodney's sacking because they never really got on that well when they were working together on a Saturday afternoon'. I was in fits of rage! I guess that was the impression that we gave on the show, but it couldn't have been further from the truth. I was immediately on the phone to Rodney's agent to explain that there wasn't any truth in the comments, but she had already been on to the station to demand a retraction and an apology. In fairness to talkSPORT, they obliged, but it was indicative of how people viewed our friendship and working relationship.

There was no way back for Rodney after that. It was the straw that broke the camel's back as far as Sky were concerned. He had sailed too close to the wind too often at that point. It was a difficult situation because that controversial attitude was exactly what Sky had originally wanted from Rodney and that's what he delivered. Sadly, Rodney couldn't stop himself from going too far and that was his flaw.

VERDICT: Guilty.

15

'Unbelievable!'

Eleven Facts You Didn't Know About Chris Kamara. And One You Probably Did.

FACTFILE: CHRIS KAMARA

BORN: 25 December 1957

CLUBS: Portsmouth (1975-7),
Swindon Town (1977-81),
Portsmouth (1981), Brentford
(1981-5), Swindon Town (1985-8), Stoke City
(1988-90), Leeds United (1990-1), Luton Town
(1991-3), Sheffield United (1992-3, loan),
Middlesbrough (1993, loan), Sheffield United
(1993-4), Bradford City (1994-5)

HONOURS: (Leeds United) League
Championship 1991

INTERNATIONAL CAPS: (England) You've got to
be joking.

1. He was a rather good footballer, actually. (That didn't come from me, OK?)

From what I can remember, Chris was quite a rugged player during his career with Portsmouth, Swindon, Portsmouth (again), Brentford, Swindon (again. Notice a pattern here?), Stoke City, Leeds, Luton, Sheffield United, Middlesbrough, Sheffield United (I told you) and Bradford City. Of course, 'rugged' could always read as 'late', or even 'clumsy', but Kammy assures me that he wasn't a dirty player. By all accounts, any reckless challenges he may have made were down to speed, or lack thereof. He wasn't the fastest player in the world, but he got to the ball as soon as he could, which invariably was about five minutes late.

On the pitch, he would absolutely give his all, however, and by the end of his career Chris suffered from quite a lot of injuries due to his competitive nature. There were one or two triumphs along the way, though I doubt burglars would find too much of note in his trophy cabinet. Still, Chris was at Leeds under manager Howard Wilkinson and won the Division One title in an impressive side that included Gordon Strachan, Mel Sterland and Eric Cantona. It's not uncommon for him to become quite misty-eyed when he recalls those glory days in Yorkshire. I know he wishes he'd spent more time working with Howard Wilkinson simply because he learned so much from him on the training ground.

I don't really remember seeing Kammy play that often, which illustrates an interesting point. He was a real engine-room type of footballer and I was always aware of him – like a lot of limping forwards, I'd imagine – but he wasn't a George Best player where you can recall great goals and flashes of skill. Yet he's carved out an amazing career for himself as a TV football expert, which is a credit to him. I guess that is one of the great things about my job. I can now count some of the world's greatest players – and Chris Kamara – among my close personal friends.

2. He's a modern-day Beatle.

Kammy is one of the most recognisable people in football, which isn't surprising given his distinctive hair and 'tache. How he keeps that fantastically permed barnet in shape, I'll never know, but with the curls and the muzzy, he sometimes gets mistaken for Lionel Richie. Still, I didn't really gauge the extent of his popularity until we went to Japan and Korea for the World Cup under our own steam in 2002. There were three of us – myself, Chris Kamara and Ian Condron, the producer of *Soccer Saturday*.

We'd just gone as fans, but for Chris it became an entirely different experience and it was soon apparent that everybody recognized him wherever we went. Groups of England fans would shout out as we walked down the street. We were hassled for autographs. And a lot of the time we would have to pretend we were looking in shop windows to avoid recognition, and bearing in mind we were in Japan, we didn't have a clue what we were looking at most of the time. Sometimes it could get a bit too much. It was like hanging out with a badly-dressed Justin Timberlake.

3. He's Soccer Saturday's most competitive man.

I remember we did our *Soccer Saturday* Superstars event a few years back for a Christmas special. The first event was scheduled to be swimming. Well, Kammy was despondent. He told me he couldn't swim.

'Have you ever seen a black man swim, Jeff?' he moaned.

Naturally, we all thought he had given up before the competition had even started, but when he turned up to race he had a silver cap pulled tightly over his head and a pair of slinky Speedos on. All over his body he had written the words, 'Unbelievable, Jeff!', and the minute he got into the pool he was brilliant. The bastard could swim like a fish and he came second only to Alan McInally. Later, he claimed he'd been having lessons.

Talking about taking things too seriously, during our aforementioned trip to Japan the weather was hot, very hot. We were drinking a fair amount of 'liquids' to keep ourselves refreshed, particularly in the early hours of the morning, and so to stay in shape we used to go for road runs during the day. On one occasion we were all a bit the worse for wear. Nevertheless, we still went running with Kammy in the morning and, as always, it was a real struggle to keep up with him. But it was about to get worse, much worse. I don't think it was intended to humiliate us, but Chris suddenly decided to hop for the last couple of miles. Even then, we couldn't keep up! I dread to think what any locals must have thought if they saw us – it must have looked ridiculous. Maybe they thought it was some kind of European ritual. Either that or, 'Why is Lionel Richie hopping down the road?'

4. He's a karaoke demon.

Kammy is a singer, and he loves it. In Japan we couldn't get him out of the karaoke bars. He's pretty good, too – he once appeared at the Birmingham Symphony Hall and did a charity gig there. He even sings in a jazz club in London, and among the numbers he regularly performs are 'Stuck in the Middle', 'Honesty' by Billy Joel, 'Brown Eyed Girl', and Barry Manilow's 'Mandy'. As you can see, it's a wide range.

Recently we did a Christmas Special aping *The X Factor* called *The Y Factor* and he was brilliant in it. He didn't win, but he was fantastic. Still, I remember during that particular show, former Palace player and *Soccer Saturday* panellist John Salako sang 'Don't Let The Sun Go Down On Me', and was also excellent. Afterwards he came up to me and said, 'Jeff, that was one of the greatest days of my life. I've always wanted to be a singer. Now maybe I can.'

I could almost detect a tear in his eye. I said 'John, this is *The Y Factor*, it's not *The X Factor*. There's no Simon Cowell here.' Sometimes our panellists can get a little carried away.

5. He's a fearsome practical joker.

On one night during the 2002 World Cup, we were staying in Kyoto, the cultural capital of Japan. We'd decided to go out for a meal and a few drinks. It got to 11 o'clock and, after dinner, Kammy and I thought we'd try to find some adventure, so we strolled up a side street. Outside one bar we noticed lots of motorbikes parked up and inside there were a group of young people, all Japanese. This appeared quite promising because they'd all thrown their keys into a pile in the middle of the table, so we decided to go in out of curiosity. Having ordered a couple of drinks we sat with them, but it quickly became apparent to them that we could speak nothing in the way of Japanese and they could speak no English, but for 45 minutes we had a pleasant time, laughing with each other and at each other (though we never found out what the keys were doing there).

With the fun and games over we decided to call it a night, but as we left, Kammy lurched into me. I nudged one of the motorbikes parked outside, which then tumbled off the side of the road, its handlebars smashing into the back window of the car parked alongside. It was right outside the bar where these kids were drinking and it was clearly one of their motorbikes. Worse, it was also one of their cars. We panicked. All the stories in the Japanese press at the time were that the English hooligans were coming to town and would cause trouble. We had single-handedly proven the headlines right. Simultaneously, I looked at Kammy, Kammy looked at me and we both shouted, 'Run!'

It was like something out of *Only Fools and Horses*. We began to sprint, past the bar, past the local police station, and into our hotel lobby. I said to Kammy, 'That was lucky, but nobody will ever find us.' I felt bad, but quite relieved.

Chris looked concerned. 'Oh yeah, tall black moustachioed man and short fat Geordie smash car window,' he said. 'There's thousands of them in Kyoto, isn't there?'

My heart sank. He was right, because even in Kyoto people would recognize Kammy and his handsome sidekick. We sat in the hotel foyer the next day nursing hangovers and feeling like wanted men. Every time a policeman came around the corner, Kammy jumped out of his seat in fear, figuring that we'd been rumbled.

The next night at three in the morning, I got the phonecall we'd been dreading: a stern sounding Japanese voice on the other end of the line wanted to ask me a few questions regarding a vandalized car downtown.

'Hello, Mr Stelling. This is the Head of Kyoto Police here.'

I thought, 'Oh no, Kammy was right, they've got the moustachioed black man and short, fat Geordie.' After five minutes of sweating and imagining the horrors of a Japanese prison, the voice said, 'I'd like you to report to the station and ask for Captain Kamara.'

The cheeky sod had stitched me up a treat.

6. He has the ear of football's most-respected names.

Kammy is amazingly influential within football circles. This often comes as a surprise to people when you tell them, but if you're with Kammy and his phone rings, it really could be anyone, from an agent or a current Premier League manager to someone from the ruling bodies or a sponsor. Everybody speaks to Kammy on just about anything because he has a high profile, but his expertise and knowledge of the game are also very impressive.

Among others, Kammy has close connections with Middlesbrough, Paul Jewell and Steve Bruce. I know that during the 2007/08 season, then-Chelsea boss Avram Grant wanted to take him out for dinner. He's on good terms with just about anyone of note within the game. The main reason? He understands football. He's played the game at a high level and has managed at Bradford and Stoke. He also understands the business side of things. I know for instance that he recommended Jérémie Aliadière to Middlesbrough. The club then bought him for £2 million from Arsenal, which was an absolute steal.

7. He didn't realize just how much he used the phrase 'Unbelievable!'

Unbelievably, Kammy claims he was unaware that he used the phrase 'Unbelievable!' so much. He reckons we realized before he did, but I don't know where and when it took hold. I believe him, because we once went down to Fratton Park where there had been an amazing turn of events in one match. Chris was reporting on the game and I teed him up to deliver his catchphrase:

'Chris, there's only one word to describe that. What is it?'

'Fantastic, Jeff!'

He missed the cue because he actually didn't know there was a cue. It's since become a word in the English vocabulary that is intrinsically linked with him. What football fan hears the word 'unbelievable' without thinking of Chris Kamara?

8. He's the nation's most indiscreet man.

When he goes to football grounds as part of his match-reporting duties, managers, players and coaches will talk to him in a way they wouldn't talk to me or a standard reporter. They'll discuss all the nuances of the game. Some of them will even tell him tactical switches and team line-ups, even though he is the most indiscreet man I know. Before any match he reports on, he'll probably chat to the backroom staff and management. He'll be told – in the utmost confidentiality – the starting line-ups of both teams. He'll often promise not to breathe a word to anyone, especially not a live audience of millions. Not that this means anything to Kammy. During the pre-match build-up he'll often turn to the camera and say something along the lines of, 'Jeff, I can't tell you the teams,

I've been sworn to secrecy, but Wigan are unchanged from last week and Lucas Neill plays for West Ham.'

9. He's been approached to manage some pretty big names in football.

I know that Chris has had plenty of offers to go back into the game as a manager. He's been offered several management jobs, and there's even been talk of a Director of Football role at one Premier League club. I think Chris believes that if he could do TV and management, then he would go for it, but you can't do both. The commitment is too great. I also think he'd be reluctant to give up what he has achieved at *Soccer Saturday* and Sky in terms of reputation, recognition and financial rewards. Furthermore, given the current life-expectancy in football these days, it could only be a very brief return to the game.

10. He could have been an admiral in the Navy. Well, maybe ...

Chris actually started his career in the Royal Navy, when his first club, Portsmouth, came calling. He was serving in the forces, though it was clear he was a pretty handy footballer and he soon switched trades. Who knows? Had things worked out differently, one of Her Majesty's Ships could conceivably have been managed by Commander Kamara, though I suspect he would have been more Captain Birdseye than Admiral Nelson.

11. He has a TV in every room of his house ...

... even his steam room. Not that I've ever been in Kammy's steam room.

12. He sometimes talks a load of nonsense.

Don't believe me? Enjoy the following examples ...

'Has anyone gone close?'
'No, Jeff, but there have been a couple of near misses.'

'He's up like a kangaroo!'

'Not only has he shown him the red card, but he's sent him off.'

'It's end-to-end stuff, but it's all at the Forest end.'

'The atmosphere here is thick and fast.'

'The ball has just crept either side of the post.'

'For Burnley to win, they're going to have to score a goal.'

'There's only one man to thank for that goal – Alan Shearer. And they've also got to thank the referee, Alan Wiley.'

Unbelievable, indeed.

16

Cocoa, Pipe And Slippers (Né Champagne) Charlie

FACTFILE: CHARLIE NICHOLAS

BORN: 30 December 1961
CLUBS: Celtic (1980-3), Arsenal (1983-7), Aberdeen (1987-90), Celtic (1990-5), Clyde (1995-6)
HONOURS: (Celtic) Scottish League Championship 1981, 1982; Scottish Cup 1995; Scottish League Cup 1983; (Arsenal) League Cup 1987
INTERNATIONAL CAPS: (Scotland) 20

If you hadn't guessed it by simply studying *Soccer Saturday* (religiously, with affection), Charlie Nicholas is a bugger – a real one-off, and a top-of-the-range wind-up merchant. I suppose this is a blessing of sorts because with all the gags and jokes, he's a perennial source of laughs, usually at my expense. Don't believe me? Well, next time you watch the show, if you're not being dragged around Habitat that is, take note of how often he pokes fun at my svelte physique and athletic ability. Elsewhere, whenever there's a commercial break, Charlie will be glued to one of the tellies in the studio (not the one he's supposed to be watching), betting slip in hand as he studies another 'dead cert' romping home to last place at the three twenty at Kempton, regardless of what's going on in the programme at the time.

In fact, he's a bloody nuisance with the tellies. Look beyond those five handsome devils on the studio panel and you can see the Sky Sports research team beavering away like an army of stat-obsessed worker drones. The eagle-eyed among you will have also noticed that there's a TV on pretty much every desk in their office, which hasn't gone unnoticed by Charlie. During any lulls in the show, he'll start hammering the buttons on a remote control that he's had hidden beneath his desk for years. From there, he'll constantly flick the TVs from channel to channel, much to the general bemusement of Sky's research platoon. One minute they're watching a live feed from a Premier League game. The next, they're staring at Harold Bishop's portly figure on the *Neighbours* omnibus. It's all very confusing for them and nobody's really worked out who's been up to mischief. Well, until now.

This image as a practical joker doesn't come as too much of a surprise. I guess with his styled hair and fancy threads, Charlie would like to think of himself as a Blues Brother for the 21st century. He'll walk into the *Soccer Saturday* office in designer jeans, designer sunglasses and designer T-shirt with a shout of 'Morning!' at the top of his lungs. Still, if asked in the pub, as I am sometimes, to summarize his character, I'll describe him as a diamond geezer, even if he does insist on wearing that stupid, diamond stud earring. I keep telling him he's too old for that kind of thing, but he won't listen. Still, it's all part of the exuberant showmanship that arrives in bundles every week.

The first act of theatre that Charlie delivers to our Saturday morning – after wowing us with his fancy dress sense and acerbic humour, that is (I'm sorry, I know sarcasm is the lowest form of wit) – is the details of his 'Bet For The Day'. Anyone who knows him will tell you the same thing: Charlie is desperate to be a millionaire. Actually, I'm not so sure he isn't one already, so let's say he's desperate to be a multimillionaire, but worryingly his financial master plan for financial success hinges on a rock-solid, credit-crunch-proof exercise in 'mathletics'. Actually it doesn't. Instead, he'll pick a 20-team accumulator, where all 20 results have to go in his favour. A cool million-quid cash bonanza awaits at the end if he gets it right, which he never does.

The more worldly-wise among you (and Paul Merson) will know that the odds are stacked against him. And heavily. In fact, Charlie's bet always sinks without trace, usually by Friday evening in fact, when his first 'winning' team crashes to a 4–0 defeat and wipes out the entire flutter. You can't knock his unwavering belief, though. As Winston Churchill once said: 'Success is about going on from one failure to the next without losing enthusiasm.' Or something like that. Charlie has clearly taken note, because with that first, crushing defeat, he'll point to his crumpled betting slip and show you his stake (never more than a pound) and the potentially mind-boggling, but ultimately unlikely, winnings (like I say, always in excess of a million). With a swig of wine, he'll then predict a change in fortunes for the following week. Sadly, I don't think he's ever scored more than five correct results, so his Roman Abramovich days are probably a long way off.

Thinking about it, Charlie has enjoyed quite a flamboyant career thus far, so maybe scooping a handsome win at the bookies wouldn't be completely beyond the realms of possibility. Certainly, he enjoyed something of a charmed life as a player. At the tender age of 19, he made his first-team debut for Celtic in 1980. By 1983, he became a goalscoring sensation, grabbing 50 goals in the 1982/83 season (don't get too excited, they were only scored in Scotland) while scooping the Scottish Footballer of the Year and Scottish PFA Young Player of the Year trophies for his mantelpiece, which I gather was cluttered with hair products and bottles of Blue Stratos at the time, given his status as the sport's hottest football pin-up long before David Beckham made a nation of mums swoon with his sarong and silly haircuts.

In hindsight, his showy attitude was probably Charlie's biggest problem. He was reportedly offered playing contracts by both Liverpool and Manchester United, turning them down for an £800,000 transfer to Arsenal and the lure of the capital. After a few glasses of wine he's told me that this was probably the biggest mistake of his career. He probably wasn't thinking about that when the club gave him a guided tour of his fancy new digs in North London, positioned, as they were, above a casino. Even better, it was open all hours. Charlie's romance with the bright lights of London was off to a flyer. Good grief, could you imagine Arsène Wenger housing one of his prodigious signings in such a place? Bryan Robson, maybe, but certainly not Arsène Wenger.

It was from here that his career hit the skids a little. Charlie only scored 11 goals in his first season at Highbury, though two came in a win against Spurs, so that modest figure was glossed over by the fans. Worse, he picked up the name 'Champagne Charlie', such were his exploits at home. Well, at home by the casino's roulette wheel. There he gathered a reputation for liking a glass or two of the good stuff and a girl (or two), but before you start tut-tutting, I'd like to stress for friendship reasons (though the words here on this rather wordy fax on my table at Winchester's northbound service station read, 'legal reasons') that this has totally changed. Charlie is very much the family man. In fact, his lawyer would prefer it if you dropped the 'Champagne' tag and all referred to him as 'Cocoa, Pipe and Slippers Charlie'.

Joking aside, I remember the headlines, the earrings and the Farrah Fawcett haircuts like every other fan from that time, but I don't remember his goals. Charlie shouldn't be too offended, though. At times the Stelling brain is a sieve, and I guess that this is as good a moment as any to admit that I don't really remember much about anything when it comes to football games from the good old days. It's a shocking admission, I know. I guess in my position as anchorman of *Soccer Saturday*, I should be a database of goals, scorers, penalty saves and results from a time before Frank McLintock was born, but I'm not. There are more football gaps in my knowledge than the Newcastle back four.

Worse, when it comes to recalling player's careers, I have a terrible memory. I even have trouble remembering performances, cup wins and match-winning strikes. To my shame, when fellow panellist Tony Cottee asked me to pick out one of his goals - 'No, *your* favourite goal, Jeff' - for a DVD he'd been putting together, well, I scratched my head for days, but I couldn't think of one. I said,

'Tony could you pick out a goal for me, I'm embarrassed to say that I can't think of any.'

He wasn't pleased. 'Cheers Jeff,' he said, crestfallen. 'I've scored however many hundred goals and you can't remember one.'

I told him not to take it too hard, before pointing out that I could probably remember some of his penalty misses if that would cheer him up.

I've digressed slightly here, but it dovetails neatly into a nice excuse for not recalling Charlie's career in glorious technicolour, HD and surround sound, because what Charlie did on the pitch was almost secondary to what Charlie did off it. Image was everything. In fact, somewhere among the works of Chaucer, Shakespeare and *Viz* in my drawer at work, I have a wordy tome called *Footballers' Haircuts* which carries a picture of Charlie looking resplendent with an extravagantly blow-dried hairstyle. More disturbingly, he's posing in a pair of rather snug Y-fronts. It really is enough to make Freddie Ljungberg blush, but it didn't matter at the time, because for some reason, the ladies loved him. Then again, those were probably the same sort of ladies who lusted after David Essex and wore all-in-one, DayGlo shell suits while wobbling their perms along to Mad Lizzie's workout on *TV-am*.

Who am I kidding? I'm only jealous. And who wouldn't be, given his opulent lifestyle?

Was Charlie a drinker? Yes. Was he a womanizer? Yes. Was he a gambler? Have a guess.

I can only do two of these things (and not particularly well), though for my own ego I won't reveal the weak link in my playboy image. Charlie, however, played a blinder at all three, as well as being a good player. I think at the time he was often compared to George Best on the pitch, which was a heavy burden to carry in some respects. I think at the time he was often compared to George

Best off the pitch, too. So it's understandable that he's more than happy to joke about his former reputation. In one show, he even confessed on air: 'Jeff, we would sometimes go out and have fights. There would be a fracas, there would be girl problems, and there would be drink problems ...'

'But enough of last night, Charlie,' I interrupted before he could explain himself. 'What was it like when you were at Arsenal?'

However, if you were to judge him by the fancy cover, you'd probably have him down as a flash pundit, big on mouth and lacking in substance. In reality he's a very sharp guy, and a relatively straight outlet of info on the show. When it comes to talking about football, he says things as he sees them. He might be off the mark, but there's rarely a throwaway statement, or an ill-considered comment for shock effect.

I know that if we ever need a sensible response to anything, I'll always go to Charlie first. He knows his stuff, he knows football, and he still works with a lot of people in the game. He's big mates with Jerome Anderson, who is one of the biggest agents in the Premier League, which gives Charlie the inside track on some of the biggest stories in football.

He can also be tough and uncompromising, which helps in the show's sometimes-heated debates. This mean streak isn't confined to the studio either. I remember we were sitting in the Marriot in Heathrow on a Friday night before the show. This used to be one of our old haunts for a drink or two, but that night a couple of guys came over for a chat at the bar. That was fine; we like that kind of thing for a while – it passes the time when you're waiting for Kammy to turn up after his karaoke night. After a while we excused ourselves because we wanted to talk about the show the next day. Anyway, five minutes later, they came over and wanted to join us again. I would have been uncomfortable with it, but wouldn't have had the front to say, 'No.' Charlie is a different animal, however.

'No, we do mind,' he said. 'We've spent some time with you, now go away.'

He did it firmly but fairly, and I was impressed. It takes a certain kind of character to act that way, but he was right to do it.

Cut through the flash exterior and Charlie knows how to play the TV game, however. I suppose he delivers those Laurel and Hardy-esque comedy one-liners in a similar manner to Rodney Marsh. The difference between the two is that Charlie isn't quite as abrasive. He knows where the line is and doesn't cross it. I remember watching one match where I cut the cameras to Charlie.

'Honestly, this could be 10-0,' he said.

I said, 'Charlie, you are exaggerating.'

'Jeff,' he laughed, 'I've told you a million times, I do not exaggerate.'

Of course, like all panellists, he can plant his foot in it on occasions. In one famous faux pas recently, he was talking about Ryan Giggs' neverending career. The panel were having quite a serious conversation about what a great servant he had been to Manchester United. Mid-conversation, Charlie blurted out, 'Of course, Sir Alex fathered Ryan Giggs.'

An eerie silence fell over the studio as the realization of what he had said sunk in. I couldn't help myself: 'Well, that's one heck of a headline for the Sunday newspapers to get their teeth into, isn't it Charlie?'

He dissolved into tears, knowing that what he'd really meant to say was that Alex had acted as a father figure to Ryan Giggs.

There are moments when Charlie can surprise you. During the 2007/08 season, for example, we were talking about the players that Arsenal might consider selling during the coming summer. I turned to Charlie on air and asked his opinion.

In a flash, he said, 'I reckon they should sell Adebayor.'

I couldn't believe it. Adebayor had tallied up in excess of 20 goals at that stage. I said, 'What?! He's their top scorer.'

'He's not pulling his weight,' he argued. 'He's not been playing nearly as well in the second half of the season as he was in the first. They should get rid of him.'

Charlie had just come back from a weekend in New York. 'Mate,' I said, 'I thought you'd come back from New York, not from therapy.'

Because he's so knowledgeable, it makes it all the more fun when Charlie gets things wrong. During the 2007/08 campaign, Wigan's pitch was absolutely shocking. It was also coming under some fire from the panel. I said, 'Yes, Wigan's pitch is shocking, but do you remember the pitch at Birmingham when [former Birmingham manager, then-Wigan manager] Steve Bruce was there? It was diabolical. What must his garden be like?'

Clearly, Charlie hadn't been listening. 'And if you remember rightly, Jeff, the pitch at Birmingham was terrible too when Steve Bruce was there.'

He'd been on another planet for 30 seconds and we slaughtered him. Sometimes, it's easy to take the piss out of Thommo, Merse or Le Tiss, because they get tongue-tied quite regularly. Charlie isn't quite so easy a target. When it does happen, though, it's an occasion to be cherished. A bit like one of his goals.

Note to appease legal eagles and miffed former Scottish playboy strikers:

Seriously though, ladies and gentlemen, the Champagne Charlie image doesn't ring true these days. When it comes to talking about football – or anything for that matter: wine, women, song – Charlie is as intelligent as they come. Not that it always shows on the programme. Still, he's happily married with a family. He invests in property abroad – I hear he has an annual pass to Legoland in France, which he's forever bragging about – and the Nicholas lifestyle is a far cry from his days residing above and below a London casino. Be warned, though: he does pay his bets in Scottish £20 notes. Try passing those over the bar in a Hampshire pub.

17

'Sit Down, Pinocchio!'

FACTFILE: PHIL BERNARD THOMPSON

BORN: 21 January 1954
CLUBS: Liverpool, Liverpool, Liverpool, Liverpool, he may have played for Liverpool (1971–84), Sheffield United (1984–6)
HONOURS: (Liverpool) Nearly as many cups as Roy of the Rovers – League Championship 1973, 1976, 1977, 1979, 1980, 1982, 1983; FA Cup 1974; League Cup 1981, 1982; European Cup 1978, 1981; UEFA Cup 1973, 1976; European Super Cup 1977
INTERNATIONAL CAPS: (England) 42

Viewers, there's a little-known fact about Phil 'Thommo' Thompson, former Liverpool legend, European champion and England captain; one that involves his attire on an average *Soccer Saturday* afternoon. Anyone watching the show for the first time might think that with his smart suits and fancy ties he cuts quite the sartorial dash for our studio cameras. But if one were to zoom in for a shot beneath his desk, viewers would be surprised to see him wearing a pair of 1983/84 Liverpool shorts, as worn in the European Cup Final against Roma.* It's quite an unpleasant sight, especially with those legs.

For those of you familiar with the show, though, this revelation isn't entirely shocking. Thommo is arguably the most biased of the *Soccer Saturday* panellists; more so than Frank 'put your Arsenal rattle away' McLintock and George 'United' Best ever were, though maybe not as bad as Paul 'I really can't stand Tottenham' Merson. He's Liverpool through and through. He bleeds red. Rumour has it that there's a photo of Bill Shankly in every room in the Thompson household.**

On one hand this can be a good thing: I like a bit of passion on the show. On the other, there have been moments where his bias has gone too far. I can recall matches where Liverpool have been losing, sometimes spectacularly, and at a point where a watching Thommo should have been praising (not to mention expertly analysing) the opposition's performance, he's instead reserved his time on air for a dissection of Liverpool's weaknesses. Of course, this has led to some rather one-sided post-match evaluations,

---

*Of course, Thommo isn't really wearing the shorts from the 1983/84 European Cup Final. He's actually wearing the trackie bottoms.

** This also might be a little fib.

which, I'd imagine, has resulted in a number of foul-mouthed tirades up and down the country.

There is a balance, however. Thommo's loyalty isn't simply one of blind faith. He's more than happy to criticize Liverpool if he feels upset at the way they're playing or handling their business affairs. Certainly, he's been as embarrassed as anyone regarding the purchase of Liverpool by current American owners George Gillett and Tom Hicks, not to mention the subsequent controversy and supposed behind-the-scenes arguments. He wasn't afraid to say so, either, though initially he was very supportive of the takeover. As the atmosphere turned sour at Anfield, however, he began to express his discontent. Since then, it would be fair to say that Phil has been one of those supporting a fans' buy-out of the club along with ace Liverpool supporter Dr Rogan Taylor. The pair of them were even looking at the models of clubs owned by supporters abroad. Thommo is very keen on that idea and I know he's been to a lot of the meetings to discuss plans.

Elsewhere, the Gareth Barry transfer debacle during the summer of 2008 was a particularly sensitive issue for Thommo. The way in which Liverpool publicly vocalised their desire to sign the Villa midfielder could have been viewed as being deliberately unsettling. It certainly wasn't in keeping with the gentlemanly traditions installed at Liverpool by managers such as Bill Shankly and Bob Paisley. Villa manager Martin O'Neill definitely believed so and criticized the club. He claimed, 'That's not the way that Liverpool used to do things.' Thommo was in agreement. He felt Liverpool shouldn't have conducted their business in that manner and said so on the programme.

These opinions are fundamental to the show. But Thommo also has a distinct advantage over his *Soccer Saturday* peers when providing an expert opinion, given that he's worked at Anfield in both a playing and coaching capacity. Currently in his second spell on the desk, his two stints sandwiched an assistant manager's role in supporting former manager Gérard Houllier which lasted for six years, though his appointment in 1998 was a bolt out of the blue for everyone.

As he tells it, there was a mysterious phone call from the club one afternoon. Thommo really had no idea what it was all about. Houllier had just been appointed and Thommo figured that maybe Liverpool were looking to bring in some old faces to work with the youth team or to oversee the club's scouting networks. This was just an educated hunch, however, because he had never met Houllier before. Shortly afterwards, he was called over to chairman David Moores' house for a meeting with all the top brass. Before he knew it, the board were asking him to rejoin the club as right-hand man to the new gaffer.

Thommo couldn't believe it. I think he was expecting a minor position in coaching at best. He had even told his wife that, while he'd love to get back into football, he'd really only expect to do something on a minor level. Coaching the reserves, he reckoned, would probably be too big a leap. When he heard of Liverpool's designs, well, he had to work hard to stifle his disbelief. And if you've ever seen Thommo on the touchline or sitting on the *Soccer Saturday* panel, you'll know just how difficult that must have been.

When I heard he'd got the job, I was absolutely chuffed for him. Liverpool could not have selected a figure more in-tune with the values of the club. Still, their gain was our loss. After he'd relayed the news, I remember writing him a letter, which I had never done for a panellist before. In it, I told him what a nice bloke I thought he was and what a privilege it had been to work with him. I really hoped it would go well for him at Anfield.

As a player for Liverpool, Thommo was a star. He had a great Shirley Temple hairstyle – a fantastic perm. He once scored a cracking own goal for England against Wales. But bloopers aside, I remember him as being part of a fantastic defensive set-up at Liverpool. He was a great captain and a far better player than people often give him credit for. He was assured in that back four, but was also good enough to play in midfield, too. If you look at the number of caps he earned for England, you soon realize that Thommo was a quality player. Yes, he was in a bloody good club side, but you don't get the caps if you haven't got the ability. Rodney Marsh used to refer to back-four players as 'dopey defenders', but there was nothing dopey about Phil Thompson in the way he played the game or the way he presents himself now.

Sadly, though not altogether unsurprisingly, our relationship changed shortly after his coaching appointment at Anfield. Once you become involved with the mechanics of a football club, the media can feel like an obtrusive nuisance, especially at a club as high-profile as Liverpool where everyone has an opinion on how the team should play, or what players should be brought in or sold. And especially when dealing with a media influence as intrusive and ubiquitous as Sky.

Thommo's loyalties altered, and rightly so. We became the enemy. Our attitude didn't waiver, however: we weren't going to give Liverpool an easy ride just because one of our mates was now sitting in the dugout. Likewise, he wasn't going to jeopardize his position at the club by giving us inside info. But after a year or so of Thommo working at Anfield, we ran a feature that really soured the relationship between Liverpool and *Soccer Saturday* and threatened to ruin our friendship forever.

At the time, during the 2002/03 season, it would have been fair to say that the club had made a handful of unsuccessful transfers.

Yes, Houllier had brought one or two impressive names to Anfield such as Emile Heskey and Gary McAllister, but there were a number of costly stinkers, too, such as Igor Bišćan who had cost £5.5 million from Dinamo Zagreb ... but the list went on, and on, and on. This, twinned with the fact that Liverpool hadn't been playing too well, meant that the management team were in the firing line.

In January that season, we ran a savage piece on the show, criticizing Houllier's costly transfer mistakes. We spliced together supporter's comments and criticisms, newspaper headlines and short interviews with pundits and ex-players. As this was going on, a roll-call of Houllier's signings and their transfer values ran down the screen. I think we may even have played 'You'll Never Walk Alone' as the background music. So it was harsh stuff, but at the same time it was factual and balanced – we listed the good signings as well as the bad, and the feature simply reflected the opinion of the fans. Well, that was my defence anyway.

On the day of this feature, Liverpool were playing away at Southampton in a five-fifteen kick-off. Somewhere in a south coast hotel, the Liverpool squad – along with Houllier, Thommo and their backroom staff – had just finished lunch. All of them were settling down in front of the TV and *Soccer Saturday*, just to kill a bit of time before they made their way to the ground. As 'You'll Never Walk Alone' came through the speakers, the list of shame began to trickle down the TV screen. A deathly silence descended on the team. By all accounts, Gérard Houllier felt so crushed that he had to leave the room. It must have been incredibly humiliating for him to sit there and watch such damning criticism in front of those players. And imagine the reaction of the players highlighted on the list of shame – how must they have felt? It was hard-hitting stuff.

When I heard afterwards, I felt very bad for both Thommo and Gérard Houllier. Liverpool won one-nil and Heskey got the winner, but by all accounts they should have had five. In fact, Thommo has since told me that they used our feature as a motivational tool before the game. Gérard Houllier said, 'Well, if that's what they think of us, we'll show them otherwise.' And they did. So I'm taking some credit because it had a positive impact. And if Gérard is reading this book, then I'd like him to know that that was the intention all along. Who am I kidding?

To say our relationship with Liverpool and Phil was frosty from then on was an understatement. I'd heard that both Phil and Gérard were upset and I can't remember talking to Phil after that. Eventually, the pair would leave the club. Almost immediately we contacted Phil and asked him to rejoin the panel. To be honest, I didn't think for one minute that he would, simply because I figured he might have felt betrayed – I was worried that it might have been the end of a beautiful friendship because we massacred them. Surprisingly, he decided to come back and we were delighted to have him with us again.

This incident highlighted an interesting part of life as a *Soccer Saturday* panellist: just because somebody is your mate, it doesn't mean they're immune from criticism if things go wrong at their club. In the same way, they'll get a pat on the back if things go right. Over the years, I've met a lot of people in football. While I don't want to criticize the people that I like, if things go pear-shaped then you have to. For instance, former Derby boss Paul Jewell is a friend of the show and I like him a heck of a lot – he makes me laugh, he's a top bloke and a man's man – but when Derby were struggling at the end of the 2007/08 campaign and the beginning of 2008/09, we had to ask the question, 'What is he doing?' You just have to hope that people understand when they get criticized.

As for Gérard Houllier, I bumped into him at the League Manager's Awards not long after he'd lost his job. We started to chat and, feeling so embarrassed about the whole affair, I apologized profusely and probably somewhat awkwardly. To my relief he was fine and said, 'Look, I totally understand. I didn't understand at the time, but now I do.' He was absolutely gracious and diplomatic which, in hindsight, made me feel even worse.

These days, Thommo is into his second spell on *Soccer Saturday* and he's great for the show. He's passionate, he's opinionated, he's terrific. And, more importantly, he's very easy to wind up. The great thing about Thommo is that he takes the banter very well (there's plenty of it as well) and he's always happy to give it back. For example, he often makes out that I'm a Liverpool-hater. I always say, 'Phil, but I like Liverpool. Well, the Everton part anyway.' (I'd like to point out to any reading Liverpool fans that I'm not a Liverpool-hater.)

However, the main thrust of Thommo-baiting is reserved for his rather prestigious hooter. It's his nose, rather than his gob, that threatens to overshadow, quite literally, the entire *Soccer Saturday* panel. Not that he's bothered. The title of his autobiography – *Stand Up Pinocchio*, a reference to the terrace chant of 'Sit down, Pinocchio!' which rang out whenever he jumped around Liverpool's technical area – sums it all up really. Thommo is rather proud of his prominent features, but the boys are happy to rib him regardless.

I remember one morning in make-up when Thommo arrived with a healthy tan. We all knew that he had a place in the Canary Islands, so fellow panellist Paul Walsh said, 'You've been out in the Canaries I see then, Thommo?'

It seemed an innocuous question and Thommo responded, 'No it was just a sunbed, to be honest.' Cue fits of stifled giggles.

'A sunbed?' replied Walshy, disbelievingly. 'How the bloody hell did you get the lid down?'

Joking aside, Thommo really comes into his own when commentating on the Liverpool games. It's not unusual to see him throwing his headphones down in frustration, as he did following John Arne Riise's injury-time own goal in the semi-final of the 2008 Champions League against Chelsea. Or even punching Frank McLintock on the arm as he did when Liverpool knocked out Arsenal in the same competition. Still, nothing tops Liverpool's embarrassing exit from the 2008 FA Cup against underdogs Barnsley. I'm sure Liverpool fans (again, it's nothing personal) will be irate to read this, but the fact is, we were deliberately poking fun at Thommo and it was hilarious.

Weirdly, the moment was made all the sweeter by the fact that Thommo wasn't actually commentating on the game – we'd given that responsibility to Matt Le Tissier. Weeks previously, Le Tiss was commentating on the FA Cup tie between Liverpool and non-League 'no-hopers' Havant and Waterlooville where, unbelievably, Liverpool had gone a goal down. At Anfield. As you can imagine, Thommo was absolutely beside himself with embarrassment. It didn't make for pretty viewing for anyone of the red persuasion, least of all Thommo, who then had to endure Paul Merson's fits of laughter afterwards. For everyone else it was a gift from above.

Not to rub salt into Thommo's wounds, but anyone wishing to view these clips can probably find them somewhere on the internet (I hear YouTube is your best bet). But for those of you without a computer (really?!), here's a transcript of both incidents. Now, bear in mind the scene: it's close to the end of the game against Barnsley, Liverpool are being rocked on their heels by a lower-league side. Thommo is squirming ... and the rest of us are loving every bloody minute of it. But first, that Havant and Waterlooville goal.

LIVERPOOL 0 HAVANT AND WATERLOOVILLE 1

MATT LE TISSIER: Goal! Goal!

PAUL MERSON [laughing]: No!

JEFF STELLING: We're going to the commentary because there has been a goal. And you know which way it's gone. Unbelievable, to paraphrase Chris Kamara. Matt Le Tissier!

MATT LE TISSIER: Oh my god [Thommo has his head in his hands at this point]. Oh, Havant and Waterlooville are one-nil up. And it's Pacquette who's got the goal, I think, Jeff. And it's unbelievable! [Pointing to Thommo] Get the camera on that man there. It's one-nil to Havant and Waterlooville! There was a corner ... There are people crying in the stands ... Inswinging corner and Pacquette has been left five yards out on his own in the box ... He's just headed it down and it's gone in. It's one-nil to Havant and Waterlooville!

And then, weeks later ...

LIVERPOOL 1 BARNSLEY 2

JEFF STELLING: Big, big, big shout in front of the Kop at Anfield ... a penalty shout for Barnsley.

[Off-camera] PAUL MERSON: That's a definite penalty, by the way. A certain penalty.

MATT LE TISSIER: Oh my god, [referee] Martin Atkinson, you've bottled it! That was a penalty all day long. Brian Howard got himself in a good position ... he's shot, he's scored! [*Soccer Saturday* panel erupts] Goooooooalll – two-one to Barnsley! And that's justice by the way because he should have been given a penalty just now, Jeff. The referee bottled it in front of the Kop, but he's got possession again, 25 yards out ... great left ... I told you he had a great left foot before the show [Phil Thompson shakes his head disbelievingly]. He struck it with his left foot, it's beaten the keeper at the near post; what a finish to this game. Unbelievable!

JEFF STELLING: Simon Davey is telling his side to keep calm. You're having a laugh! They're going crazy. Crazy at the moment! A wonderful strike from Brian Howard. His 11th of the season. He hadn't scored in his previous eight. He's saved his best right until the final seconds of the game.

How Phil managed to keep calm at that moment, I'll never know. Maybe this unswerving passion for Liverpool is his Achilles heel. I know that rival managers often used to rile him on the touchline to gain some sort of advantage when they were playing at Anfield. The most notable of these was when former Sheffield United manager, and good friend of mine, Neil Warnock took to baiting Thommo during their clash in the 2003 FA Cup.

That afternoon, Thommo was doing what Thommo does best: preparing to blast into orbit with rage, frustration and passion. Meanwhile, Warnock was winding him up like crazy with a few well-aimed jibes. Thommo was going ballistic in the other dugout. It was like watching the Chuckle Brothers going to war. I think they may have nearly come to blows. It was a funny sight, and since then Neil Warnock has been invited into the *Soccer Saturday* studio at the same time as Thommo, but it would be fair to say that those two didn't exactly exchange business cards, or manly hugs, afterwards.

It's this passion that makes Thommo such a great addition to the *Soccer Saturday* panel, though. Where would we be without his bias, tantrums and prominent hooter? Certainly the show is far better for having him back with us, though he is a loss to coaching. It would be interesting to see whether he gets back into football, but I think he enjoys his work with us too much. You can't blame him. Why put yourself in the firing line when you can have so much fun shooting the bullets?

18

The Magic Man

FACTFILE: PAUL CHARLES MERSON

BORN: 20 March 1968
CLUBS: Arsenal (1985-97),
Brentford (loan) (1987),
Middlesbrough (1997-8),
Aston Villa (1998-2002),
Portsmouth (2002-3), Walsall
(2003-6), Tamworth (2006)
HONOURS: (Arsenal) League Championship
1989, 1991; FA Cup 1993; League Cup 1993;
European Cup Winners' Cup 1994
INTERNATIONAL CAPS: (England) 21

Anyone looking for a clue as to why Paul Merson became a fallen hero during his playing career should recall those formative years at Arsenal. The writing was on the wall for Merse from the beginning, especially when considering the troubles that would dog him later in life. While his career was a rush of great goals, fantastic matches and game-winning performances, he was plagued with personal addictions: drugs and gambling for the most part. Merse reckons there are some games that he can't remember playing in, even today, mainly because he was pie-eyed during the 90 minutes on the park. He recalls being so pissed in one game that he fell over. Not under a challenge – there was no one near him – he had simply tried to run, and fell over in not-so-splendid isolation!

The reason for his spectacular shame could be pinpointed to another *Soccer Saturday* panellist, however. When he joined Arsenal he was assigned a mentor to keep him in check. I guess the coaching staff could see that this wide-eyed kid might need a bit of guidance in the big smoke of London. This idea is still popular today. I hear John Carew at Villa keeps an eye on Ashley Young – the idea being that the junior player can pick up good habits while staying on the straight and narrow. The only problem was, when Merse started breaking into the Gunners' first team, they twinned him with 'Champagne' Charlie Nicholas. Is it any surprise it all went pear-shaped?

But while Merse carried that hedonistic streak away from the game, he never held the swagger and arrogance of someone like Mark Bosnich or Adrian Mutu. Merse was just playing the silly little boy act. Somehow, he pulled it off with an innocent, vulnerable charm that remains with him, even now. When he confessed to his problems at an Arsenal press conference – sitting alongside his manager, George Graham, the tears rolling down his face – the majority of football fans felt genuinely sorry for him.

It would be wrong to remember him simply as a hedonist, however. On the pitch, Merse was a maverick, a creative genius who could unlock defences with his tireless running and creativity from midfield or attack. He scooped a few medals as well, most notably with Arsenal where he grabbed a couple of championships, an FA Cup and a European trophy. His drug, drink and gambling problems became public in 1994, though once again, I'd like to make it clear to Charlie's legal team that I'm not really inferring it was his fault.

Merse later moved to Boro for a whopping £5 million, which was the most any non-Premier League club had paid for a player. He then went on to Villa and Pompey, where he helped to kick-start Harry Redknapp's revolution. It's for this reason that Harry has such an affection for him – his skill and vision shaped the club's success in the Premier League. The coaching staff certainly appreciated this and became very protective of him. They knew that if they wrapped Merse in cotton wool and afforded him some privileges, he would deliver for them every weekend.

For example, they would only get him in for training once or twice a week, then they'd let him go home. He was even given extra holiday time if he needed it. Harry tells a great story of when Merse came into his office one day and said, 'Harry I need a bit of time this week, I want to go into a bit of rehab.'

Harry was fine with the situation. He knew Merse was being honest with his problems. He also knew that when they got him on the pitch he would give him his all, so he allowed him to go. He said, 'All right, Merse, right you are son, go and sort yourself out.'

A week later, Harry got a call from a mate of his in Barbados. He said, 'All right, Harry, one of your boys is out here.' Harry was confused and wanted to know which one. 'Paul Merson,' said his mate.

'No, no, no. You've got it wrong,' laughed Harry. 'I spoke to him last week and he's gone into rehab.'

'No, he hasn't, Harry; I can see him across the way. He's sitting at the bar.'

When Merse came in the following week, he was as brown as a berry. Harry called him into the office and said, 'So how was rehab then, Merse?' Merse shrugged, and that was about as far as it went. I think he may even have scored the following week.

These days, Merse only has one gambling problem: he's rubbish at it. He'll come into the office on a Saturday, crack a few jokes, tell a few stories and have us roaring with laughter. Then he'll turn to me conspiratorially and ask, 'Do you fancy East Stirling against Forfar today, Jeff?'

'Er, what, Merse?'

'East Stirling against Forfar,' he'll say. 'It's just that a lot of Forfar players are away working today because they're part-time, so it might work in East Stirling's favour.'

You have to wonder how he knows things like that. Well you don't, because I can tell you: he's making phone calls here, there and bloody everywhere, trying to get the inside track that might help him with any bets he plans to make. Not that they do. You can bet your last dollar that Forfar would have won that game.

I guess the nearest thing I could get to Merse in terms of bad luck is the former snooker player Willie Thorne. Willie and I are good friends and we used to cover snooker tournaments on Sky together. By far, he was the unluckiest gambler I knew – in the history of the universe, most probably. There were times when I would have 10 quid on a horse and Willie would have considerably more on another. The pair of them would come down the last flight, locked together in a steeplechase. Willie would be thinking, 'Please let my horse win!' Meanwhile, I would be thinking, 'Please don't let mine win!' It used to break my heart watching Willie gamble. You knew he was going to lose his money in the most unfortunate and unlikely circumstances.

There was a classic moment when we were at one snooker event, trying to pass the time. As you can imagine, covering these tournaments is quite a slow-moving process – you never really watch the potting of every ball. There were always bookmakers located in the venues and we would have a bet or two. One day, we were wandering around the bookies. Willie had received a great tip and decided to put on a very big bet. We watched the race and, lo and behold, his horse was streaking ahead.

It was clear at the last, probably 20 lengths in front. We were all delighted for Willie because it looked like he was about to have a massive win. Then, all of a sudden, the weight cloth on his rider's saddle fell off. The minute that goes you know the horse is going to be disqualified. When you finish a race you have to weigh the same as when you started. If you don't, you're out. A lost weight cloth meant you were very much out, and Willie knew it.

His face was ashen. Up until then, the horse had jumped every fence in the race. It was 20 yards from the line and he was 20 yards from picking up some seriously big bucks, when a sheer stroke of bad luck had kicked him in the swingers. To put it in perspective, I don't think I've ever seen a weight cloth fall away from a horse before or since. As soon as the horse crossed the line, a steward's inquiry was called. A girl with us said, 'Don't worry Willie, it might still keep the race.'

I think she meant well, but anyone who's been in that situation will tell you it's best to keep your mouth shut. The horse faced automatic disqualification. Luckily for her, Willie's jaw was drooping somewhere on the floor among the ripped-up betting slips, which meant he was unable to answer.

And that's the problem with Merse. He has exactly the same level of misfortune. God, he's unlucky! He doesn't gamble that much these days, and he keeps himself to himself in terms of when he has a big bet, but I know for a fact that he backed Harry Redknapp to take the Newcastle job in the 2007/08 season and lost a lot of money. He had a big stake on it, because he had excellent inside information that Harry was going there – by all accounts he was definitely, definitely taking the Newcastle job. In fact, Merse only just managed to put a bet on before the bookies stopped taking stakes on it because Harry was such a clear favourite.

I'd also been told that Harry had decided he would go there, so I figured it was a shrewd bet. But of course, Harry slept on it and changed his mind. That's fair enough. It's not Harry's responsibility to think, 'Well, some people have put money on me going to Newcastle, even Merse, I'd best go.' He had to make the correct decision for himself. Merse wasn't bitter about it, though; he knew that Harry had to do the thing that was right for him, even though he was cursing his luck that he had missed out. Again.

It's been so bad for Merse that I even remember one of the girls in the office saying to him, 'Paul what's the biggest bet you've ever had?'

He thought about it and after a while he revealed that it was £10,000.

She said, 'Was it a winner?'

And he laughed and said, 'Nah, you've got to be kidding – my biggest winning bet was £10!'

I think he must have lost a hell of a lot of dough in his time. On one show, we were discussing the fortunes of Southampton on the last day of the 2007/08 season. Merse and co. began talking specifically about what the board had done with all the money they'd made from the sales of Kevin Phillips, Peter Crouch, Theo Walcott, Gareth Bale and Kenwyne Jones. Matt Le Tissier, the expert on all things Southampton, said, 'I don't know, but apparently the club are losing £39,000 a week!'

Merse laughed next to him and chipped in with, 'Me too.'

It was a brilliant flash of the self-deprecating humour which we all love him for. It would be very easy, given the personal problems that he's had in his life, to feel sorry for him, but Merse is such a nice character that you don't. Everything seems to wash off him, and his enthusiastic vulnerability increases his popularity. I know when he started on *Soccer Saturday* there were doubts about him. He was not particularly articulate and people felt that he wouldn't be able to contribute to what is, ostensibly, a chat show, but he does, and his patter and insights work very well.

He comes onto the panel and he speaks his mind. In that respect, he's very similar to Rodney. He's forthright, but he's forthright in a much more innocent way than Rodney ever was. Whereas Rodney would sit there and ponder on something before coming out with a savage comment, Merse will just blurt it out. Sometimes even with a tooth, which happened once when he was doing one of his match reports. It was unbelievable. One minute he's yapping on, the next an incisor has dropped out of his mouth. He was whistling away for the rest of the show – it was as if he'd developed a lisp. Luckily, Noreen, one of our floor managers, had the foresight to find the tooth among the cables and wires on the studio floor and pop it into a glass of milk, which preserves it in the hours before you reach the dentist's chair. (No, not the kind used by the England team before Euro 96 – a real dentist's chair. And if you're unaware of what I mean, Google it. You may see some of our panel in action.) Immediately after the show he was making appointments to see an emergency specialist.

Merse with a full mouth of teeth can be scary – his use of the English language is creative to say the least. When it comes to him being forthright, you know when he's about to have a dig at somebody because his criticisms are always preceded by, 'I ain't being 'orrible, but ...' It's also handy to have a Merse-to-English dictionary handy, because sometimes I do not have a clue what he's talking about. With this in mind, I have provided some examples, with translations, so you can get a faint idea of his vocabulary. Hopefully it will improve your *Soccer Saturday* 'experience'.

'He's off the Judi Dench!'
Translation: It looks like they're bringing Jermain Defoe off the substitute's bench.

'It came straight from the Jack Horner!'
Translation: The ball went in straight from a corner kick.

'Oh, he's hit the beans on toast!'
Translation: An Emile Heskey shot has hit the woodwork.

'It's getting a bit Lionel [Messi] now!'
Translation: It's not going so well at the moment.

'He's about as useful as a fish up a tree!'
Translation: He really isn't contributing to the game at all.

'It's all gone a bit Jonathan Ross ... the last resort!'
Translation: Manchester City are throwing everything at Boro in a desperate attempt to salvage a point.

Then of course there are the occasional blunders:

On Manchester United:

'Ronaldo has done about eight leg-overs.'

Er, don't you mean step-overs, Merse? That's good, even by
    his standards ...

**When Fulham went three-two up against Manchester City in
    2008:**

'Oooooh! What a goal! WHAT A GOAL! Oh, that was
    amazing!'

Who scored it, Merse?

'I don't know!'

Charlton 2 Watford 0:

'There is absolutely no way that Watford are going to get
    back into this.'

The game ended 2–2.

On referee Steve Bennett:

'I'm 100 miles away from the incident and can see it's a
    handball. He's two yards away and he's got it wrong.'

Merse's refreshingly different turn of phrase makes him a popular
pundit with the viewers, but he's not so popular in one corner of
the world. I know fans at Walsall regard him less than highly after
a tempestuous managerial spell there, which is a shame because
he's regarded as a legend by the fans of his other clubs. To prove
this point, we were presenting *Monday Night Football* together on
Sky. The game was Macclesfield versus Walsall in an FA Cup first
round replay, and I remember it well because the winners were due

to play Hartlepool in the next round. I also remember it because it was a shocking game.

Merse had arrived in our studio, which was positioned about 30 yards away from the Walsall end. Before the kick-off, the first three or four Walsall fans came into the ground and spotted him immediately. Cue a burst of: 'Paul Merson, what a wanker, what a wanker! Paaaaaa-uuuul Merson, what a wanker, what a waaaaan-ker!'

From the minute we went on air, Merse was flashed various fingers and inappropriate gestures, and subjected to all sorts of abuse. It was hilarious. And Merse could not understand why he was getting so much negative attention.

'How do they know I'm even here?' he said. 'Have they all got great eyesight or something?'

Unbeknown to him, the producer of *Monday Night Football*, a guy called Steve Tudguy, had been interviewed for the match programme and mentioned that Sky's official guest for the night would be Paul Merson. This quote was accompanied by a bloody great picture of Merse alongside it. All the way through the match – and it was embarrassing in the end – the whole Walsall end were singing, 'Paul Merson, what a wanker, what a wanker!' because they'd been tipped off by one of our producers.

By the end of the game, the joke had worn thin. Merse was really peed off about it and I'm not surprised. One of the stewards really should have done something.

I think he's more annoyed at the fact that he's played for all these great clubs and the only fans that give him any stick are from Walsall. That must be irritating. He's loved everywhere else and even when he played for England he was popular. He tried his best at Walsall and he wasn't the first manager who failed to turn it around there. He won't be the last, either.

THE MAGIC MAN

It's also a shame because Merse is a really nice bloke and didn't deserve that treatment. Certainly, he's different from anyone else on TV. I think what makes him perfect for the show is the fact that he was a great player, but he had his vices and troubles like so many of our other panellists – Rodney Marsh, Bestie and Charlie Nicholas among them. But they say, that in all walks of life, geniuses tend to be flawed. Clearly footballers, especially Paul Merson, are no different.

19

A Big Fish In A Small Studio

FACTFILE: MATT LE TISSIER

BORN: 14 October 1968
CLUBS: Southampton
(1986-2002)
HONOURS: Heaviest member
of the *Soccer Saturday*
panel
INTERNATIONAL CAPS: (England) 8

When Gordon Strachan managed Southampton (2001–4), he made an astute observation about the south coast city. 'Southampton is famous for three things,' he said, 'the *Titanic*, yachting, and Matt Le Tissier.' He wasn't too wide of the mark, either. For all his post-football work and national media celebrity – well, as much as you can get from being a panellist on *Soccer Saturday* – it's while wandering through the streets of Southampton that Le Tiss turns from mere mortal into football deity.

This should come as no great surprise, really. Despite recurrent criticisms of laziness and an apparent weight problem throughout his career, Matt was a phenomenon as a footballer, and probably one of the most exciting ball-playing midfielders in the country. He was also a one-club man, and though there was recurring interest from Spurs, Manchester United, Chelsea and AC Milan among others, he decided to stay with the team he first joined as a schoolboy. This unswerving loyalty, twinned with an eye for the spectacular goal, made him a terrace hero. So much so that Southampton-based airline Flybe recently named a plane after him. And before you ask, no, it wasn't a jumbo jet.

Since then, there's been talk of an even bigger acknowledgement. In the same way that Liverpool's airport is named after John Lennon, or the title of JFK has been bestowed upon New York's bustling international airport, there have been high-level discussions about Southampton's modest terminus being renamed The Matt Le Tissier International (two titles which didn't sit together that regularly when he was a player, it has to be said), though many fans think that this is too small a gesture. 'It's not enough!' a number of them have wailed on internet forums.

I think the fact that he was a one-club man is what makes Matt such a great addition to the *Soccer Saturday* panel. If he'd spent his career trailing the motorways as a journeyman, or played for one of the big Premier League clubs, then somewhere along the way he would have made himself unpopular with a large number of fans. As it was, by staying at Southampton he was a) regarded highly by large numbers of the football community because his club were hardly perennial winners, and b) hated only by Pompey fans, and who really cares about that?

Regardless of his prodigious talent, he was a lazy so-and-so on the pitch. Matt would never run any further than he had to, which was probably why he always scored those goals from 25 yards rather than inside the penalty area. If he could be bothered to run an extra 10 yards he'd have been in the box more often, but why bother when you can fire one in from just inside your own half? In fact, as if to prove his laziness, Matt once admitted to us that he loved it when the Premier League drug testers arrived at training. If you were randomly selected for screening, they would make you sit in a room for the rest of the day. This meant no more hard work.

'It was great,' he said. 'They would come in during the middle of training and I'd be thinking, "Pick me, please pick me," just so I wouldn't have to do any more work in the session.'

There are other legendary stories regarding his physique, though I'm sure they're not entirely true. One of them involves a former Southampton coach who flew into a panic after realizing that there was a 'bucket meal two-for-one' deal on offer at the local Kentucky Fried Chicken. Apparently, the unnamed Southampton gaffer rang the store manager, pleading with them not to serve Matt unless he could prove he really was with a mate!

Of course, we give him a lot of stick for his size and lazy demeanour. A couple of years ago we were talking about Craig Bellamy on the show. Bobby Robson was playing him out of position on the left wing when he was at Newcastle. Bellamy absolutely hated it and was making a massive fuss in the press. Le Tiss said, 'I've got absolutely no sympathy with him whatsoever. I played on the left wing a lot at Southampton and I didn't like it, but I just wanted to be on the pitch, so I just got on with the game.'

This seemed an out-of-character display of enthusiasm from Matt. 'That must have been a double then,' I said. 'Out-of-position and out-of-shape.'

Eight England caps were not enough of a return for a player of Matt's talent. He has said on more than one occasion that, if he were Italian or French, he would probably have earned a higher number of international appearances. Foreign coaches were more likely to have appreciated his unpredictable ability. The fact that he played for an unfashionable club like Saints probably didn't help, either. If you ask Le Tiss now, he'd probably say that, yeah, he would have claimed more caps if he'd played for Spurs or Arsenal, and maybe he should have made the move when he had the chance. There were opportunities for him, particularly at Spurs, but he never took them. I suspect that deep down in his heart he has some regrets that he didn't make the move.

Still, I always found it strange that Glenn Hoddle didn't utilize Matt as a player when he was the England manager. They were very similar in so many ways – scorers of fantastic goals, players with tremendous vision and imagination, creative thinkers – yet when it came to picking his 1998 World Cup squad, Matt was omitted, even though he'd scored a hat-trick in an England B game the week previously. Around this time, I've heard that there was a press conference involving Matt. He was asked what he thought the reasons were for his exclusion from the international party travelling to France. He shrugged his shoulders. 'It's probably because I don't play for Spurs,' he said. Even now, you shouldn't ask him about Glenn Hoddle, unless you want your ears chewed off.

In that respect, he fills the flawed genius role established by so many of our other panellists. Matt wasn't a hedonist, but he was certainly regarded as a maverick player – 'a luxury player' was the term commonly used to describe him – alongside the likes of George, Rodney, Charlie and Merse. As a pundit he's a different animal entirely. Initially I didn't think he was an obvious choice, because he didn't seem to be the most talkative of players in interviews. He expressed himself brilliantly on the pitch with those wonderful goals and amazing glimmers of skill, but not off it. You never saw his name in quotes. He was never one for the limelight. Still, we tried him out and we immediately appreciated his personality.

It was apparent, straight away, that Matt was very different from Rodney, who he was effectively replacing. Matt had been on the show with Rodney on several occasions. When our resident big gob was sensationally fired, Le Tiss became a permanent fixture on the *Soccer Saturday* team. It was clear to everyone that these were giant shoes to fill under any circumstances. Furthermore, Matt knew he was never going to be a motormouth in the same way as his predecessor. We were also aware that he wasn't going to be as controversial as Rodney, or as difficult, but then again we didn't want him to be. We wanted Matt to be himself.

This was the right decision. What we immediately understood with Le Tiss was that he had a lovely self-deprecating sense of humour which worked very well on the telly. It's a much gentler form of wit than the others, but it often makes me laugh out loud. Hopefully it works for the viewers at home, too. I remember while we were talking about his time at Southampton he brought up the 'big fish in a small pond' theory. Apparently Matt quite enjoyed being a big-name footballer at a modest club.

'You must have been quite a big fish,' said Charlie.

'Er, yeah ... a whale,' laughed Le Tiss. 'No, no, hang on, that's a mammal.'

In 2008 he dropped himself in it while we were chatting during a commercial break. I'd been talking about music on the show and decided to rattle off some pop-related stats.

'The last time West Brom won at Old Trafford was in 1984 when Shakin' Stevens was in the charts with 'This Ole House',' I said to camera.

During the ads Matt leaned over to me. 'I'm not sure if that's true, you know. I think the single might have been out in 1981.'

He even texted a friend during the break to confirm the fact. 'I knew I was right!' he said, when the response came back. 'He was my idol as a kid. I had Shaky posters all over the wall. I loved that record. It was one of the first I ever bought. I had all his albums. I saw him in concert, twice.'

Merse began nudging him. 'Don't tell him, don't tell him!' he said.

Tears of laughter were running down my face. As soon as we were back on air, I apologized for making the mistake and then turned my attention to an unsuspecting Le Tiss. 'So, Matt, you're quite a big Shakin' Stevens fan?' Poor Matt had to tell the story again, until Paul Merson enquired whether his house had a Green Door. He could have confessed to snorting cocaine or being an alcoholic, but a Shakin' Stevens fan? It takes a brave man to admit to that vice. A very brave man.

He's not afraid to speak his mind, either. What he does bring to the show, as well as calories, is a general calmness. He delivers information incredibly well. He's eloquent, he's to the point and he's brief. I never have to tell him to shut up in the same way that

I have to tell Thommo to shut up. He doesn't pull any punches, either. In the past, he has been massively critical of Emile Heskey, mainly due to the England man's lack of goals. Elsewhere, he's incredibly critical of referees, for whom he has no time whatsoever. He was also very dismissive of Steve McClaren when he was in charge of England. But hey, that's a pundit's life. He wouldn't be on the panel if he couldn't be pointed in his opinions.

Meanwhile, Matt is also aware that very few of his Southampton peers, if any, matched his technical ability. This fact would make it very easy for him to criticize many of his former team-mates. However, he is genuinely supportive of players he's worked with, like James Beattie or the kids in the Southampton side, such as David McGoldrick. Having said that, I don't think he's ever been afraid to criticize an old team-mate. For example, Brian Howard, now at Sheffield United, was with Le Tiss for a while at Saints. He may even have cleaned Matt's boots as an apprentice. When Barnsley, Howard's club until recently, were having a fantastic run, I asked Matt whether he had the ability to make it at the very top.

'I'm not sure,' said Matt, 'because the one thing he hasn't got is a turn of pace. He hasn't got that extra yard of speed that you need to be successful in the top flight. You can't get that from working hard, either.' I always wondered how Matt would know that.

I think the most impressive part of Matt's *Soccer Saturday* game is his demeanour. He never panics when he's in the studio or under pressure. He's calm and collected, with seemingly all the time in the world, which was the way he behaved on a football pitch, where he had an unswerving faith in his own ability. But to describe him as flawless would be wrong: on one occasion he nearly caved in under the pressure when, at the end of last season, we insisted that he come in to report on the Southampton versus Sheffield United match. The game was highly charged. It was the last weekend of the season. Saints had to win and results had to go their way elsewhere for them to stay up.

Of course, it turned out to be a really dramatic fixture. Southampton won three-two after going down to 10 men. For a while, Sheffield United were battering them. Matt got very carried away and forgot the logistics of the game.

'Saints have got all 11 men back in the box!' he yelled.

'But Matt, they've only got 10 on the field!'

He threw his pen to the desk when Sheffield United scored. He punched the air when Southampton came back into it. I've never seen him sweat so much. He was perspiring throughout, and he was more excited, more animated, than at any time during his career. And I include his playing days, not just his media work, in that. So, despite his generally calm exterior, there can be glimmers of exuberance, which are all the more exciting because they're so rare.

If there is one flaw, though, it would be Matt's fidgety nature. God, is he noisy in the studio! If he's not playing with his phone, he's rustling biscuit wrappers and munching on chocolate bars, all of which adds to his public image as a greedy-guts. They say that the cameras put 10 pounds on you when you work in TV. If that's true, I reckon Matt must have three on him at all times. Not that he cares. The annoying truth is, despite the snacks, crisps and KFC meal deals for two, he could probably still play us all off the park today if he really wanted to. With a football at his feet, the man was a legend. With a packet of crisps in his hand, a scruffy shirt and the *Soccer Saturday* headset, he's an expert pundit in the making.

20

Uncle Frank

FACTFILE: FRANK McLINTOCK

BORN: A long, long time ago.
Before stats were invented, in
fact
CLUBS: Leicester City
(1957-64), Arsenal (1964-73),
Queens Park Rangers (1973-7)
HONOURS: (Leicester City) League Cup 1964;
(Arsenal) League Championship 1971; FA Cup
1971; Inter-Cities Fairs Cup 1970
INTERNATIONAL CAPS: (Scotland) 9

UNCLE FRANK

It's highly likely that a large number of you, dear readers, might not be too familiar with the work of our very own Frank McLintock. So I think it's high time to honour the great man with a brief appraisal of his fantastic career.

In the beginning, Francis (he later became 'Frank') was a tasty wing-half (that's old-people-speak for midfielder, kids) with Leicester City until Arsenal manager Billy Wright thought he would suit the playing style of his nifty Arsenal team in 1964. Wright was, er, right. Frank played for the Gunners for the next nine years, moving from midfield into the centre-half position and skippering the side to a number of trophies, including the League and FA Cup double and the Inter-Cities Fairs Cup of 1970. He also picked up the Football Writers' Association Footballer of the Year award in 1971.

If you were to compare him to a modern player, think of John Terry. He was also an incredible grafter: Frank played over 700 games for his club sides (combined). He was also regarded as something of a gentleman. In 1972 he even scooped an MBE, which was no mean feat in those days. So if you're ever watching him on the telly and wondering, 'Who the hell is this guy?' well, now you know.

You probably won't see much of Frank these days, mainly because of his age. When he left the show, it was deemed that he was a generation or two apart from the footballers our audience were more familiar with, and so he was edged off the panel for some newer, shinier models. Well, Paul Merson and Matt Le Tissier anyway. But for a while he made up a quarter of our *Soccer Saturday* dream team alongside Rodney, George Best and Charlie Nicholas.

And what a pleasure it was to have him on, because he was often a great laugh, often unintentionally and sometimes even controversially. Many years ago, when David O'Leary was doing great work as a manager, probably around the time when he was managing Leeds United, Frank's sense of humour nearly went too far. David was always on the telly because he was tall, dark, young, smiling and softly-spoken, and he was always praising his kids. Anyway, on the panel one morning I turned to Frank for his opinion, knowing full well that he probably would have encountered O'Leary through his Arsenal connections. I said, 'Frank, everybody loves David O'Leary – he's a talented manager, he's tall, good-looking, quiet, articulate, pleasant, intelligent ... but he must have a dark side?'

'Oh yeah,' said Frank in a flash. 'He's a paedophile.' And then he laughed.

The thing was, I wasn't laughing. This had gone out live on air. In fact, I remember gasping with horror. But Frank was still laughing mainly because he thought it was so bloody funny and also because he hadn't looked across at the panel to see all of us, open-mouthed, looking at him in disbelief. It's one of those gags that goes down well in the pub (and I have to stress to Mr O'Leary's lawyers that I am not, in any way, inferring that he is a paedophile or suggesting that people should be making jokes about him in a pub), but on a hugely popular and award-winning football show? Well, it's a no-no.

I had to make an immediate apology. I said, 'Of course, Frank McLintock is joking and Sky disassociates itself from that remark.' He was lucky. Had he said that joke three or four years later, Frank probably wouldn't have made it to the end of the show, let alone returned to Sky in a commentating capacity, especially in the light of what happened to Ron Atkinson over at ITV when he made a racist remark about Chelsea player Marcel Desailly, unaware that his mic was still switched on after a Champions League match in 2004.

UNCLE FRANK

I don't think we got a single email complaining about Frank's gag. And it didn't offend anyone in the office or even David O'Leary. Everybody knew it was just his sense of humour – which might not have been to everyone's taste – and it wasn't vindictive or malicious. It was actually pretty funny when you think about it. But that's the thing with Frank, he doesn't really have it in him to upset anybody, whereas Rodney Marsh or our other argumentative panellist, Alan McInally, could start a brawl in an empty room. Frank couldn't wind up anyone if he tried.

Certainly not Sir Alex Ferguson, that most tempestuous of characters, who, for some reason, Frank believed that he'd upset with some comments on the show. He got into such a tizz about this affair that I was even asked to make an apology on his behalf at the League Managers Association Awards a few years back. Once Frank knew that I was going to be in the same room as the Manchester United gaffer that night, he started to badger me.

'Will you see Alex there?' he asked one morning.

I told him that I probably would.

Frank got all excited and said, 'Look, if you see Sir Alex, can you say to him that I send on my regards and I'm really sorry if I've done anything to offend him.'

Anyway, on the night, I was sat next to Alex, drinking fine wines and eating fancy canapés, and I seized my opportunity to pass on Frank's message: 'Anyway Alex,' I said between mouthfuls of delightful pastry and smoked salmon, 'Frank sends on his regards.'

Sir Alex beamed. 'Ach, Frank, he's a lovely boy isn't he?'

I thought, 'Well that wasn't the reaction of someone who's had their nose put out of joint'. So I continued: 'And he's also asked me to tell you that he didn't mean to offend you in any way.'

Sir Alex looked confused. 'Offend me? Frank could not offend anybody. He could not offend anybody if he tried.'

So, god knows what he had worked himself up about, but that incident goes to show what a gent Frank was. Fergie clearly had a lot of affection for him, as a lot of people in the game did, and still do.

This love stems from the fact that Frank was an absolute legend throughout his career and there are few players that could match his reputation as a footballer. Sure, we get players on the show and all of them need to have won something significant to qualify for 'legend status'. Thommo is an excellent example – he's lifted more silverware than one of the great train robbers. But there are very few people in the game to have won a lot and still managed to remain popular in the public eye. Even if you've won very little it can still be hard to remain popular with everybody. If you look at Marshy, for example; he has a lot of critics within the game. But Frank? Well, you couldn't find anyone who didn't love Frank.

This didn't extend to his time on the pitch with his Arsenal team-mates, nor in the dressing room when he was captain of the club. By his own admission, Frank was capable of threats and physical action in the dressing room, but only if it was needed. He was a big, fit fella when he played, and I'm sure he would have been more than happy to pin somebody to the wall should they need some extra motivation during a game. He was a winner in so many ways, which was the difference between him and Rodney, who was a born joker. I remember Rodney telling me that during one match for England, Sir Alf Ramsey wasn't best pleased with his lethargic approach to the game. He yelled, 'If you don't pull your weight, Marsh, I'm going to pull you off at half-time!'

Marshy gave him a cheeky smile and said, 'Pull me off? Blimey, at City we only get an orange.'

Don't get me wrong, though, Frank wasn't without his moments. For starters, he was probably one of the most politically incorrect people I have known, not because he was being vindictive or horrible, but because he came from a totally different era. When there was a particularly full-chested floor manager working in the studio on a Saturday morning, he would say, 'My darling, you're both looking particularly well this morning.' In fairness, people were never offended by it, because it was Frank and it was obviously harmless.

Still, he almost fell foul of the PC brigade when we were talking about Premier League managers being sacked, one after the other. Frank remarked that it 'was like *Ten Little Niggers*', a reference to the Agatha Christie novel where the book's protagonists are killed off one by one (the book has since been renamed *And Then There Were None*, though today it's being sold as *Ten Little Indians*). It really landed him in hot water and there was a bit of an uproar, but Frank wasn't aware of the change in the book's title and so that's how he referred to it. He got a lot of stick and grief from some viewers, and they had every right to their opinion, but he didn't receive any sort of warning or reprimand from Sky because everybody knew that it wasn't an intentionally-offensive remark and because Frank didn't want to offend anybody – black, white, male, female, tall, short, fat, thin, or size zero.

He was always one for getting tongue-tied on the show, however, usually with hilarious consequences. His pronunciations of foreign players' names were often so wide of the mark that they were like a Darren Bent volley. He would refer to Jens Lehmann as 'Jens Lemon', though this malapropism wasn't entirely inaccurate. And if Aliadière was playing for Arsenal (now Boro), he'd tie himself in terrible knots. More hilariously, as Rodney Marsh would attest, Frank was easier to wind up than Thommo. And Marshy would revel in it. During one show, Frank foolishly claimed, 'Well, I could be repeating myself here, but I think that

Alan Curbishley, along with Martin O'Neill, are the two best young managers in the game'.

Rodney, being Rodney, couldn't help himself and fired back, 'Frank you're repeating yourself.' He would never let him get away with anything.

But Rodney had a strange rivalry with Frank . They were good friends, but Rodney loved to wind him up and, like Thommo, he used to refer to him as a 'dopey defender', even though Frank was a Double-winner with Arsenal and a fantastic player – one of the greatest to have graced the game. Unsurprisingly, given his leadership experience, Frank could stand up for himself. He was intelligent, articulate, witty and certainly not cowed by Rodney, so they had a fantastic on-screen spark. Rodney, no matter how hard he tried, couldn't pull the wool over Frank's eyes. There was also a certain respect between the two because they'd played against one another.

Looking back, if Frank had one flaw, it was that sometimes he could be too nice. Whereas Rodney would not pull any punches if he was about to criticize somebody, it was often hard to get Frank to say anything bad about anybody. Still, he was passionate – he used to get really carried away on the show, especially when it came to talking about Arsenal – and he had his beliefs about football. One thing he used to claim was that footballers from his era could play in teams today, which is not a popular theory in the modern game. Many experts think that footballers from an older generation wouldn't be as fit or technically-gifted as the players we have in the Premier League now. It's also a widely-held opinion that a lot of them probably wouldn't stay on the pitch long enough to find out because they'd have been sent off after the first 10 minutes, such was the physicality of the game back then. But Frank was adamant. He reckoned players from his generation could be just as effective as the players competing now. I for one wasn't going to argue with him, not with his weighty reputation. Or his MBE.

Sadly, he doesn't do the shows too often these days. I know he came back for one or two Arsenal games in the Champions League, which he loved, but I think he gradually appeared less and less on the show just as a way of changing the programme's image. Sometimes you have to freshen things up. I knew that the golden era period of *Soccer Saturday* which featured Bestie, Marshy and Frank needed to change at some point, especially as times were moving on, but I personally thought he was moved out a shade early, to be honest. I still think he had something to give. It's also a worry because it means at some point they're going to want to get rid of me to bring in some new young, thrusting presenter. Though who could fill these shoes? Actually, don't answer that question ...

21

Introducing The Best (and Worst) Of The Rest

Reckon you've got what it takes to be a *Soccer Saturday* presenter? OK, hotshot, on any given Super Sunday, test your mettle by settling down in the living room with the loudest Scot you can find positioned on your left (to represent our very own Alan McInally, of course), and a rattle-waving Scouser (Thommo) to your right. Bring in a dashing, witty friend to play the role of anchorman. Flick on the telly, push the volume button to full blast and ... away you go!

Left ear: 'JEFF! YOU WOULDNAE BELIEEEEVE WHAT'S HAPPENING!'

Headphones (Alan Parry): 'And, ironically, in the football commentator sense of the word, John Terry also plays for Chelsea, though surely that's coincidence, or even circumstance, not irony. I really should check the dictionary definition ...'

INTRODUCING THE BEST (AND WORST) OF THE REST

Right ear: 'JEFF! LIVERPOOL MUST SCORE, THEY MUST,
    OOOOH! I DON'T BELIEVE IT, HE'S HIT THE BAR! IT'S A
    TRAVESTY THAT LIVERPOOL AREN'T 15–0 UP!'
Studio: 'And now, over to our debut panellist for a razor-sharp,
    fact-packed tactical analysis of the first 10 minutes of the
    game ...'

What do you mean you haven't been able to concentrate properly?
It's not as easy as it looks, is it? Which is why it's a pretty tough job
finding suitable candidates to join the *Soccer Saturday* panel. It's
also the reason why our selection process is so rigid: new guests
have to be contemporary. In the studio, they have to be able to
talk about what's going on in front of them while shutting out the
surrounding noise. Then they have to deal with me. During match
reports they need to be able to be succinct and entertaining on
camera. All in all, it's a pretty tough gig.

Nevertheless, we've been pretty lucky with the panellists we
currently have on the show, not to mention the ones that have been
and gone. You're probably already familiar (or bored) with the regular faces, plus I've already embarrassed them in previous chap-
ters, unless, of course, you're reading this on the loo, in which case
you're probably flicking idly from chapter to chapter and missing
out on vast, informative chunks of prose in the process (tut, tut).
Anyway, some of the names I'm about to introduce you to – irreg-
ular guests, the night-shift workers, the on-the-road reporters –
you might not be so au fait with. But each one is a little (or large)
football legend in their own right. And they've also got the medals
to match their mouths. Well, apart from John Salako, that is ...

NAME: **Gordon McQueen**
BORN: 26 June 1952
CLUBS: St Mirren (1970-2), Leeds United (1972-8),
Manchester United (1978-85)
HONOURS: (Leeds United) League Championship 1974;
(Manchester United) FA Cup 1983
INTERNATIONAL CAPS: (Scotland) 30

On the pitch, Gordon McQueen was a giant of a centre-half who rarely took prisoners. Off it, he had a fearsome gob to match: on signing for Manchester United from Leeds for £495,000 in 1978 he reportedly said, 'Ninety-nine per cent of players in this country dream of playing for Manchester United. The other one per cent are liars.' Today, he has an equally terrifying reputation with the *Soccer Saturday* crew, though much of this comes from an incredible drinking prowess that leaves the rest of us in his wake.

I guess we shouldn't really be surprised. Much of this 'talent' comes from his size and his training – he once shared a dressing room with Bryan 'Hollow Legs' Robson and Viv Anderson at Old Trafford, fearsome boozers, the pair of them. But on the occasions we do socialize, more often than not at our end-of-season bash, Gordon is always the last man standing, despite our best efforts to keep up with him.

There are two infamous stories that serve as a warning as to why it's unwise to embark on a big night out with Gordon. Number one: it was recently rumoured that he had to have an operation on his ankle. Before he could go under the knife, he was required to take a medical for insurance purposes. A doctor enquired how many units of alcohol he drank and Gordon informed him, accurately and honestly, that it was probably around the 30-unit mark. Well, the doctor was quite impressed – it was obviously a little over the safe limit of 28 units, but not by too drastic an amount.

'Thirty units a week, Mr McQueen?' said the doctor. 'That's not bad at all. Not bad at all.'

'No, no, no, doc,' responded Gordon in his thick Scottish brogue. 'Thirty a dee.'

Number two: after a few drinks, Gordon McQueen can eat raw eggs. Not cracked and poured into a glass, Rocky Balboa-style, but whole, uncrushed shell and all, like a wild, ravenous mongoose. Honestly, it's a stomach-churning art that has to be seen to be believed, but with a quick flip of the head, a medium-sized egg has disappeared down his gullet in a flash. Even David Attenborough would be impressed.

I'm not quite sure how this peculiar talent came to light, but no Christmas bash is complete without The Gordon McQueen Raw Egg Challenge. A few drinks are sunk, an office junior (or John Salako) is dispatched to the kitchen to grab some eggs, and contenders young and old step up to the plate to match Gordon's record of four eggs in one sitting. I don't think anyone has come close, not even Matt Le Tissier. Which is just as well because it's a vile sight and every time I hear him utter the immortal words, 'Fetch the eggs ...' my heart sinks and my stomach flips over like Robbie Keane doing a somersault.

Regardless of these outbreaks of high jinks, Gordon is a much-respected figure within the game. As well as occasionally appearing on the *Soccer Saturday* panel, he doubles up as a scout for Boro, so it's obvious he knows his onions. He's also a lovable character – if you were to ask the guys on the panel who their favourite other pundit was, they would all say Gordon. Unanimously. Though perhaps this stems from the fact that sometimes they could not really understand a word he was saying (I think even Sir Alex Ferguson would have a job). For all I know he could be making an offensive comment about Mrs Stelling every time he wanders past and I just haven't realized it yet.

That said, he makes for a cracking reporter with a terrific sense of humour. We once sent him out to interview Juninho when he was at Middlesbrough, which made for a brilliant piece of TV, firstly because we shot Scotland's favourite giant walking along a bank of the River Tees with Boro's favourite Hobbit (I think Gordon was at least two feet taller), and secondly because Juninho referred to him as 'McQueenio' throughout the interview. It was fantastic, though it's unlikely the Brazilian would have been quite so accommodating had McQueenio been 10 pints to the good and reaching for a pack of Sainsbury's free range.

NAME: Andy Goram

BORN: 13 April 1964

CLUBS: Oldham Athletic (1981-7), Hibernian (1987-91), Rangers (1991-8), Notts County (1998), Sheffield United (1998), Motherwell (1998-2001), Manchester United (2001 loan), Hamilton Academical (2001), Coventry City (2001-2), Oldham Athletic (2002), Queen of the South (2002-3), Elgin City (2003-4)

HONOURS: (Rangers) Scottish League Championship 1992, 1993, 1994, 1995, 1996, 1997; Scottish Cup 1992, 1993, 1996; Scottish League Cup 1993, 1994; (Queen of the South) Scottish League Challenge Cup 2003

INTERNATIONAL CAPS: (Scotland) 43

I have to admit that, on hearing that former Scotland keeper Andy Goram would be joining us in the Sky Sports studio, the Stelling buttocks clenched with fear. Don't get me wrong, I haven't got anything against the lad, it's just that a) it has been widely reported in the media that Andy had been treated for a mild form of schizophrenia, although Goram has never gone on record to confirm or deny the stories. There was even a famous terrace chant doing the rounds while he was playing which went: 'Two Andy Gorams, there's only two Andy Gorams ...' and I wasn't sure how serious his condition would be; and b) to describe him as potty-mouthed would be an understatement.

When he came in for the midweek shows, I was greatly relieved that he didn't utter the 'F' word once (one fewer than me during our respective careers, eagle-eyed viewers will have noted), though he seemed to come close on occasions. Ultimately, though, he was a rare guest, mainly because he made Gordon McQueen sound like Prince William, and he was fraught with complications. For example, you never knew where to send the appearance cheque. If you sent it to his home address or placed it straight into his bank account, he was worried that his wife would get hold of it.

We had to take a punt on Andy, like we do with all our pundits. You can't really audition people before they get on the show, because there's no way you can practise the live environment. I think the best way to manage new panellists is to throw them in at the deep end, on air. So with people like Andy Goram, we'll tend to put them on in the midweek games when the viewing figures are lower. If they work out in that environment, we'll bring them back in for the Saturday afternoon show, which is a little more hectic.

We have got it wrong on occasions, and one that didn't work out was the ex-Forest and Leeds player Paul Hart. Yes, he was a lovely man and very articulate off-camera, but when he came down for the midweek show he seemed to freeze. It just goes to show that it's a difficult business and not everyone can do it. There you are, watching a match and focusing on what's going on in front of you. Before you know it, I'm jabbering in your ear asking for an eloquent match report. It's quite a juggling act and Paul only managed to do it once, and he realized almost immediately that it wasn't for him. The next day he sent us a fax reading, 'Great show, great fun, shame I was crap.'

NAME: Tony Cottee
BORN: 11 July 1965
CLUBS: West Ham United (1982-8), Everton (1988-94),
West Ham United (1994-6), Leicester City (1997-2000),
Birmingham City (1997, loan), Norwich City (2000),
Barnet (2000-1), Millwall (2001)
HONOURS: (Leicester City) League Cup 2000
INTERNATIONAL CAPS: (England) 7

I've never seen a *Soccer Saturday* panellist break down in tears at the misfortunes of a former club, but former West Ham and England striker Tony Cottee has come close. Very close.

The emotional event took place at the end of the 2002/03 season when West Ham were on the verge of relegation to Division One (now the Championship). As is typical, their fate was to be decided on the final day of the season: The Hammers were away to Birmingham and fellow relegation candidates Bolton were at home to Boro. West Ham needed to win and Bolton had to lose if they were to stay up. But it wasn't going their way as the afternoon ticked on and, as it became clear that West Ham weren't going to get the result they wanted, Tony became more and more depressed. Even though he's played for loads of clubs, West Ham are his team and he takes defeat very badly. He takes relegation even harder.

West Ham drew 2-2 and by the end of the game Tony was on the brink of tears. I had never seen a man quite so upset by a football match. I found it really touching, but maybe because Hartlepool have that effect on me every week. I also remember thinking that the atmosphere really changed in the studio that day

– it wasn't the usual *When Harry Met Sally* cacophony of grunts and groans. The mood was really flat because of what was happening at West Ham. And to make matters worse for Tony, Rodney 'Kofi Annan' Marsh was delivering the commentary on the Bolton-versus-Boro game with a less than UN-acceptable level of diplomacy. He was enjoying rubbing the result in as Tony sank in the quicksand of despondency. It couldn't have been an easy afternoon.

The only other pundit to have come that close to breaking down was probably former Millwall assistant manager Keith Stevens. Keith had just been sacked, but he was Millwall through and through – a former player and manager – and still very much in love with the club. We figured it would be good to get him into the studio for Millwall's fixture against Southend. He talked very well in the build-up to the game, but as the game kicked off, Millwall very quickly went a goal down. Then two. Then three. Then four. They were eventually walloped seven-nil. At the end of the match, I couldn't get a word out of him. He was so depressed at what had happened that he clammed up. It was an awful moment.

Tony's emotional state was a rare lapse in composure, but it made for great TV. Usually he's the perfect pro. I like working with him because he's feisty, he's intelligent, he's been around the game and he knows the clubs well. He has a lot of great contacts within the game, and he's still very much respected. I also like working with him because he has a passion for the sides he's represented. We used to get pundits to commentate on teams that they played for because it added a sense of drama to our coverage. So, for example, Alan Mullery would always cover Spurs games, Charlie Nicholas would follow Arsenal, Phil Thompson would cover Liverpool and so on. For some reason, we've recently moved away from that, which is driving Thommo to insanity because he has to keep his eye on two games whenever Liverpool are playing. I'd like to point out that this was a decision from above and I'm still not sure if it works. I liked the drama and passion the old arrangement brought to the studio. But then, if it prevents an outbreak of sobbing then maybe it's for the best.

NAME: **Paul Walsh**

BORN: 1 October 1962

CLUBS: Charlton Athletic (1979-82), Luton Town (1982-4), Liverpool (1984-8), Tottenham Hotspur (1988-92), Queens Park Rangers (1991, loan), Portsmouth (1992-4), Manchester City (1994-5) Portsmouth (1995-6)

HONOURS: (Liverpool) League Championship 1986; (Tottenham Hotspur) FA Cup 1991

INTERNATIONAL CAPS: (England) 5

When you think about it, Paul Walsh should be a bit of a Jack-the-Lad character on *Soccer Saturday*. His pin-up good looks, swashbuckling style of play for Liverpool and Spurs, and that Farrah Fawcett *Charlie's Angels* haircut, made him a hit with the ladies and a hero to the fans. The reality, though, is that Walshy is a very serious character. And, like Tony Cottee, he can get quite upset when results don't go his way, but only if he doesn't win the office sweep, or accumulator.

He also gets upset if the boys take the mickey out of him – which they do all the time, and it's usually about money. I remember he once came in on Grand National day and a few of the girls were running a sweep – £1 per horse. Now, Walshy had only brought in

40 quid, and given that it costs £20 to enter the office accumulator and £20 for the office sweep, he didn't have another penny on him. Eventually he borrowed £2 from Thommo so he could have some horses in the Grand National. And the lads have never let him forget it.

The one thing that strikes me about Walshy is his hairstyle. Sometimes I'll shake my head in despair – he looks like a Bash Street Kid with his spiky barnet. This is a bit of a smokescreen, though: on-camera he's generally pretty straight. And he can infuriate me sometimes, mainly because he doesn't understand the meaning of the words, 'Be brief!' or 'Keep it short!' Instead, he'll generally give a long-winded description of a goal rather than a short account, much to the frustration of the producers.

Paul's a regular for us now and he's settled in well. He's not a joker like the others, certainly not like Matt or Charlie, and sometimes he can dig himself into a bit of a hole with his predictions. There was a funny moment before the Manchester United-versus-Boro game during the 2007/08 season. The whole panel had gone for a United win, but they could tell from my huffing and puffing that I didn't think the same way. Walshy piped up: 'So, Jeff, who do you think is going to win, then?'

'I think Boro could get a draw or even win it,' I said. And I meant it, too.

He couldn't get his head around this. 'How can you possibly say that?' As I started to explain, he interrupted: 'What could you possibly base that on?'

That got me started: 'Well, Walshy, I'm basing it on the fact that they've taken four points off Arsenal, they have the best results against the top four clubs out of any side not in the top four and they raise themselves for games like this. They also have a terrific record against Manchester United. That's what I'm basing it on.'

[Cue smug look on the Stelling chops as I prove I've been doing my homework.]

Paul greeted this expert, well-researched and deliciously-delivered info by telling me I was talking rubbish. So when Boro drew against United, having played them off the park, I could hardly contain my glee. We even replayed his comments a week later. Sadly he wasn't there to defend himself, but he tends to take those things very well.

NAME: John Salako
BORN: 11 February 1969
CLUBS: Crystal Palace (1986-95), Swansea City (1989, loan), Coventry City (1995-8), Bolton Wanderers (1998, loan), Fulham (1998-9), Charlton Athletic (1999-2001), Reading (2001-4), Brentford (2004-5)
HONOURS: None
INTERNATIONAL CAPS: (England) 5

Poor old John Salako. He's a lovely fella and an excellent addition to the *Soccer Saturday* mob, but sometimes, just sometimes, he says the daftest things. Generally we use him as an on-the-road reporter these days, though he did utter one of the greatest lines in *Soccer Saturday* history while reporting on a Reading game from the gantry in 2007.

'Jeff,' he yelled. 'I can't believe it. There's been a goal and Reading have conceded at the worst possible time – the 37th minute.'

We all looked at each other: How could the 37th minute be the worst possible time to concede? The 45th, yes (it's never nice to go into the dressing room having just leaked a goal), and most definitely the 90th. But the 37th?

Then again, John is prone to blunders like that. As a player, he was a pretty tenacious beast. As a pundit, he's occasionally liable for the odd howler or own goal. A case in point was when we were talking about Boro's form in 2007/08. For some reason, they weren't scoring a lot of goals and John linked their lack of fire-power to an absence of creative force in their midfield. Good point, John, I reckoned. So I said, 'OK, who would they look at if they were to invest during the transfer window?'

'Well, if I was them, I'd look at Mo Sissoko from Liverpool.'

I flashed him a glance to check he wasn't joking. Judging by the look on his face, he wasn't. I thought, 'Creative midfield player? Sissoko has a lot of qualities, but he ain't creative.' And nobody was going to let him get away with it, either.

Despite these blips, I know he's very interested in the game. He's just completed a referee's course, not because he ever wants to be a ref – I mean, who would? – but because he wants to understand the game a bit better, which is a great idea. He's a lovely guy, and a good-looking fella, which is a bit annoying because all the girls love him, and I'm not a man to be overshadowed in the Hunk of the Year stakes.

NAME: **Alan Mullery**
BORN: 23 November 1941
CLUBS: Fulham (1958–64), Tottenham Hotspur (1964–72), Fulham (1972–6)
HONOURS: (Tottenham Hotspur) FA Cup 1967; League Cup 1971; UEFA Cup 1972
INTERNATIONAL CAPS: (England) 35

There's one story that defines England, Spurs and Fulham legend Alan Mullery. Surprisingly, it's not how he man-marked Pelé during England's clash with Brazil in the 1970 World Cup finals, or how he lifted the UEFA Cup as Spurs skipper two years later. Instead, this tale takes place at a BSkyB party for a large number of the staff who had been made redundant. Mullers was part of the punditry team who, along with a raft of other big names (for shame they will remain nameless here), were invited to join us for limp sausage rolls and warm beers at the leaving drinks party.

As the evening wore on, it was obvious our so-called celebrity friends and colleagues weren't going to show (no shame there, more limp sausage rolls for me), all except for Alan Mullery who arrived to wish us luck and thank us for all the work we had given him. It was a small gesture, but one that showed Mullers to have that bit of extra class. It forever marked him down as a stand-up gent.

He was from an older era, but he was great for the show because he was opinionated and considered. Mullers was also a brilliant acquisition because of the things he had done throughout his career – winning trophies, marking Pelé for England, as well as managing a host of teams including Brighton (as well as Hove

Albion), Palace and QPR. Because of his link to an older generation, however, he is one who is brought out for *Soccer Saturday* on
rare occasions. Generally he'll appear when we do match reports
on Sky Sports News, but it's always a pleasure to have Mullers on
the panel.

NAME: **Dave 'Harry' Bassett**
BORN: 4 September 1944
CLUBS: Wimbledon (1974-5)
HONOURS: None
INTERNATIONAL CAPS: A big fat zero

Harry's one of those people who always has to be in work, whether
it's management, coaching or doing TV stuff with us. He's always
up to something - I believe he's even involved in the League Managers Association these days. But the real beauty of having him
on the telly with us is that a) he's a character and he's achieved a
lot in the game as a manager, and b) he's never short of a word or
two. He loves a chat.

He's been on the show quite a few times, but I recall one particular occasion when he had us in fits of laughter. I can't remember exactly which game it was, but it involved Chelsea. Of course,
Didier Drogba was up to his usual antics - throwing himself around,
falling over at the slightest hint of a breeze - and Harry was up in
arms. You have to bear in mind that for a while he was the gaffer
at Wimbledon alongside legendary loonies such as Vinnie Jones
and John 'Fash The Bash' Fashanu. Anyway, Harry was losing his

rag at Drogba's trickery and, in a fit of pique, he yelled (and why he came up with this, I'll never know) 'Didier Drogba goes down easier than my daughter!'

Now, what he meant by this was that Drogba was playing like a girl. The way he delivered it came loaded with so many other connotations, however. I looked at him, open-mouthed. Harry stared at the screen oblivious to what he had said. To make matters worse, we actually work with his daughter, Carly, in the Sky Sports offices. She's a beautiful blonde. And now I can never look at her in quite the same way again.

NAME: Alan McInally

BORN: 10 February 1963

CLUBS: Ayr United (1980-4), Celtic (1984-7), Aston Villa (1987-9), Bayern Munich (1989-92), Kilmarnock (1993-4)

HONOURS: (Celtic) Scottish League Championship 1986; Scottish Cup 1985

INTERNATIONAL CAPS: (Scotland) 8

Good grief, Alan McInally can be a fearsome character, which is probably what stood him in good stead when he was clattering defenders during his playing career. But what really sets The Big Man apart from your usual battering ram of a striker when he appears in the *Soccer Saturday* studios is his sense of humour. If he didn't have one, it's highly likely I would have had my well-groomed head forced into a camera or two after a few gags, especially when I recently revealed his middle name to be 'Bruce'. Alan wasn't even on the panel that day, but he was still enraged enough to call the studio live on air. Despite the hundreds of miles separating us, I was quaking in my shoes.

He has every right to carry a bit of gravitas: Alan has had a pretty distinguished career, having played for Celtic, Aston Villa and Bayern Munich. In fact, if you go to Munich (for the sights, not the beer festivals of course) and walk down the street with Alan, he generally gets mobbed. He's an absolute legend over there. He's an absolute legend on the show, too, because he gets fired up and he loves nothing more than a fiery debate. Just like Rodney Marsh, though, what happens on air stays on air. At the end of the afternoon any arguments we may have had are always forgotten, even if the pair of us have been going at it like cats and dogs.

The one thing you may have noticed about Mr McInally is that he's a tactless and shameful name-dropper. You'll be talking about Bolton Wanderers and before you know it, CLANG! 'Well I was on the phone to Gary Megson this week ...' You'll be discussing the emerging talent at Aston Villa and, CLANG! 'I bumped into Martin O'Neill the other day ...' He can also be a bit clumsy with his words. I remember him describing Cristiano Ronaldo as 'one of the most unique players in world football'. I thought, 'Come on, Big Man, you're either unique or you're not.' Bless him. Maybe he headed too many footballs during his career. Or just footballers, for that matter.

The one time we did upset him was when we were recording the *Jeff, Rodney and Friends* Christmas special several years back. The idea was to bring all the panellists into the show for the day to talk about their highlights of the season. As they filed in, we realized that there wasn't enough room in the studio to accommodate them all, so some bright spark came up with the idea of having a subs' bench outside, and from there we would bring the boys in one by one. Somebody else had the bright idea of leaving The Big Man until last. And then when the recording got underway, Matt Le Tissier had the even brighter idea of not letting him in at all – for comedy value, of course. There was nothing vindictive about it all, and I have to say that at the time, I thought it was a good idea. In retrospect, maybe it wasn't.

Given that it was a Christmas show, it was bloody freezing out there in the Sky Sports car park. In fact it was snowing. As the cameras rolled on (and on), The Big Man sat bravely in the cold. To his credit he played along with the joke admirably, reading a copy of the *Racing Post* as, one by one, the other guests had their turn in the studio warmth. 'Any moment now,' he must have thought, 'it's going to be my turn and I can get a nice cup of tea.' And then, the bombshell. As our time drew to a close, I cut back to the substitutes' bench: 'Anyway, time to bring in our last guest ... Oh, hang on, I'm just being told we don't have any more time. Goodbye!'

Well, Alan was livid. Livid. He got up from the bench, stormed through the snowdrifts and into the studio where he planned on having an almighty showdown with me and the producers. Unfortunately, he kicked in the door and burst into the wrong studio, which was completely empty. It wasn't until afterwards, when he was having a drink with Chris Kamara, that it turned out that he was really upset by the whole incident. Kammy came up to me and said, 'He's a little miffed, Jeff – unbelievable, I know, and he realizes that it was a great idea, and a very funny idea, but you probably should have told him. At the very least, he could have put some thermals on.'

In hindsight, I guess we should have warned him. Alan is theatrical enough (though if you're reading this, Alan, I am in no way comparing you to a 'luvvie') to have pulled off the element of surprise. But, then again, it was bloody funny. And, of course, I apologized profusely afterwards. On the phone, mind.

NAME: Alan Smith
BORN: 21 November 1962
CLUBS: Leicester City (1982-7), Arsenal (1987-95)
HONOURS: (Arsenal) League Championship 1989, 1991; FA Cup 1993; League Cup 1993; European Cup Winners' Cup 1994
INTERNATIONAL CAPS: (England) 13

Alan Smith - what a trouper! We sent him off to do the North London derby at White Hart Lane in 2006 - Arsenal versus Spurs, one of the biggest games in the Premier League. It was a murky day and Smudger was up in the gantry above the Spurs fans, which was fine. He managed to deliver the team news and other bits and pieces of info before the game with no problems at all. But when we cut to him later, the view had got murkier still, so we had to put the TV lights on him. As we were to find out very quickly, this marked the beginning of a personal nightmare.

First of all, picture the scene: a North London derby at White Hart Lane where tensions are high, when a former Arsenal striker starts reporting for the telly, his frame illuminated by banks of TV lights. Well, you can imagine the reaction. 'Al-aaaaan Smith, what a wanker, what a wanker,' sang the crowd. At first the chant was a mild murmuring. After 30 seconds, the entire ground seemed to be singing it, and it was so clear on the broadcast that I had to say at the end, 'Alan, I see that you've brought your fan club with you.'

The problem was that every time we cut to Alan for a match report, the Spurs fans would start up again. As soon as the TV lights came on, it was as if we were cueing up the crowd, but bless him, he got through it with a smile on his face. The same couldn't be said for the Spurs faithful, because they lost, so Alan had the last laugh, too.

PART 3

BEING

JEFF

22

In The Beginning

If legendary movie director Martin Scorsese were to make a biopic of my life (and I'd like to imagine a suave Robert De Niro representing me during my *Soccer Saturday* years), then the opening scene would resemble the sweepingscript work of his Mafia masterpiece, *Goodfellas*. The cameras zoom in on a younger, trimmer version of myself, resplendent in an ill-fitting suit while cutting rather a sharp dash with my lustrous hair. I'd be sitting on the steps of my Hartlepool house, mentally emulating Frank Bough, who was my hero at the time, but I'd like to stress at this point that my admiration for Bough was because of his role as *Grandstand*'s unflappable anchorman, rather than the shameless S&M antics that came later. Being exposed in the national press as someone who wears ladies' underwear at sex parties is not something that I've ever aspired to. (Probably best to talk to the other members of the *Soccer Saturday* panel on these matters.)

As we settle into our seats, the camera pans back. Cinema-goers will have me down as a man of humble beginnings with a 'go-get-'em' attitude as the opening fanfare of Tony Bennett's pop classic

'Rags to Riches' pumps from the speakers (or maybe something by Genesis). Beyond the crunch of popcorn and the unmistakable groans of yawning adults, I utter the immortal words: 'For as long as I can remember, I always wanted to be a broadcaster.' Cue a montage of glamorous girlfriends (I hear Uma Thurman is a fan of the show), fists slammed onto desks in high-powered meetings, and one-liners delivered expertly to camera. It'll have the critics drooling.

The truth is, for as long as I can remember I have always wanted to be a broadcaster. My big opportunity came in local radio when, as a cub reporter for modest rag the *Hartlepool Mail*, I scored a job at Radio Tees in 1977. I'd got a taste for journalism when I was about 12 and I began writing letters to the local paper. The star letter got a pound by way of a prize, which was a big deal in those days. Every time I wrote in, I got the star letter, which was fantastic. I thought, 'I really like the idea of this. Seeing my name in print is great!' It wasn't until I got a job at the *Hartlepool Mail* that I realized the only reason I was winning the star letter prize every week was because I was the only one writing in.

When it came to academics, however, I was hardly Stephen Fry material – or even Frank Lampard (nine GCSEs, including one in Latin. Wow!). After school I came out with a handful of O-levels and A-levels and I was accepted by a couple of universities, though they were in Belfast and Hull and I didn't know which was the worst option, to be brutally honest. I knew that I wanted to work for the local newspaper, and the editor, Maurice Brady, gave me a job straight away. I hardly set the world alight at the West Hartlepool Grammar School for Boys, but I was pretty good at English and creative writing, though I was never top of the class at anything. When it came to maths, I was usually somewhere towards the bottom. Miraculously, I passed my exam, though even today I still can't get the hang of the *Countdown* numbers game.

IN THE BEGINNING

Funnily enough, my maths teacher was a semi-professional footballer called Jimmy Douglas, who once played for Hartlepool. I remember one day he walked past my garden after my O-level results came out. He said to me, 'Jeff, of all the things in my career, the goals and suchlike, nothing has surprised me more than you passing your maths O-level.' I thought, 'Join the club, mate.'

My mum and dad were hardly journalistic. My dad, Andy, was a steelworker all of his life. I would meet him after work when he was covered in all sorts of crap, pushing his bike along the street. He would work from six in the morning until two in the afternoon, and he was always determined that, no matter what vocational path I chose, as long as it wasn't the same as his, he'd be happy. He didn't push me in any direction whatsoever. He was very forward-thinking and he was a staunch union man and Labour supporter. He could have had an absolute fit when, as a wet-behind-the-ears 18-year-old, I voted Tory in my first-ever election. It was beyond the pale, but he took it really well. I learned the error of my ways myself as time went on.

My mum, Nora, was a housewife, though she had been a nurse. I had two brothers – Tony and Peter. Tony went off to work in chemical plants on Teesside. Peter, meanwhile, went to Portsmouth Poly, as did my sister, Susan, who sadly died when she was 37. She just woke up one day and – bang – keeled over. Losing her was a big shock. She was the closest to me because we were the closest in age. I was the youngest of the litter, but completely against the grain when it came to our respective career paths.

Looking back I have absolutely no idea how I got the gig at Radio Tees, but the producers at the station were finding their feet in what was a relatively embryonic format at the time. They needed bodies on the end of microphones. I was 23 years old, with nothing in the way of broadcasting experience, but I had one or two journalistic qualifications with some local knowledge, so I was a) trained and sufficiently qualified, in theory, b) an expert on the area and c) cheap. It made me the perfect candidate.

Once ensconced in the studio I was absolutely wetting myself with excitement, even though for six days I wasn't even on the airwaves. But then my big break happened. It was a Saturday morning and I was playing football in the park with my mates. Suddenly, in the distance I could see my mum running towards me waving a telegram. A telegram! It tells you a lot about my age, and the scene was like something from *Last of the Summer Wine*, but there was nothing in the way of gentle humour on the paper:

```
= BERNARD GENT ILL — STOP — PLEASE GO TO
ELLAND ROAD IMMEDIATELY TO COVER LEEDS
    UNITED VERSUS MIDDLESBROUGH — STOP =
```

I couldn't believe it. For those of you under the age of 40, this game was a big deal at the time because it was a clash in the old First Division. It had a derby feel, too, so it was a huge responsibility for me to be covering the outside broadcast. Feeling a surge of adrenaline, I grabbed the telegram out of my mum's hands, picked up my ball and ran towards the house to gather my journalistic savvy. There was one snag: though I could drive at this point, I didn't actually have a car. In a flash of underhand inspiration, I rang my then-girlfriend.

'Hello darling, how do you fancy an afternoon in Leeds for a bit of shopping?' I crooned. It worked. She was very excited by the prospect of hightailing it to the city and perusing the boutiques while holding onto the Stelling arm. It was only when we were well on our way that I informed her that I wouldn't be carrying the bags and would instead be sending match reports from the Leeds United game. I don't think she was best-pleased.

In a frosty huff, she drove me to Elland Road. It was only then, once the initial excitement had passed, that I realized that I actually didn't have a clue what I was doing. I didn't know where I was going, how to get into the ground, where to get my pass, or who to ask for when I got to the ground. I didn't have any official Radio Tees identification. And I had absolutely no idea how to do the match reports when I eventually got into the ground. All these simple questions were firing around my mind. Which office did I collect my ticket from? Where was the best gate to approach? Was I in the right queue? And where was the press room? Unsurprisingly, I didn't get anything more than a sigh of support from my long-suffering girlfriend.

Through trial and error I somehow managed to get into the ground and made my way to the press box. There I was, completely wet behind the ears, in a room full of established national journos, all of whom knew one another and were locked in an intense debate about team selections and training-ground gossip. Meanwhile, I stood there like an 11-year-old in short trousers on the verge of peeing myself. I was in a complete state of confusion, but from my experience of listening to Hartlepool's away games on the wireless, I knew that at certain points during the game I would have to use a telephone to call in my reports to the radio station.

There was only one problem: I couldn't find the bloody telephones in the press box and had no idea of who to call. Thankfully a guy from the *Evening Gazette* in Middlesbrough took pity on this knock-kneed cub reporter and showed me where to pick up my phone and where to plug it in. I think he may have even handed me a copy of the local phone book so I could call Radio Tees. It was a real baptism of fire.

It was also one of the most terrifying experiences of my broadcasting career, because I had no idea of the basic rules of reporting. I certainly knew nothing of the logistics or techniques that I should have been using to relay information succinctly and precisely (as I do on a second-by-second basis every Saturday, loyal viewers), and looking back I was completely naïve. I guess this is why I sympathize with Paul Merson when he has to flap his way through a match report. Still, it was a great game for me. Leeds and Boro played out a 2-2 draw, but it was one of those fixtures where there was plenty of action to report.

In hindsight, this was a blessing, even if it didn't feel like it at the time. Having never been on the air in my entire life, I was suddenly the main port of call for the station, not that I had any idea what was going on or what I was saying because I was so bloody nervous.

There was also the added problem that I didn't really know that much about Middlesbrough or Leeds. I was a Hartlepool boy and that's where I spent most of my Saturday afternoons. In those days the blanket coverage of football that exists today was unimaginable, so a number of the players on show were a complete mystery to me. It was also a massive hindrance that footballers didn't have their names printed on the back of the shirts like they do today. It became apparent very quickly that recognizing the players was going to be a real job.

Thankfully, I quickly discovered a sense of camaraderie among the press corps – if I was unsure of a player's name, or if I'd missed something while running to the loo, then I only had to ask. In a flash, one of the other journalists would tell me what had happened, complete with names, ages and relevant player profiles, thus helping and heaping shame on me in equal dollops. I'm sure somewhere along the way I may have been duped by a smart-arse, but generally everybody was really helpful. Despite the trials and tribulations, I'd got through the game with relative ease.

There were more shocks to follow. When I went into work on the Monday morning, I was asked if I wanted to do a report every weekend. Staff in the station excitedly told me how good it had sounded, but in reality I think I was just rattling off a load of gabbled nonsense with one or two facts thrown in. Nevertheless, this really was the start of my broadcasting career. Bernard Gent's illness had given me a massive break, which I'm still thankful for today. Strangely, I don't think the girlfriend shared my overflowing enthusiasm.

Radio Tees was good fun. The working conditions were basic, but the great thing was that it was a news station and local radio was an emerging medium. Working on a local, independent channel was a very new thing back in the late 1970s and very exciting, too, particularly because there was more emphasis on local news, though principally it was a music station.

When I walked into the office for the first time, I knew nothing about the radio world, but I was in good company. Among the people employed there at the time was John Andrew, currently a BBC TV correspondent. Diana Goodman from the BBC, and Mark Mardell, the BBC's Europe Editor, were also cutting their teeth at the station in those days. I didn't realize it at the time, but I was working in an incredibly talented newsroom. Another friend of mine, news reporter Lee Peck, followed a slightly different career path and later went on to be one of the 'stars' of the second series of the TV prank show *Game for a Laugh*. Anyone who hasn't been scarred by the memory of this particular programme may recall that it also included Jeremy Beadle.

Still, I received a great education at Radio Tees. Having made the breakthrough into match-reporting, I later went on to manage sport for the station on a full-time basis. Much later, I even became their sports editor. I didn't have any staff, but I was running a sport and music show, which was a dream because I could indulge myself musically as well as editorially. It was probably one of the only sports shows around that would regularly feature Genesis between reports. It was fantastic fun and I remember sending subliminal messages out to girlfriends with the records I was playing. During pillow talk, I would tell them to listen out at a certain time in the afternoon and then play 'Who Were You With In The Moonlight?' by Dollar. It was a bloody awful record, but great fun to play.

Because of my relative enthusiasm, however, I was allowed to call the shots by then and so I began covering a lot of top-flight football. It was my first proper grounding in the game and, in those days, reporters could actually go to grounds and interview the players without too much hassle. You didn't need a club official to give you the green light, and I remember interviewing the likes of Tony Mowbray – who was a Boro hero at the time – and Graeme Souness. But Boro were quite a good side in those days and these contacts were vital to the show.

I also used to cover Sunderland and Newcastle to a lesser degree, and if I was really lucky I would get to Hartlepool now and then, though it was hardly sprinkled with glamour and stardust. Those were horrendous days for the club. They had no money, and a farmer called Vince Barker was in charge as chairman. I remember regularly phoning the manager, Billy Horner, in his office. On more than one occasion he would ask if he could call me back later. Billy would then leave his office, go to the phone box over the road and ring me back before informing me that the chairman was listening to his conversations on the other line.

IN THE BEGINNING

It was a crazy time, but despite my love for Hartlepool I began to experience itchy-feet syndrome. In 1981, I found myself heading to the bright lights and riots of London Town. My reputation was blossoming and I'd actually got a job with LBC Radio in the capital, though it was at the second time of asking that I eventually agreed to join them. I took some persuading – I was, by then, a married man and felt uncomfortable at moving to a completely alien city. Besides, Chas & Dave were very big at the time and the thought of moving to a city inhabited by cockneys was initially unnerving.

Eventually we plucked up the courage to move, though relocating to London was a bigger culture shock than we'd expected. The housing was terrible. We bought a place in the North End Road, West Kensington, and it was hardly palatial. Previously we'd lived in a lovely four-bedroom home overlooking a golf course in Billingham, and were used to the high(ish) life. Because of my 'climb' up the career ladder, we had ended up in a one-bedroom, ground-floor apartment with a shared bathroom and a slot TV which took 50-pence pieces. It was hard not to think, 'What have we done?'

The good news didn't end there. At the time there were a number of riots kicking off in the capital. Obviously, because of my job at a news station, we would often get word of when and where they were going to take place. Rather conveniently, many of them were exploding near my front door. I particularly remember one night when we found ourselves locked in our house on a sweltering summer evening. A busload of riot police were taking their positions outside with shields, protective armour and batons. It was a bit like queuing for a pie at the New Den.

You didn't have to be Rageh Omaar to realize that living in a ground-floor flat in those days was tactically unsound – you never knew where the petrol bombs were going to hit. I remember spending one evening crouched behind the front door preparing for what seemed like an imminent attack. The only weapon I had to hand was an empty bottle of whisky. If anyone tried to smash their way in – rioter or bobby – the plan was to wallop them over the head as hard as I could. It was hardly Tony Soprano home security, and I suspect I may have been drunk on the whisky before the riot even kicked off that night, but desperate times called for desperate measures.

If our new home was proving quite a shock to the system, then on air there were cultural gulfs to bridge too. I soon realized that my north-eastern dialect was at odds with what was being spoken in the capital. The station even received complaints, and there were often letters from confused listeners. One that sticks in the mind was a note that arrived on the desk of Mike Lewis, my editor, with the Monday post.

Dear Mr Lewis
Where the hell did you get that bloke with the terrible
    accent? Take him off the air!
Yours sincerely,
Mr M. Jones

It was short and savage, a bit like Dennis Wise, but Mike wrote back a diplomatic reply:

Dear Mr Jones,

Thank you for your letter regarding Jeff Stelling. He is from
the north-east, and I'm sure that in this day and age,
regional accents should be encouraged, not discouraged.

Yours sincerely,

Mike Lewis

Two days later, Mr Jones had written another letter:

Dear Mr Lewis,

Thank you for your reply. I am in agreement that regional
dialects should be encouraged. However, speech
impediments should not.

Yours sincerely,

Mr M. Jones

The radio station stuck by me regardless, but the complaints
didn't end there. One of my jobs at the time was to do a weekly
press review on air. I got this idea from something we used to do
at Radio Tees – it was basically a facetious look at the sporting week
by reviewing the media. After a month of working with this format,
I received an angry letter referring to some disparaging remarks
I had made about John McEnroe. I knew it wasn't going to be too
complimentary because it started with the words 'Jeff Stelling:
shit!' and went on to say:

How dare you insult John McEnroe? He is a genius. Are you
great at anything? In actual fact we have been wanting to write
about your horrible accent. You have the same horrible accent
as that lunatic on the darts programme when the lovely Mr Bristow is on. When you read the pools, your silly accent says "Woon"

(instead of one). You take the one a mile [this, I believe, is a derogatory reference to my prenunciation of the word 'one']. Wherever the hell you are from, you and [Ian] Paisley have the two most horrible accents, so why don't you stick your head in shit rather than speak unfit about a great tennis player, the best in the world. You are so simple, you talk about football as if it was important, a matter of life and death. How dare you speak about an Irish American when you're useless. So go and put your fucking head in the lavatory pan. Go on a trip in a barrel down Niagra Falls you simple shit.

When we hear your horrible weak voice we usually turn you off. If you were one of John McEnroe's toes you would be something. John McEnroe would think it an insult to be on a programme with you. Watch what you say about anyone Irish in future you shit. Shit, shit, shit, shit. **9**

I thought, 'Cheers, Mum.'

The final 'shit' was double underlined, by the way. It could only have got any weirder had it been written in capital letters and stamped by one of Her Majesty's Prisons. It's arguably the greatest letter I have ever received, though I'm expecting a few more after the publication of this book. But, as you can see, working in London was pretty scary, and I would rather have been anywhere else in the world. I remember applying for jobs in Bristol and Leeds, but everyone turned me down and I didn't get anywhere. In hindsight it was the best thing that could have happened to me because the job really started to take off from then, and as a sports reporter for LBC I ended up travelling the world. For some reason I became the station's athletics correspondent at the beginning of the 1980s. It was a bizarre situation because I knew very little about the sport and my inexperience started to show.

In fact, my career almost stalled when I went to the European Athletics Championships in Yugoslavia in 1981. It was a two-day event and the broadcasting techniques were hardly high-tech: we used to send in radio bulletins via telephone and would attach 'croc clips' to the tape recorder to deliver reports down the line. This worked absolutely fine, and on the first day I gathered a load of interviews that I had to send back to the station when I returned to the hotel.

Of course, Yugoslavia was still a communist country at this time and I couldn't get an outside line through the operator. I'm sure my calls were being bugged, too. It was like a James Bond movie, but without the glamorous women and fancy sports cars (this would come much later). Matters were made worse by the fact that LBC were being slightly cautious with their budget and had put me in a two-star hotel with limited facilities. As the night went on, it was obvious that I wasn't going to be able to get an outside line. By 11 o'clock that night, I had been trying for three hours. In the end I thought, 'Sod it, I'm going out.' So I left the hotel and had some dinner and a few drinks.

When I returned to the room, I had a furious row with Mike Lewis. He'd managed to track me down and was quite unhappy that I hadn't called in my reports. 'It's the biggest mistake I've made putting you in as athletics man,' he shouted. 'You should have been sitting there all night trying to get through. You've let everyone down.'

He was right, but I was still inexperienced and hadn't realized the severity of my error. Unbelievably, Mike stuck by me and I soon became a proper roving reporter abroad. I loved those foreign assignments. I had some fantastic times, and I remember going to the World Athletic Championships in Helsinki in 1983, which was a big, big deal by then. I would do a lot of the trackside interviews with athletes after they had finished competing, and it was here that I heard the most politically-incorrect interview of my career.

I was chatting to Alan Wells, the Scottish sprinter who was running for Great Britain in the 100 metres. He came fourth and I'd managed to get an interview with him as he walked away from the track. We started innocuously enough. 'Are you disappointed Alan? You've only just missed out on the medals ...' I said.

He looked at me and smiled. 'Well, I was the first white man home, wasn't I?'

I couldn't believe it. We actually put that out on air – these days we wouldn't have broadcast that at all. In hindsight, he wasn't being racist, it was just a statement of fact, but in this day and age you couldn't get away with saying something like that.

Unsurprisingly, most of the fun took place away from the athletics stadiums. I remember being out one night with two reporters called Doug Gillan and Alex Cameron. We'd been partying and, as the evening came to a close, I went back to my room for some more drinks because the booze in Helsinki was incredibly expensive and we had our own stash. Alex also decided to pop back to his room to fetch a bottle of scotch.

Doug was a real Rob Roy character with a dangling beard, and for a joke he decided to hide in the wardrobe. The plan was to spring out when Alex returned to my room with the drink. Anyway, Alex came back with his bottle of whisky, and we sat there for an hour or so and drank the lot.

'Shame,' said Alex. 'It would have been nice for Doug to have stayed up and finished this with us.'

I thought, 'Shit! Doug!' We opened the wardrobe door and there was Doug, fast asleep. It was juvenile stuff, but all good fun.

It wasn't long before I was on the move again. Mike Lewis had moved to Radio 2 which was then the equivalent of Radio 5 Live now – it focused on sport, phone-ins and discussion shows. He decided to take me with him, and I was only too happy to oblige. Once there, I was working with Peter Jones and Bryon Butler, who were the doyens of the football commentary world, long before the likes of John Motson and Alan Green came along. They really were fantastic commentators.

I also worked with a character called Peter Bromley, who was one of the scariest men I'd ever met, but the best horse racing commentator I knew on the radio at that time. He was always right (he could call a photo finish at a race before the official verdict had been delivered) and absolutely fearless to boot. Big, burly and bear-like, Peter was a throwback to something from the early 20th century. He would often wear tweed, which was a very unfashionable look. That, twinned with his incredibly high standards and fastidious nature, meant he was a man very much of another time.

For a while, I was a racing reporter alongside him and it was obvious that everyone was afraid of Peter. Most notably me. He would bellow, he would shout. He would not tolerate anything he saw as foolish. If you weren't wearing a tie you were in trouble.

I remember one day at the racecourse he came in and started bellowing:

'Stelling! I want you to ring this number – 324167.'

As it was Peter, I wasn't going to argue. He was putting me through to York racecourse, so I asked who I was calling.

'It's the clerk of the course,' he shouted 'Tell him it's a bloody disgrace! The men's toilet has no toilet paper and I've had to wipe my arse on the greyhound pages of the *Sporting Life*!'

Of course, there was no need for me to tell the course clerk. He had heard the tirade from Peter as he picked up the phone in his office.

I could see my time was coming to an end at Radio 2. I really wanted to present the show called *Sport on 2*, which is now known as *Sport on 5*. The then Head of Sport didn't think I was as good as the guy who would later go on to present it: John Inverdale. John was a good mate of mine – and he still is – but I was mortally offended by this decision. In hindsight, he was right, though. John was very good, particularly on the radio. He's still a fantastic broadcaster, and while it was hard to accept at the time, I couldn't see any way of getting past him, so it was clearly time to move on. But my next transfer was to propel me into the world of Olympians and shaggers. Anyone assuming that I'm linking you, the reader, somewhat neatly, to the *Soccer Saturday* panel would be close. But you won't be receiving the celebratory cigar. My subsequent career-hop to the breakfast telly show *TV-am* took me into the world of presenting, Sir David Frost's sofa and the back seat of Daley Thompson's chauffeur-driven car. And what a blast it was too ...

23

'I'm Not A Celebrity

... Get Me Out Of Here Anyway!'

Only the early risers and the more advanced in years among you would have caught my debut on national television and *TV-am* a couple of decades ago. It happened one weekend in 1988. I was presenting a sports round-up on ITV's *Frost on Sunday* show, as presented by legendary telly icon Sir David Frost. So, as this was the sort of early-morning programme favoured by teetotallers who weren't nursing a sore head from the night before (so none of the *Soccer Saturday* panel, then) and the politically-minded, it's unlikely any of you lot would have been drawn to the telly that morning. Not that my appearance would have lived long in the memory anyway. Well, apart from my sweater, which would probably have embarrassed Noel Edmonds. Oh, and I was perspiring slightly through nerves.

Still, I received my most impressive introduction to date, a link from Sir David, no less – the man who had once telly-whipped former US president Richard 'Watergate' Nixon.

'Ladies and gentlemen,' he purred in those distinctive tones, 'please welcome, for the very first time, Jeff Stelling.'

I visibly beamed with pride. Twenty years on, I can still remember that morning vividly, even though I was shaking and trembling with terror. I was hot and sweaty and there was no sign of my 'oasis of calm' persona (this would come much later, readers), but I managed to get through my two-minute cameo without any major disasters. In fact, I remember the floor manager and camera crew giving me a hearty round of applause once we'd gone to the commercials. It was a massive boost to my confidence.

Of course, this TV break didn't happen overnight. I first had to see out my time at BBC Radio, which I did in 1988. Somewhat foolishly, I'd handed in my notice on the eve of the Seoul Olympics, and I fully expected the Beeb to take away my press accreditation for the event, while telling me to hop it to ITV. Surprisingly, they kept me on, and so it was that I was on-hand to cover one of the most controversial moments in Olympic history, Ben Johnson's positive doping test.

Being the aggressive newshound that I was, when I first heard the news of Johnson's fall from grace I was tucked up in bed, sound asleep. It was around five o'clock in the morning that my peaceful beauty-slumber was disturbed when the bedside phone began to ring. Whoever was on the other end of the line was asking for Jonathan Marlin, head of the BBC at the time. I explained, somewhat gruffly, that they had called the wrong number and tried to get back to sleep, but the alarm bells were beginning to ring. Anyone brave enough to want to wake the head of the BBC at that ungodly hour must have had some serious news to report.

I was right. Half an hour later I received another call, though this one was more abrupt.

'Jeff,' said the voice. 'Get your arse down to the athlete's village. Ben Johnson has failed his drug test.'

This was shocking news. Johnson was, of course, the most revered athlete of his generation and any scandal surrounding him was big, big news. Tearing off my pyjamas and dressing hurriedly, I scampered down to the Olympic village with a handful of other BBC journalists to cover the event. Once there, we were only given two passes. I grabbed one and the other went to a guy who was covering the story for the Beeb's local stations. Swiftly, we went to work on uncovering the juicy gossip on Johnson's disgrace.

By now the athletes were starting to wake up and the un-believable news was spreading through the village like wildfire. My brief was to get as much reaction from the athletes about the Johnson story as possible – the bigger the names, the better – but there was a hitch. By now, the authorities were on to us and trying to get the press out of the village as quickly as they could. Thankfully, with a few deft manoeuvres more in tune with a scene from *The Bourne Identity* than BBC *Grandstand*, I managed to lose my Olympic markers and gathered quotes from some none-too-alert athletes. My partner in crime wasn't so fortunate and was nabbed almost immediately, quickly cracking under interrogation.

'What company are you with and are you alone?' snapped his 'arresting' official.

The reporter blubbed. 'I'm from the BBC and I'm with Jeff Stelling, who is sitting over there, you see? The bloke with dark hair, a suit, notepad. There, that one there. Yeah him, no, no, the one next to him,' he wailed, pointing fearfully in my direction as I shook my head in disappointment. It was hardly something out of the Andy McNab SAS handbook, though we were hardly the Water-gate crackers, Woodward and Bernstein. Still, I managed to pipe some quotes through to the Beeb and it marked an exciting end to some enjoyable times.

Looking back, I worked in a golden era for British athletics. During that time, I was covering some of the biggest names in world sport, including Daley Thompson, Steve Cram, Fatima Whitbread, Tessa Sanderson and Steve Ovett. Daley was the biggest star of the lot and he always drew a lot of attention from fans and the media, especially the Sunday newspapers. Word would often come through that the news boys had been sent out to an athletics event, and nine times out of 10 they were tailing a story on Daley, but I rarely got to interview him because he always declined. However, I remember we had to walk to these cabins in the training camp in Seoul every morning for press conferences and briefings, and as I was walking down one morning, it began peeing down. Daley always had a chauffeur-driven car to take him to and from training and, as I slowly became damper in the rain, I heard a toot of a car horn and Daley pulled over. 'Fancy a lift, mate?' he said. I was driven to training and Daley was as nice as pie.

Generally, though, there was always plenty of gossip going around the British camp concerning any number of athletes. Let's be honest, these men and women were fit, virile young Olympians and anybody looking for tittle-tattle would find plenty of it. We knew what was going on. We knew who was shagging who and suchlike, and equally the athletes knew that the media's sports corps would never breathe a word to anyone, but as soon as the news boys from the national newspapers came along it became a different matter.

Suddenly, athletics was big news and some of the stars of the show suffered accordingly. Steve Ovett, for example, was a man who was very much misunderstood among the public, especially when he was at the peak of his powers during the 1980 Olympics in Moscow. A lot of people found him to be abrasive in front of the cameras and microphones – when he talked into them, that is. At one meeting at Crystal Palace a press conference was scheduled after the event. With the world's journos assembled, Steve didn't bother turning up. He didn't even give an explanation for his absence. Anyway, I'd got wind that he was leaving the stadium and went out into the car park to find him walking to his car. Plucking up the courage, I approached him, asked him for some quotes and we had a good chat and a great interview. Clearly he was happy to talk – he just didn't want to be at everybody's beck and call during a press conference. 'If somebody wants to speak to me, then I'm happy to have a chat,' he said. 'But why should I troop up there because everybody wants me to?'

These were the best of times really, but it was around 1988 and the Seoul Olympics that I noticed a souring relationship between sportsmen and journalists. I'm not sure why, but I guess it was because so many of our athletes were household names, and with that burden comes unwanted media attention. Up until this point, we would report on events like the European Athletics Championships and after the meetings we would go out on the town with a whole host of athletes. We would even have a few beers with them – it was always a good laugh and there was certainly no feeling of 'us and them' among the press and the sportsmen. In some cases there were genuine friendships, too.

All of that changed around the time of Seoul. By then, I imagine that pretty much every athlete had been the victim of bad headlines during his or her career and nobody liked to read them.

The trust had gone, especially once the tabloids started throwing muck around – it's a problem that the modern footballer still suffers from today.

Last year I was in Spain with the Blackburn Rovers and England keeper Paul Robinson. A request came through from an English magazine asking for an interview and, as a courtesy, they sent him a list of questions they were hoping to ask. He showed them to me and one of them read, 'What do you think of Real Madrid?'

Paul, who was at Spurs at the time, said to me, 'I think that they're a fantastic club, but if I say that in the interview, the headline will be "Robbo says: Madrid bigger than Spurs" or "Robbo plea: Come and get me Madrid."'

Another question asked him to compare Steve McClaren to Sven-Göran Eriksson, which of course he couldn't do because the answer would have been taken out of context and splashed all over the papers the following day. I could see completely where he was coming from, but 20 years ago, those questions and answers would have been treated completely innocently.

In a footnote (all very Bill Bryson, I know), I have to say that the Seoul games were probably my biggest adventure to date, though it wasn't without its dramas. For one assignment, I was sent out to Japan to work at the British team's training camp in Chiba City. I was on my own, and the first thing you realize when you get to Japan is that you can't read any of the signs. I had planned on getting a cab to the training camp, but all the drivers were quoting me prices of £300 or more. Of course, I was on a BBC budget and therefore restricted to getting a train. I got to the station and after about three stops I realized that there weren't any English signs. I had absolutely no idea where I was. After every stop I would stand up and in my loudest voice shout, 'Chiba City!' Eventually I found my way there, but not before receiving some curious looks from some rather terrified Japanese commuters.

I hated it at *TV-am*. Absolutely, bloody, 100 per cent hated it.

I started there as a sports presenter, but it was the worst period of my life, bar none. Nobody on the show was interested in sport, so I was restricted to producing two 90-second bulletins per day, and that was it. Worse, the people who ran the station had no understanding of sport, so on a Saturday they would ask us to do a live sports round-up, though it took place at 6.30 in the morning when nobody was watching. It was all very frustrating.

Looking back, I guess the producers only really became interested in sport when something big or glamorous came up, such as the Derby or FA Cup Final. But even when their interest was sparked, the coverage was usually bungled or delivered in a shoddy manner. For example, a couple of days before the Derby, one of the management team approached me and told me that they wanted one of the competing horses and its riders in the studio on the morning of the race. I thought he was joking at first.

'Well that is absolutely impossible,' I said.

I was then told that Red Rum had been in the studio before, so I tried pointing out that Red Rum had been a 19-year-old horse at the time and he wasn't running any more. To bring a thoroughbred stallion into the studio would have been fraught with complications. Not that we could afford the insurance that would have been required to get the horse and jockey into the studio. So even if a horse trainer and owner were insane enough to consider our invitation on the day of the race, it was totally, utterly, completely impossible logistically.

JELLEYMAN'S THROWN A WOBBLY

Fellow Sky presenter Richard Keys was there at the time, as was easy-on-the-eye weathergirl Ulrika Jonsson, not that I was in her league – I was merely a tiny little cog on the other side of the office. And I detested it. Thankfully, the likes of Rustie Lee, Roland Rat and Timmy Mallett had just left the station, which was probably a blessing in disguise when you consider the DayGlo leisurewear he used to bring into the studio (Mallett, that is, not Richard).

In hindsight, the job should have been a dream because the sports team operated on a three-week rota. On the first week we'd work on overnight scriptwriting. We'd start at nine o'clock in the evening and that was supposed to take you until the following morning to deliver. But we only had a 90-second script to write which, with a bit of practise, we could deliver by nine thirty. The big decision was: do you go to the pub until eleven o'clock, come back and have a bit of a kip; or do you do it straight away and get to the pub for last orders and a curry? The tedium of working those nights was unbelievable, but you couldn't really bunk off and go home just in case something happened, which of course it wouldn't, because nothing sport-related happened at three in the morning. Unless it involved George Best.

The second week would involve me doing a report for the Saturday show but because the company had a policy where nothing could run for longer than 90 seconds, I was hardly challenged. In fact, I had a full week to decide what I wanted to do, where I wanted to go, when to organize the camera crew and edit it all. It's the sort of thing they would do in two hours at Sky and I soon realized that I didn't want to be sitting on my arse all the time. In 1990 I was following Mr Rat and Mr Mallett away from *TV-am* and into the fuzzy world of satellite telly. It was the beginning of a confusing era.

24

Cable Guy

(Well, Satellite TV Guy If We're Being Pedantic, But There Isn't A Hollywood Movie Of The Same Title ...)

As if by magic, along came the 'squareial'. Well, satellite TV, which had a pretty rubbish reputation in those days. It was the early 90s and I remember that the medium was pretty new and getting a lot of stick from all quarters. Not all of it was unjustified, either – the dishes were bigger than the technology you'd find at NASA and the reception was often a bit iffy. Even those grizzly old forerunners of *Soccer Saturday*, Saint (Ian St John) and Jimmy 'Greavsie' Greaves were having a pop. I believe the former Spurs striker claimed live on telly that he'd pretended to the neighbours that he had Sky by tying a wok to his roof.

He had a point, I guess. The technology felt a bit, well, hit-and-miss, but when satellite company BSB offered me an escape route from my breakfast telly hell in 1990, I jumped at the chance. Before I knew it, I was getting drunk with darts players and commentating on fencing, among other things. Elsewhere, I was flexing my muscles as a bona fide sumo wrestling expert. As Greavsie once noted, 'It's a funny old game,' though I believe he was talking about football, but this maxim could just as easily be applied to the world of television.

My journey towards the *Soccer Saturday* studios began when Ian Condron – now the producer of *Soccer Saturday* – went to BSB and suggested I try and join him. BSB was just about to launch, and I reckoned on there being quite a few opportunities for a thrusting showman like myself. I was right, too. I was being offered the job of sports presenter and roving reporter for the station, which I figured was a good result.

I was told that it would be my role to act as a stand-in for one of the three star presenters – Anna Walker, Gary Richardson and Steve Scott – should they be struck down with illness or off on holiday, but, to be honest, I would have taken just about anything to escape the horror of *TV-am*. Little did I know just how eventful my appointment would prove to be.

A week before BSB was due to launch, my new boss, Vic Wakeling – yes, the same one – called me at home.

'Look, Jeff,' he said, 'I've been looking at your showreel tape and I think I've made a mistake here. We're wasting you as a reporter. I'm going to offer you a job as a presenter.'

I laughed. I knew exactly what was happening: one of the main presenters had changed their minds. 'That's fantastic, Vic,' I said. 'Who's dropped out?'

Vic laughed and said, 'No, no, no, Steve Scott's not coming, but ...'

But? There were no buts. I didn't care what the reasons were. I was happy to have the job and it was apparent that I'd walked into a bloody good gig. Almost immediately the pressure was off, because nobody was watching BSB, which was handy because I was working on a lot of sports that I knew absolutely nothing about, including snooker and swimming. This meant I had to do a hell of a lot of bluffing, and anyone tuning in would have noticed pretty quickly that I was like a fish out of water.

I wasn't the only one. I distinctly remember sitting in the dressing room one night with beautiful co-presenter Anna Walker. We were about to host an evening of European football. By way of final preparations, the pair of us began going through all the names of teams and players to double-check their correct pronunciations. After a while, we thought we had cracked it, until we got to Dundee United and the name of their home ground, Tannadice. This was at the time when Dundee United were doing well in Europe, but Anna had obviously got a little carried away with all those Italian and Polish pronunciations, because she decided to refer to United's famous ground as Tanner-dee-chey.

In hindsight, this was a small-scale blunder. Satellite TV seemed high-tech at the time, but in reality it wasn't. In some senses it was practically steam-driven. Often you'd be presenting a sports report at one-thirty in the afternoon from a cubicle the size of a toilet. You'd be working with autocues that were foot-pump driven, like the accelerator in a car. We were positioned out near Chelsea, far from HQ, in a fabulous building with great marble towers on Battersea Bridge. This was obviously the company's downfall because they'd spent an absolute fortune on running before they could walk.

So, even though I was finding my feet in the world of satellite TV, the writing was on the wall that BSB's existence could be short-lived. There was also a poorly-kept secret doing the rounds that a battle between BSB and the other kids on the squareial block, Sky, was about to turn into a full-blown war. Expert opinion reckoned that there would only be one winner and that was going to be Sky. The date of my redundancy was even predicted by a former colleague of mine, Mike Miller, the man that got me a job at *TV-am*. Out of the blue, he rang me one day and said, 'Jeff, have a look around to see what jobs are out there because on 14 April you're going to be sacked.'

I couldn't believe it. I told my mates and thought it was complete fantasy, but I knew BSB was shaky anyway, so I managed to get some work at Tyne Tees TV, just in case. Anyway, on 14 April we were called into a staff meeting. It was horrendous because the MD of the company came in and he explained to the crew that there were one or two financial problems. My heart sank. Mike was right.

'Now, this does not mean that there are going to be redundancies at the company,' he said. Everyone breathed a sigh of relief, especially me. And than he continued: 'However, all those working on sports news will be made redundant.'

My heart sank again. It was awful. The people who weren't on the sports news team didn't know whether to laugh or to cry. Luckily I had a job to go to. I travelled to Tyne Tees, but I was only there for two weeks when my guardian angel, Mike Miller, called again. This time he arrived with even stranger news: 'Jeff,' he said down the telephone, 'what do you know about American football?'

'Nothing,' I answered.

He seemed unperturbed. 'How quickly can you learn? We're launching the World League on Channel 4 and focusing on the London Monarchs. I'm looking for a presenter. Do you want to do it?'

He offered me 13 weeks' work. It came in at double the pay I was receiving for a year's work at Tyne Tees. I couldn't turn it down, plus it was back in London. It was also the correct move. *The American Football Show* was sensational. We were working with a US production company, which was an experience in itself – the access to players, for example, was absolutely staggering. We were in the locker rooms, in their homes, and partying with the coaches. Whatever we wanted to do, we were granted access to it. It was also the first year of the World League and there would be 70,000 fans at Wembley for the London Monarchs' games, all of them able to drink beer in their seats, which made for a great atmosphere. I absolutely loved it.

What came next was a blur of opportunities and confusing adventures. All of a sudden, Channel 4 had secured the rights to show the sumo wrestling. I got another call, this one enquiring, 'What do you know about sumo wrestling, Jeff?'

I said, 'Exactly the same amount as I knew about American Football when I started.'

'Well,' said the voice, 'how would you fancy doing a documentary on it?'

All of a sudden we were covering a live 'Basho' – or tournament – at the Royal Albert Hall. The event was an absolute sell-out. My role was to say, 'Hello, here we are at the Royal Albert Hall for the biggest sumo event Britain has ever seen,' and 'Goodbye!' at the end. That was it. I had become, by accident, the official face of sumo, and I loved it. In those days Channel 4 used to run a show on the sport every Monday night. I soon realized that what I thought was a joke discipline played by Japanese fatties in cotton nappies was actually an artful feat of athleticism. I wouldn't exactly call the sumo wrestlers sportsmen, but I began to see a level of skill which I hadn't appreciated before.

The rollercoaster ride had only just begun, however. I later got a call from Eurosport, the continent-wide sports channel, which was then in its development stages. The company were launching their

British channel. They were based in Paris, but would I like to go over as a presenter anyway? Well, of course I would. I was divorced and newly single, so I was very excited by the prospect. We were based in an office on the banks of the River Seine, but the work was strange. Very strange. I don't want to be rude, but how the French can have a fantastic infrastructure in their cities is beyond me, because the organization of their TV shows was unbelievably bad.

I got over there and they asked me what I wanted to do. I told them I could do most sports, football and even sumo if they wanted, so they decided they were going to use me for athletics, but their coverage was quite hyperactive to say the least. Nothing was covered live from an event; it was all presented from a big building somewhere in Paris. From the studio I would be commentating as the events on the TV screens at home jumped all over the place. One minute I'd be covering a marathon in the glorious sunshine in the States and then I'd be commentating on the shot put from a Grand Prix event in Moscow in the snow and rain. It was ludicrous.

You'd get the start-time lists of all the events so you could plan for what you were meant to be commentating on next, but often they would be wrong and then all sorts of disaster could befall you. I remember commentating on a 3000 metres steeplechase race and I was given 12 names for 12 runners. The only problem was there were 13 runners. After a couple of laps, the bloke who was leading the race was running at a world-record pace. The only problem was, he was the guy we didn't have a name for. People were running around behind the scenes trying to find out who he was, but we didn't have a bloody clue. Thankfully, he ran out of steam, but it was purgatory for us not to have a clue as to the identity of this potential world-record-breaker.

I remember we used to work with Angus Loughran, or Statto as he was later known on late-night show *Fantasy Football League*, which also featured comedians David Baddiel and Frank Skinner. He was called in one day to commentate on an ice hockey match between the USA and the USSR. He knew nothing about ice hockey, and worse, the producers didn't have a teamsheet for him to work from. What we knew, as presenters, was that most of the time our French paymasters weren't listening in. When they were, they didn't know what we were saying. Once the game got underway, Statto started naming the Russian team ('Gorbachev, Stalin ...') and the Americans ('Reagan, Nixon, Kennedy...'). He did the entire game as Presidents versus Soviet leaders. Unbelievably we had no complaints.

I later offered to cover tennis because, after the steeplechase incident, I couldn't really trust the info we were getting from our researchers. I figured that with only two names to worry about, well, what could go wrong? Anyway, I remember finishing one match when a French controller grabbed me and said, 'Jeff, Jeff, you must go back into the studio!'

I said, 'I've finished; why?'

He said, 'We have to get someone to commentate on the world fencing championships. Our commentator hasn't turned up.'

Well, I could creosote a fence, but I couldn't commentate on the actual sport. Anyway, I was told that if I didn't do it, I would lose my job. I went back into the studio where I knew nothing about what was going on. As a result, my commentary was hardly award-winning stuff, comprising of, 'Good afternoon from Prague. That was great! What a move!' or, 'Oh my word! The crowd really appreciated that move!' I believe I finished on, 'Well wasn't he a worthy winner?' It really was appalling.

In the long term, it wouldn't have done anyone's reputation any good if Eurosport had stayed that way. We would have a laugh about the shoddy presentation in the bar afterwards, but we knew things would have to change. I had to get out. Thankfully I would have another calling when I received a message from Andy Cairns, who was head of the sports news department at Sky. It was a Saturday night. He wanted to give me a chance on telly.

I asked him when, and he told me it was for the following morning. Well, I thought about it and figured that it could be a good move for me. I decided to book a flight. It was certainly worth a go. I got back to England late that night, grabbed a couple of hours sleep and then went into Sky. I'd never been there before, so I didn't know where the sports department was. In those days it was like working for a one-man band. I got in and there was a changeover sheet waiting for me explaining what I had to do. Of course, I had no log-in details to get into a computer. I had to beg people to log me in. I then had to find the place where they kept the tapes of various news reports and edit them into a comprehensive sports round-up, but it was a system that I was totally unfamiliar with. Miraculously I got through the morning with a hell of a lot of help from the people around me, but then I had to get myself together. I presented these news reports every half an hour. It was a nightmare, but it went well enough for them to offer me a job.

Initially I didn't do what I'm doing now – I was covering a lot of other sports, though I remember getting one or two critical letters during my time on Sky's horse racing coverage:

Dear Mr Stelling,

In last week's horse racing show, you said 'as well' 43 times and 'indeed' 73 times. I would like to wipe the smug smile off your face with the toe of my boot.

Yours, Mr Miffed of Musselburgh

I thought, 'Well, that's charming,' but decided to read the letter out on air. I also read out his full name and address. We knew Musselburgh quite well at the time, and the next time I went into the town, a group of lads came up to me in the street. This was one of the first inclinations I'd ever had that I was actually being watched on telly because one of them said, 'You know that bloke who wrote a letter to you, saying he'd like to wipe your smile off your face with his boot? Well, we went to pay him a visit.' Crikey, I thought, that wasn't the intention when I read out his address, but by the sounds of things he got more than he bargained for.

I really fell in love with the job when I started covering the darts for Sky. In fact, when the PDC (Professional Darts Corporation) started, I was hosting the first of their world darts championships. The breakaway of the PDC from the BDO (British Darts Organisation) – currently the two ruling factions of darts – was pretty brutal to say the least. The PDC took all the best players and organized bigger-money events, so naturally the two sides didn't speak to each other. Tensions were often heightened. People hated each other on either side, but I was working with the players who had broken away to make more cash – the PDC. And there were some big names, too. We had Eric Bristow and Jocky Wilson, Dennis Priestley and some of the boys we have now, including Phil 'The Power' Taylor, although he was just Phil Taylor at that point, as he hadn't quite discovered 'The Power'.

I remember we were doing a launch show live from the Circus Tavern in Purfleet, Essex. It was the PDC's first World Championship, and naturally they were eager to make a big deal of the event. We were going live on air at two o'clock and I had a duo of big names with me in the shape of Eric Bristow and Jocky Wilson. I gave them a grand entrance: 'Hello ladies and gentlemen, this is a big night for Sky and darts, and how better to introduce our live coverage than with two of the biggest names in the game: Eric Bristow and Jocky ... er Jocky, er ... Brown!'

For some reason I had a mental blackout and had got the name of one of the biggest names in the game completely wrong. All these darts experts from the PDC must have been watching and thinking, 'What have we done? Let's go back to the BBC!'

It was quite a low-key event in those days - it was nothing like the Super League Darts you see on Sky today. The competitions were so poorly attended that we had to position the cameras to make the venues look full when we were reporting. We would often have one table that was packed and the rest of the hall was empty, so we would put members of the production crew on tables to fill them up. It's amazing how it has taken off since then.

It was still brilliant fun, in fact they were probably some of the best days and nights of my career. We went everywhere with the darts players: Essex, Blackpool, Birmingham. And if you're going to work in darts, you have to be able to drink a little bit. Booze was their life. I remember working with Keith Deller, who was one of our 'spotters'. What this job involved was sitting in a room and watching the body language of Eric Bristow, or whoever was playing at the time, and informing the director where he was about to throw his next dart. The cameras could then seamlessly zoom into the right section of the board. This would obviously require an expert knowledge of the positioning of the darts player's body and what number he would need to 'check out'.

Keith really had to be on the ball, but he was a fantastic spotter, though he could be a bit up and down in terms of his temperament, especially if he wasn't winning when he was playing. He was still a good player at that time and he'd had an impressive career: in 1983 he was the youngest-ever world champion, but he never achieved those heights again. Later, I got an inkling as to why this was when he had to play at midday one day in Blackpool. He lost and came off the oche with a face like thunder.

'I can't play at midday,' he said.

I said, 'Why not?'

Keith told me that it was because he'd only had eight or nine bottles of Budweiser before he played that day. Usually he would have drunk a bit more and would have competed more effectively. I couldn't believe it. He then claimed that he would normally drink 16 bottles before he went on to play.

'Keith,' I said, 'have you ever thought that this might be the reason why you haven't won anything since 1983?'

It was all good fun, though. After the darts, I presented rugby league tests and some cricket; in fact there were very few sports that I didn't do. But I was under no illusions: I was doing things because I was a working-class lad and I understood working-class sport, and the powers-that-be reckoned those sports – darts, pool, snooker, dog racing – were the ones that suited me best. I loved it, but when Sky unveiled *Sports Saturday* and employed me as their presenter, my career would change for ever. Suddenly, Saturday was the most exciting working day of the week. My life had become, to quote one of the game's great thinkers, 'Unbelievable, Jeff!'

25
Supporting Hartlepool

Throughout these topsy-turvy times, there was only one sporting constant in my life: my home team, Hartlepool United.

I think you should know that I was duped into supporting Hartlepool. OK, I know this is one of the many excuses used by long-suffering supporters of perennially under-achieving teams all over Europe, but I was genuinely conned: when I first went to Victoria Park in 1962, Hartlepool won three-nil against Stockport County. Three-bloody-nil! I thought I was in football heaven. In my dreams I visualized the same performances every week as we strode to football nirvana, kicking aside teams like empty beer cans on our pre-destined route to Wembley and the First Division. There would be trophies and glory; town-hall celebrations and open-top buses. There would be kudos in the school playground among my jealous friends who had foolishly opted to follow Newcastle or Sunderland. Except there wouldn't be any of that. After that dizzying three-nil high, Hartlepool didn't win for another six months.

I'll never forget that first game, though. It was in the mid-60s, and I was watching in the snow and the rain and the hail. Well, that's what it felt like, anyway – it was freezing. I was a schoolboy in those days and my sister used to take me whenever she could. She was five years older than me and we would stand on the terraces. Looking back, it was very unusual to see a woman in a football ground back then, not that it bothered Susan – she didn't seem to care.

She began taking me because my dad was at an age where he'd lost faith in it all. He'd tell me the stories of Hartlepool playing Manchester United in the FA Cup, a game which Sir Matt Busby would describe as one of the most exciting he had seen in his life. The Busby Babes were starting up and they'd drawn Hartlepool in the third round. Man U went three-nil up as expected, but somehow, Hartlepool pulled it back to three-all, before the Reds got a winner in the 90th minute. Typical.

Dad would always tell me about the great players of the past, but he didn't want to go any more. I was seven or eight years old and really wanted to see the games, so Susan took me. Victoria Park had a wide-open stand in those days. It was constantly lashed by the smell of the docks and the harsh sea, and it was bitterly, bitterly cold for both of us. If we had had any money, we could have gone into the temporary stand which was erected just after the First World War. Even in the 1960s it was the only stand with a roof at Victoria Park. But we couldn't really afford it, so I would stand in the snow and the rain and the hail, shivering as we lost again, and again, and again.

What stuck in my mind that first fateful day was the performance of a lumbering giant (I know, we've had a few of those in the team during my time) called Willie McPheat. I remember thinking, 'What a name,' when I saw him on the teamsheet. I also remember thinking, 'What a player,' when he scored twice against Stockport and we grabbed both points (only two for a win in those bygone days). Then I remember thinking, 'What a wally,' when I fell into the trap of believing that this would happen week in, week out, only for my hopes and dreams to be cruelly dashed. Still, I was young and naïve. Willie McPheat had never scored two goals in a game before, and he would never score two goals in a game for us again, and Hartlepool were about to embark on their journey of six miserable, winless months.

But by then it was too late. Like Matt Le Tissier on chocolate digestives, I was hooked. I knew Hartlepool were never going to be world-beaters, but it got to the stage where I had to keep going. I needed to see if they could win again. Later, Brian Clough took over in the dugout and things got a bit better, but obviously I loved them because they were my hometown club. I'm not going to get on my soapbox here, but I believe if you can support your local club then you should, even if you follow another bigger team as well. Sadly, I don't have a bigger team to fall upon for comfort in hard times, just Hartlepool United.

I guess if I'd been born in Manchester I might have supported City or United, but I think supporting a smaller team helps my position on *Soccer Saturday*. If I went on about United or City during the show the whole time, or Liverpool or Chelsea for that matter, then it might get on the nerves of a lot of viewers. Hartlepool aren't considered to be too much of a threat to the Premier League pecking order, or the Championship for that matter. And fans of the show know that if I had been born in Mansfield or Rotherham I would go on about them just as much. Though it must be quite galling if I'm waffling on a bit when we win, I just can't help it.

This, then, is the perfect moment to admit that, yes, I have abused my position of power and gloated on live telly. I'm not proud of it, either. There have been several seasons where Hartlepool were involved in relegation or promotion scraps, usually concluding on the last day of the season, and maybe I haven't been as diplomatic as I should have been when the results have gone our way. I remember a few years ago we had to draw with Bournemouth to get into the League One play-offs. Bournemouth, meanwhile, had to beat us to nick our spot. As you can imagine, it was a pretty nerve-shredding affair.

We had pictures coming into the office all afternoon – Bournemouth had gone one-nil up and all you could hear around the ground was a resounding chant of, 'Are you watching, Jeff Stelling?' When Hartlepool equalized, I couldn't help it. I looked into the cameras and said, 'Yes boys, I'm watching.' It was terribly smug, but nobody at the ground could hear me say it, so it wasn't doing too much harm. I guess it was the sort of banter you want to hear at a football ground and I feel like I'm contributing in some small way.

When I'm in the studio on those important afternoons, it is frustrating that I can't get to the game. But then, other Hartlepool fans would probably express relief at this. By all accounts, I'm a certified Jonah – a jinx – and we always lose when I go to Victoria Park. I can't accept this charge, though. Surely I'm not being held responsible for our dismal record over the last 100 years? Anyway, it's not true. I've seen Hartlepool win. Well, once or twice anyway.

Nevertheless, maybe my absence from the games is a blessing. There's the very real concern that I might bring shame upon myself and Sky Sports when I'm following Hartlepool. It's not a totally unfounded fear, either, as anyone who saw me when I once went to watch Hartlepool play at Leyton Orient will confirm. I was there with snooker impresario and Orient director Barry Hearn and snooker legend Steve Davis, who is a big fan of the O's. Premier League jobsworth Rob Styles was the referee (in his early days) and I watched him book every single Hartlepool player apart from the goalkeeper. To add insult to injury, he even sent one of our players off (and all of this before the 'Respect' campaign). It was unbelievable and a terrible display from a Premier League official-in-waiting.

As the teams came off directly below us, I couldn't help but shout, 'You're a disgrace! You're a bloody disgrace!' several times in the direction of the referee. I was so close to him that he could look up at me and witness the hatred in my eyes. Worse, I was in the directors' box, so I was embarrassing everyone there as well. Even today, I'm very ashamed at my behaviour. But having said that, a few years later I bumped into Rob Styles at Southampton. By then he was a Premier League ref and, like all refs at one stage or another, I think he'd taken some stick from the *Soccer Saturday* panel.

'The reason you don't like me is because of that game at Leyton Orient,' he said. 'You've never forgotten it.'

I said, 'That's partly it, Rob. The other part is that you're crap.'

It was all tongue-in-cheek, but it shows that a good referee always remembers. Unless they're Graham Poll.

There are times, though, when I'll do anything to watch Hartlepool. Back in the days before *Soccer Saturday*, I was working on the snooker for Sky in Bournemouth one weekend. The session we were covering finished at five to three, so I ordered a cab which was waiting for me outside the NEC to take me to Dean Court. I worked out it would take 15 minutes to get there, so with my studio suit and make-up still in place, I went straight to the ground. Once through the turnstiles, I stood in the Hartlepool end behind the goal with a solid bunch of supporters and smiled. Work was over. I was in heaven. But the smiles would only last for a short while.

At that stage, *Soccer Saturday* didn't exist. Nobody knew who I was. Worse, nobody knew why I was wearing a layer of foundation and eye make-up, while doing my best impression of David 'cheap as chips' Dickinson with a distinctly orange complexion. Almost immediately, I heard a voice say, 'Hey, look at him, he's got make-up on.' My stomach began to knot. I could sense a fight-or-flight moment coming on. A few more shots were fired across the bows. My eyeliner began to run with the sweat of fear that was forming on my brow.

Suddenly, a voice yelled, 'Let's have him!' as a gang of burly lads made their way towards me. I was horrified. I didn't want to get beaten up by my own fans, especially as I was in make-up. Thankfully, there was a lifesaver nearby. My cousin, David – who is about six foot nine – spotted the fracas and shouted out, 'Hey, it's our Jeff, he's one of us! He's all right.' As the kerfuffle calmed down, I had to explain to people why I had make-up on. I spent the rest of the afternoon having pictures taken with them. Today there must be some funny snaps on Facebook of groups of burly Hartlepool fans posing alongside a cowering man with a face like a nectarine.

I think the club appreciate the profile I bring to Hartlepool. Well, I hope they do. We certainly haven't had any fallings-out that I can think of. These days Hartlepool is a very well-run club, so I haven't got any problems in that sense, but it hasn't always been like that, as I discovered in my junior reporting days at Radio Tees. As I've said before, when Vince Barker was the chairman he ran a very strange ship. I once heard a story where manager Billy Horner went into the boardroom to write the team line-up down in chalk, just for the chairman's information. Ten minutes later Vince Barker came in and wiped out five of the names and changed the team. Would Roman Abramovich behave in such a manner? Actually, don't even answer that one.

My greatest moment as a Hartlepool fan? Well, I'd like to say getting to the play-off final for League One, but it wasn't that great because we lost. It was frustrating because a win would have meant a season in the Championship, which would have been beyond everybody's wildest dreams. Still, it was a great day for all the fans, me in particular. I was in the dressing room at Cardiff's Millennium Stadium with the players beforehand. The chairman even asked me to come on to the field if we won, but I declined that offer. It would have been the players' day, not mine.

The fact that we were two-one up with six minutes to play against Sheffield Wednesday (and blew it) still makes me feel sick. In the run-up to the game, I was fed up hearing Wednesday fans say, 'You've done well to even get this far, but we're a big club and we belong in the Championship.' Patronizing buggers. But over the 120 minutes they deserved to win. It would have been nice to shut a few of them up, though, in the nicest possible way, of course.

Another great day came with another defeat, which sounds strange, but please bear with me. We lost two-nil to Tranmere in the second leg of the play-off semi-finals that same year. We'd already walloped them at home two-nil, but at their place we found ourselves two-nil down and it was like the Alamo. Somehow we survived and got through extra time, which we didn't deserve. To add to the injustice, we beat them in the penalty shoot-out.

As this drama was unfolding, I was at home watching the game fretfully on the telly with one of my sons, Robbie. It got to the shoot-out and Ritchie Humphreys stepped up to take a penalty. Now, Ritchie Humphreys missed a spot-kick in the play-off semis a couple of seasons previously against Cheltenham, so my heart was in my mouth. Back then it had been the decisive kick of the shoot-out, and in a slice of misfortune, his shot had hit the bar and bounced down into the goalkeeper's arms. It was the penalty that cost us the game.

Anyway, this time around, he didn't miss. It was a real Stuart Pearce/Euro 96 moment which proved his bottle and shredded my nerves. Everybody in the ground was screaming. In my Winchester living room, I screamed and screamed, too, which must have made quite a racket because my wife and my two other boys came racing down the stairs in a fit of panic. They thought I was being attacked by an axe-wielding burglar. Immediately the phone started to ring and the texts began buzzing through, which is always a great experience for a fan when your team have won. It was brilliant and a great occasion, which was bizarre considering we'd actually lost the bloody match.

Thankfully, my wife Lizzie is an understanding woman when it comes to my tryst with Hartlepool. She's a London girl, so I took her to Victoria Park on our second or third date. I figured it would be best to test the water in the relationship's early flourishes. She was pleased with that; I was even more delighted, though we lost to Rochdale three-one, and we were absolutely shocking over the 90 minutes. I think it may have rained, too. Not that Lizzie was bothered – she had a meat-and-potato pie at half-time which she rather enjoyed. I can only imagine it's the reason she's stayed with me for so long, because the entertainment wasn't so great. Still, that was 10 years ago and she hasn't been back since – not even to the ground. I think it must have put her off football considerably. And the pies in our local supermarket are so good that I guess there's no need to travel to Hartlepool for a meal.

There have been times when I've been glad I haven't travelled to Hartlepool myself. The team have certainly embarrassed me on the telly on more occasions than I would care to recount. Early in the season a couple of years ago, we had to play Peterborough away. Unbelievably we were four-nil up after 53 minutes.

'This is fantastic,' I shouted. 'Four-nil up in 53 minutes. Still, there's plenty of time for them to come back. The last time we were four-nil up, we lost six-four against Wrexham. But that's not going to happen, is it?'

Of course, this was the kiss of death and the videprinter began to do its best impression of the Grim Reaper: Peterborough 1 Hartlepool 4; Peterborough 2 Hartlepool 4; Peterborough 3 Hartlepool 4.

By then, the rest of the panel were absolutely pissing themselves with laughter. My heart was in my mouth. Surely we weren't going to blow a four-nothing lead? Luckily, we scored a fifth goal shortly afterwards, and I was relieved. But I must admit, it's very hard to concentrate on the show during afternoons like that, especially if you're involved in a relegation scrap or a promotion battle.

I remember we had to beat Forest to stay up one year and they were pushing for promotion. I didn't fancy our chances, but against the odds, we were leading two-one. With the game winding down at 10 to five – and with moments left – I could see the game on one of the TV screens. Forest had made a break and were straight through on goal. Meanwhile, I was trying to read out the full-time scores without losing my cool. Nobody could work out why I was losing concentration, and thankfully the ball was fired wide, but the irony was that results elsewhere conspired against both teams. We were still relegated, and Forest didn't go up.

The weird thing is, I've been stopped many times by people in the street asking me how Hartlepool are doing, which is always better than fielding questions about Kammy's moustache. Sometimes fans of the show will tell me that Hartlepool have become their second team, just because of my patronage, and I'd like to think that I've done my bit in the recruitment drive for new fans. There's even a group of students from Newcastle who now follow Hartlepool whenever they can, simply because they watch *Soccer Saturday*. I've stopped off at M6 services and a shop assistant will say, 'How are Hartlepool doing?' It's good that word has got around, but fans of other clubs must think it's a right pain in the arse that I mention them so often. Just thank your lucky stars that I don't behave quite as badly as Phil Thompson.

26

'One From The Bottom And Two From The Top.'

How I Got The Countdown Job

So why, I hear you ask, curious reader, should I want to overload myself with another presenting shift at the *Countdown* studios if I already have the greatest job in the world? The truth, I guess, can simply be put down to greed: if you eat a McDonalds at the weekend, there's nothing wrong with taking a Burger King during the week. I am joking, of course (I don't eat burgers, as you can tell by my lithe physique), I just felt that a change of scenery would do me good, providing I could still maintain my role at Sky.

To be fair, the rumours of my appointment had been flying around for years, and generally the rumours were by-and-large true. *Countdown* was something I'd been linked with before Des O'Connor got the job, but there was no real substance in it at that time. But later, during the summer of 2008 when Des announced he would be going, the show's producers approached my agent and asked if I'd be interested in doing it.

I wasn't so sure at first. I didn't really know if it would be my thing and I certainly didn't want to give up *Soccer Saturday*. Anyway, we decided to roll with the idea regardless. I even went to a few meetings, just to get a feel for the role.

Given that the show was something of a national institution, it was unsurprising that speculation should be rife surrounding the new appointment. Names were being bandied around the papers with the usual gossip – there were even people like Christopher Biggins being mentioned. I wasn't even sure I was really in the frame until the producer and executive producer asked to meet me in London. I did, and I thoroughly enjoyed being wined and dined by them – they were big fans of *Soccer Saturday*, and they were paying – so I thought I could definitely work with them.

At that point, though, there were obviously other people in the running, there was no question about that, but for some reason, my potential appointment caught the imagination once it was announced. One night, the *Sun* newspaper rang me and said, 'You know you've definitely got the job, don't you?' Apparently it had been leaked by the *Daily Mail* that it was a two-horse race between myself and Alexander Armstrong of the comedy duo Armstrong and Miller. The paper described him as an ex-Cambridge chorister and the 'graduate, plummy-voiced individual from the Pimm's advert'. Apparently he was battling for the job against 'the gritty north-eastern sports journalist'. They tried to compare and contrast us, which was very funny – I'm not gritty. Some people would argue that I've never been a journalist either.

When the *Sun* rang again – this time to get a quote for their story – my wife answered the phone. At that time, no offer had been made to me by Channel 4, so I didn't really want to talk to the press.

Lizzie did a sterling stalling job: she wouldn't put the journalist through to me. She may have even told them that I was out, but she passed on every detail as the conversation rolled along:

'Oh, he's got it has he?'

I mouthed the words, 'Where did they get that from?'

'What makes you think that? Oh, I see … You're running the story on Tuesday are you?'

I panicked. After they called, I got straight on the phone to my agent, Robert. We then heard that a high-ranking TV source from Channel 4 had said that I'd got the job even though no firm offer had been made. Anyway, the next day we decided the best thing was to find out what the guys from *Countdown* wanted. They weren't able to tell us at that point, but by then we knew what the commitment was: I would have to be recording five 50-minute shows a day for three days a week if I accepted the position.

This would mean an immense effort on my part. The travelling distance was huge for starters – I would be driving five hours to Leeds and five hours back again. I thought, 'We've run with this, but there's no way I can do it. It's too big a commitment.' I'd even got out of bed that Monday morning feeling absolutely bloody knackered. I took my kids to school and I thought, 'Would I really want to drive to Leeds now?' And the answer was no.

Even though the job had not been offered, I had decided that, if it was, I wouldn't take it. We rang the *Sun* straight away to tell them that there was no truth in the story, but they said, 'We're going to run it anyway.' And they bloody well did:

6 SKY Sports legend Jeff Stelling is set to become the new host of hit telly quiz Countdown.

The sharp-witted *Soccer Saturday* frontman will replace retiring presenter Des O'Connor.

Stelling, who has become a cult hero on Sky's six-hour footie results service, was linked with *Countdown* in 2005 after the death of legendary host Richard Whiteley.

But bosses hired Des Lynam instead because he was seen to have a higher profile. O'Connor later took over, but quit this year, as did brainbox Carol Vorderman.

Hartlepool Utd fan Stelling, who writes in the *Sun*'s Saturday football pull-out *Super Goals*, is said to be "loving" the idea of hosting *Countdown*.

One telly source said: "He'd be perfect. He's quick-witted, clean-cut and is bound to be a hit with housewives."

Stelling, 52, will be offered the Channel 4 job, but will NOT quit *Soccer Saturday*.

A *Countdown* source said: "We are confident of getting him."

Dad-of-three Stelling is renowned for his hilarious quips on the Sky football show.

When Guylain Ndumbu-Nsungu scored for Sheffield Wednesday, he joked: "Local boy makes good."

Whenever a player named Stephenson nets, he says: "I bet that was a rocket."

And each time Hartlepool's James Brown scores, Stelling produces a James Brown doll which sings "I Feel Good". **9**

My picture was placed beneath the Page Three girl (always a nice place to be), but I knew the appointment wasn't going to happen. Then, of course, my phone exploded. People wanted to congratulate me. I spent all of Tuesday and Wednesday telling them that the story wasn't true. Friends, intelligent people some of them (so not Thommo, then), were even asking whether I'd be helping to choose the new Carol Vorderman. Well, I told them that it certainly wasn't going to be my missus because she can't even spell 'Countdown', let alone anything else.*

After a while the fuss seemed to die down and the 2008 season got underway. A couple of months later, I changed my mind. There I was sunning myself, Charlie Nicholas-style, on a beach in Portugal when another call came through that *Countdown* still wanted me to present the show. I thought about it and agreed in theory, but only if the recording schedule could be altered to suit my Sky TV commitments. Clearly, circumstances had changed. Alex Armstrong had gone for the screen test at Channel 4, but I'm not sure how it had gone, and he pulled out of the running. The producers spoke to me again and told me they were still interested in getting me involved.

My misgivings still focused on the schedule. But we negotiated and what I didn't realize was that the people who worked for ITV Productions – the company who shoot the show – weren't exactly overjoyed with the schedule themselves. They have to film a year's worth of shows in a four-month block, which is very hectic as you

---

*A NOTE FROM LIZZIE STELLING: 'I'd like to point out that I can spell, as Jeff well knows. I send him off to the supermarket with the family shopping list every week.'

can imagine. They were much happier at the thought of spreading it out over the course of the year.

With that in place, we got together and did a run-through of the show with 'the New Carol Vorderman', Rachel Riley, who is great. She's also drop-dead gorgeous. The *Guardian* described her as having a Gwyneth Paltrow look to her, which I thought was spot-on. This dry run took place because the producers wanted to get a feel for me and what I was like in the flesh and to see what the chemistry would be like with Rachel. The company had organized a photo shoot immediately after the practice run. Not wanting to put any pressure on me, I was told that there wouldn't be any photographers afterwards if it didn't go well!

Thankfully, we did the photo shoot and filming got underway in mid-December. After a couple of rehearsals we went to Leeds to record the first 15 shows in three days. It's all well and good doing rehearsals when you only have the cameras to worry about. Doing it in front of a live audience of students and older folk – all of them *Countdown* fanatics – is a very different experience. I had a fantastic time. During the first week, some members of the audience arrived wearing Hartlepool scarves and shirts, which I thought was brilliant. On the day of the first show I even got a bouquet of flowers from Carol Vorderman. It all started very well, but then it's a relatively simple gig for me: Rachel does the maths, Dictionary Corner work out the words, the producers produce and I just press a button which starts the *Countdown* clock.

The first shows we did were the 'Champion of Champions' tournament. All the people that were competing had obviously been on the show before and all of them, it would be fair to say, could be considered *Countdown* nuts. On the second day, one of them came over to me during a quiet moment and said, 'I just wanted to thank you for saving *Countdown*. We were all worried about what would happen to the programme if it got into the wrong hands. Now I know it's safe.' I found it really touching. Clearly the show was very important to this guy, as it is to a lot of people.

In fairness, there are a couple of similarities to the *Soccer Saturday* studio. Although you don't actually have a panel, we do have bodies in the studio – there are a couple of contestants, Rachel, Dictionary Corner and a guest – so there are five people you have to work with, but it is a refreshing change from working with shouty footballers. But the great thing about working on *Countdown* is that I'm a new face and Rachel is a new face, but the game hasn't changed at all. It's a national institution, so why should it? I still can't do the bloody conundrums. I am useless. I can do some of the maths and I can pick out some high-scoring words, but the conundrums are a complete mystery to me. In fact, regular Dictionary Corner guest Richard Digance said to me, 'Jeff, there's only one football team with a name made of two nine-letter words: Sheffield Wednesday – which is a double-barrelled conundrum.' I'm not holding my breath that either of those words will come up any time soon.

27

'Der-der, der-der, der-der-der-der, BONG!'

(My Life In The Countdown Hot Seat)

I've learned two things since parking my backside in the *Countdown* chair. Number one: the only nine-letter word Phil Thompson knows is 'LIVERPOOL'. Number two: the public can be as fickle as a Manchester City chairman when it comes to their favourite daytime telly show. And no, I'm not talking about *Deal or No Deal*, thank you very much.

From the moment I took on the *Countdown* job, I knew it was going to be a tough challenge to follow the likes of Des O'Connor and Des Lynam, both of whom had previously sat in the hot seat. Trailing the legendary Richard Whitely's footsteps was an even grander task because he was such a fantastic presenter. The *Countdown* faithful held him in high esteem, and rightly so, as he presented the show from 1982 to 2005. But even though two presenters had taken on the job after his death in 2005, Richard's presence still loomed large when I signed up.

So I have to admit, I was overwhelmed at first. In the first few programmes it showed too, so much so that quite a few people immediately emailed Channel 4 to complain about my presenting style. Well, there's nothing like giving the new boy a baptism of fire, I thought – any football manager will tell you that. Still, the treatment was pretty harsh, even by Wimbledon's standards. For those of you too young to remember, the Dons of the 1980s used to burn the clothes of the club's new signings. *Countdown*'s fans were just as savage as Vinnie Jones and co.

'Jeff Stelling is so boring he might as well be a cardboard cut-out,' wrote one 'admirer'. 'Channel 4 should stop trying to replace Richard Whitely with celebrities who aren't as funny as he was.'

It hurt, but that was only the beginning. Another fan, going by the name of 'Slack Rocker', took the insults one step further. He reckoned I had an 'unconvincing bonhomie and a leery smile through what look like borrowed teeth'. He then went on to claim that presenter and former Tory MP Gyles Brandreth should be given the job, which tells you just about everything you need to know. For a while I wondered if Rodney Marsh was behind the attack, but sadly the criticism was genuine.

However, compared to Rachel Riley, my glamorous assistant, I'd had it easy. In the opening weeks of the show her inbox was flooded with insults from hardcore viewers. Some took offence to her easy-on-the-eye appearance (one sourpuss compared her to a 'hooker'. Unbelievable). Others reckoned her maths wasn't as good as that of *Countdown*'s former co-host, Carol Vorderman. That was nonsense too. As anyone who's worked with Rachel will attest, she's as sharp as a tack with the numbers. She was just finding her feet as a presenter. I think a lot of people overlooked the fact that, at 23, she was still very young to be taking on such a substantial role.

It wasn't just the viewers who were putting the boot in. Every day there seemed to be a negative article in the *Daily Mail*. For some reason they seemed particularly keen on knocking the show and I soon noticed that all the unflattering comments had been written by somebody called Liz Thomas. I'm not sure what her problem with the programme was exactly – maybe she was a *Soccer Saturday* widow, I know there are plenty of them out there. Anyway, one of her stories claimed the *Countdown* ratings were falling, though evidence presented by Channel 4 seemed to contradict this. Still, never let the facts get in the way of a tasty headline.

None of this helped me, of course, and I initially felt quite nervous in my new job. The show exposed a lack of knowledge in the words and numbers department, and I seemed to be the only one in the studio without a specialist skill. Rachel, despite the criticism from a small minority, was a complete whizz with the numbers; in Dictionary Corner we had Susie Dent, a proven master of the nine-letter words and their definitions. Meanwhile, the contestants were red hot.

To the trained eye, my only job was to press the bloody button that started the *Countdown* clock – all 30 seconds of it. And while I can tell you (with some pride) that I do this for every round of the show, it's sometimes hard not to feel useless and insignificant. Basically, I'm a wally with a stopwatch, though at least now I have some sympathy for the much-criticised fourth official.

Thankfully, the negative criticism didn't last for long, and these days I'm starting to feel a bit more relaxed in the role. The healing process was helped by a cracking production team and some great guests in Dictionary Corner, many of whom I've helped to bring onboard. We've had the likes of snooker legend Steve Davis and cricket commentator David 'Bumble' Lloyd. The producers were so desperate one week that we even invited Matt Le Tissier into the studio. When you're working with people of that calibre, *Countdown* is always a laugh.

I remember Bumble told me one of my favourite stories of late. It featured Albert and Gladys, a couple from his local pub who drank there every night, though I suspect they might be fictional. One evening, the pair of them had a huge row and stormed out. The following day Albert turned up alone, so the landlord asked him, 'What happened pal? Where's Gladys?' Albert looked despondent. 'She's gone, she's left me,' he said. 'She's taken the lot, she's cleaned me out. She's even taken my satellite dish and extensive Bob Marley collection. It's terrible. No woman, no Sky.'

If you're groaning at that one you might want to prepare yourself for another 'joke' from comedian Tim Vine, a regular in Dictionary Corner. 'A man walks into a butcher's shop and says to the bloke behind the counter, "I bet you a tenner you can't reach the meat on the top shelf." The butcher looks at him and shakes his head. "Sorry, mate, I can't take you up on that. The steaks are too high."'

When it comes to *Countdown*'s greatest guests, there can be only one winner though: US telly legend Jerry Springer. Over the years Jerry has built quite a controversial reputation. His hit confession programme (imaginatively titled *The Jerry Springer Show*) often featured cross-dressing dwarves, kissing cousins and sex pests. Thankfully, I deal with similar characters on the *Soccer Saturday* panel every weekend, so the pair of us got on very well.

Even so, I was quite concerned when Jerry arrived. Firstly, he was such a big name that I wasn't quite sure how he would fit in. And secondly, it quickly became apparent that he didn't really know that much about *Countdown*. He'd been asked to come into Dictionary Corner and I think he must have agreed without doing his research. He didn't have a clue what was going on when we started the *Countdown* clock for the first time. More worrying for us was the fact that Jerry looked exhausted when he arrived. We were in make-up – a touch of guyliner here, a dab of lippy there – and I looked across at him.

'Christ, Jerry,' I said. 'You look bloody knackered.'

He just shrugged his shoulders and sighed. 'It's a way of life, son,' he said. 'A way of life.'

He wasn't kidding. As I walked along the corridor to start filming, I could hear a massive commotion breaking out among the audience. When I arrived at the studio floor Jerry was standing in front of the crowd. All of them were on their feet shouting, 'Jerry! Jerry! Jerry!' as he regaled them with jokes and anecdotes. From that moment he was the consummate professional. It was as if he'd flicked a switch and moved into 'Presenter mode', and the *Countdown* audience were eating out of his hand. It was sensational stuff, but god knows where he'd got the extra energy from.

By this stage I was used to an unruly commotion at *Countdown*. At first we recorded the show at a Leeds studio, but we soon shifted our workspace to Manchester, where I found myself working alongside a presenter just as controversial as Jerry – the one and only Jeremy Kyle. For those of you unfamiliar with daytime telly, *The Jeremy Kyle Show* is every bit as raucous as *The Jerry Springer Show*. It often features topics such as 'He Likes To Do It In Public!' and 'Your Brother Is Your Husband?' as troubled souls bare their private lives in front of an audience that wouldn't look out of place at Millwall, circa 1981.

On telly it was terrifying stuff. The problem for me was that we were now working in the studio next to Jeremy and his oddball audience. I can tell you that in the flesh they're even more horrific. It's certainly an uneasy sensation looking at the audience

queues for both shows. Every afternoon a busload of mild man-
nered, educated *Countdown* fans stand alongside a gang of what
look like suspects from *Crimewatch*. Unsurprisingly, the elderly
ladies and gents keep a tight grip on their handbags and wallets.

Behind the scenes it's even riskier. At the studio the name of
each presenter is printed on their dressing room door. Well, everyone apart from Jeremy, that is. My theory is that he's naturally concerned about the prospect of the brother/husband from 'Your
Brother Is Your Husband?' taking umbrage to one of his comments
and exacting revenge backstage. On paper this seems like a wise
move, except Jeremy's dressing room is next door to mine. Most
nights I'm woken by a nightmare where the aforementioned star
of 'Your Brother Is Your Husband?' wanders backstage to exact
revenge – except he takes it out on the wrong guy.

The wrong guy being me.

If you were to ask a man on the street to describe the audience in
the *Countdown* studio, he'd probably compare it to the British
Legion or that other great institution, the Post Office queue. Maybe
that was the case a few years ago, but these days we seem to get
quite a lot of students. I even get my fair share of *Countdown*
groupies. I'd like to stress that *Countdown* groupies are very different from Kings of Leon groupies. They only ever want autographs and even then they're usually presents for other people.
I've lost count of the number of times I've scribbled the words 'To
Mum' across a picture of my 'leery smile' (cheers, Brighton's 'Slack
Rocker'). Sometimes it's worse. Sometimes I have to scribble 'To
Gran, all my love, Jeff. X'. And that's a real kick in the 'borrowed
teeth' (again, © Brighton's 'Slack Rocker').

Despite this, I've always felt comfortable in front of the *Countdown* audience because you can bounce off them quite nicely.

Often it's like having a more intelligent version of Thommo, Le Tiss, Charlie and Merse alongside me. They groan kindly at my jokes and they're forever giving me presents such as jam, Jaffa Cakes and homemade biscuits, not that you could ever tell from my rippling physique. I was even presented with a painted portrait by one fan, complete with an ornate, Tate Gallery-style frame. The boys at *Soccer Saturday* claimed it looked like Sebastian Coe, but I was very flattered. It now hangs imperiously in the *Soccer Saturday* office to remind the panel of who's really in charge around the place.

Sometimes our audience can go one step further with their generosity, as proven by 2009's Valentine's Day show. I'm not usually a fan of this particular calendar event, mainly because I never get any cards – which I suspect will come as a shock to all of you (and will probably be picked up by some gleeful hack at the *Daily Mail*) – and in the days running up to it, Rachel was inundated with notes and flowers. Sure enough, I didn't get a thing. I moaned about it on the telly shortly afterwards and the crowd 'Awwww-ed' in unison. I figured that would be an end to the sympathy.

Imagine my surprise when a card arrived at the *Countdown* studios a few days later. It was from a lady who claimed that she had 'never had a Valentine in her life' and she wanted to take me out for dinner. At the bottom of the page she mentioned her age. My Valentine was 89, which was very sweet, but I declined on the grounds that a) I'm happily married, and b) I would never romance someone in the same age range as Frank McLintock.

Our contestants can be just as quirky. Some of them are very chatty, out-going and garrulous, but then there are others who have absolutely nothing to say. One guy claimed the most memorable moment in his life was winning a trip to Canada. When I asked him what was memorable about it, he shrugged his shoulders and told me he couldn't remember. Another reckoned the most exciting thing about his life was that he lived on the same road as Jeremy Clarkson. He'd never met or even seen Clarkson. He just knew that he lived there. Bringing these people to life can be a dry business sometimes.

One exception to the rule was the 2009 champion, Chris Davies. Chris was a man of few words in real life; in *Countdown* terms he was a man of plenty. I'd never met a contestant like him before. There was absolutely nothing he couldn't put his mind to – letters, conundrums, numbers. Apparently he was some kind of Rubik's Cube whizzkid as well. On the show he was a star and not only did he regularly deliver nine-letter words, he knew the definitions of all of them, which a lot of contestants can't actually do.

On the flipside, Chris was very shy. It was hard to get him to open up on air, but by the time he'd won the Grand Final everything had changed. Because of his fame on *Countdown*, Chris had scored a girlfriend. He was confident and outgoing and he'd developed into a more rounded person. Somehow, our humble little show had brought him out of his shell. I just hope and pray that, one day, *Soccer Saturday* can do the same for John Salako.

28

The Real Jeff Stelling

(In A 1980s-Style Football Interview)

As you can imagine, I've read quite a few footballers' autobiographies. And while I've thoroughly enjoyed some of them (no, Thommo, not yours), I've always winced with embarrassment at the moment a so-called star gives the reader a glimpse into their personal life (cats, golf handicap, a love of diamond-encrusted underwear). So, instead of boring you with my personal life (cats, golf handicap, diamond-encrusted underwear), I've instead decided to answer the questions from an old *Match* magazine interview with former Liverpool and Scotland defender Steve Nicol, replacing his answers with my own. Hopefully it'll afford the 'Stellingettes' – or is that 'Stellingette'? – an insight into my spare time without boring you all to tears. Like Thommo's book tends to do (only kidding, Phil).

Name:

Jeff Stelling.

Nickname:

Chopper Stelling, after my days as a ruthless full-back. Or Jaffa Stelling, because when I was a kid I used to carry an orange rucksack to school, and I was very fat – it made me look like an orange.

Position:

Right-back.

Clubs:

The *Hartlepool Mail* in the Hartlepool Sunday League, BBC Radio FC in the Octopus League, so named because there 12 twelve teams in it. Obviously there were eight originally, but it just grew. I was long-serving at both of those teams – I didn't have as many clubs as Chris 'Peter Stringfellow' Kamara.

Strengths (as a player):

Tenacity. Strength in the air. Not. Swearing. Buying the first round in the pub afterwards.

Weaknesses:

Jesus, how big is the page? Not tall enough. Not fast enough. I was very much in the Kenny Sansom (Arsenal) mould, but without the pace. I didn't score a lot of goals, either.

I play a bit like ...

Kenny Sansom. Or maybe Phil Thompson, but with more grace and style.

Greatest goal:

I can hardly remember it, but it was against a team called ILPS and we were two-nil down. It was pouring with rain, and I ran 60 yards to score a diving header in the mud. Nobody, except me, knew who had scored it because the ball was in the net, I was in the net and when I got up I looked like the Creature from the Black Lagoon. I was caked in mud. It was something of a surprise to everyone on the pitch, but it kick-started a three-two revival.

Have you ever been sent off?

Yes, just a couple of times. Once for *Hartlepool Mail* which was grossly unfair. I was marking a fantastic player and I was having one of my best-ever games, but it meant me sticking to him like glue. He got very pissed off with me and swung a punch. I swung one back and that was the end of it, we were both off. I'm not exactly Gary Lineker.

I present a bit like ...

Former TV scientist Magnus Pike, what with all the frantic arm-waving. Or maybe hairy botanical TV expert David Bellamy.

Career highlights:

Winning the Sports Journalists' Association's Broadcast Journalist of the Year in the first four years of the awards. It's only been running for four years and so far I've been the only winner. I'll probably get booed if I win it again. There's quite a prestigious list of nominees: Gary Lineker, Claire Baldwin, John Inverdale and Jim Rosenthal among them. All the press boys vote for it.

Career lowlight:

Working at *TV-am*. Without question.

Best player played with:

Steve Hodge, formerly of Nottingham Forest, Spurs and England. He was a still a great player when I played with him in a game four or five years ago. There were a whole host of us in the team – Micky Quinn, Steve Hodge, Alvin Martin and Gary Stevens. Barry Fry managed us. All the players we were up against were in their mid-30s. Barry put me up-front with Micky Quinn and the two of us were like a small elephant stampede. With 10 minutes to go, Barry shouted out, 'Substitute!' and both Micky and I ran towards the touchline. 'No, Jeff,' he said, 'not you; you're staying on.' I know he was torturing me deliberately. But Steve Hodge stood out, he was fantastic.

Best player worked with:

Bestie; there was no comparison really. He was different class.

Current car:

Jaguar XF.

Favourite films:

It's a Wonderful Life, which I can't see too many times;
Schindler's List; *There's Only One Jimmy Grimble*.

Favourite books:

Rothmans Football Year Book 1961, 1962, 1963, 1964, 1965, 1966, 1967, 1968, 1969, 1970, 1971, 1972, 1973, 1974, 1975, 1975 (I bought it twice by mistake), *1976, 1977, 1978, 1979, 1980, 1981, 1982, 1983, 1984, 1985, 1986, 1987, 1988, 1989, 1990, 1991, 1992, 1993, 1994, 1995, 1996, 1997, 1998, 1999, 2000, 2001, 2002, 2003, 2004, 2005, 2006, 2007, 2008* ...

Favourite TV programmes:

The X Factor, Ant and Dec's Saturday Night Takeaway, Question Time, Our Friends in the North.

Favourite three-course meal:

Oysters to improve my sex drive; golden bream, as cooked by Jorge from Azul, a restaurant outside Albufeira in Portugal, followed by raspberry-ripple ice cream.

Favourite holiday destination:

Barbados and Mauritius. Not at the same time.

Most embarrassing moment:

I was hosting the launch of the Premier League's version of 'Respect' in Sunderland at the start of this season. It was part of a three-way live TV broadcast – Richard Keys and Eamonn Holmes were in London and Manchester. We had refs (such as Mike Riley), chairmen (Boro's Steve Gibson among them) and players on the stage. I had to interview several – Julio Arca, Shay Given, Dean Whitehead and Ian Ashbee.

All was okay until I reached Ashbee. Focusing intently on him, I didn't realize where the stage ended and tumbled off inelegantly! Cue gales of laughter. Apparently, Gary Neville was watching in Manchester and had to wipe away tears of mirth. Ashbee helped me back up, only to have me berate him for tripping me. 'That would be a red card,' I urged Riley – though we all knew no one had touched me. The next day my fall from grace made headlines in most of the national press, thereby guaranteeing the campaign maximum publicity. The Premier League even wrote to thank me for my eye-catching presentation!

Dream date (apart from the wife or Chris Kamara):

Cheryl Cole. People in the *Soccer Saturday* office think I'm obsessed with her. Which I am, of course.

My tombstone would read:

'I don't feel good.'

29

Frequently Asked Questions

(At Cocktail Parties)

On the rare occasions that people don't say, 'Hey, that looks like the football bloke off the telly, only he's a lot shorter,' and actually approach me, then they'll usually ask one of several questions ...

Here, Jeff, how tall are you? You're shorter than you look on the box ...

I'm average height! I'm five foot seven and three quarters. The three quarters of an inch is very important. I'm taller than Tony Cottee for definite. I don't know why people make so much of my height. If I'd been born in Guatemala I would be regarded as a giant, but unfortunately I was born in Hartlepool, so I'm average height. And no, I don't sit on a cushion, but my seat is cranked up quite high.

Here, Jeff, have you got Georgie Thompson's number? Or Vicky Gomersall's? Or even Kirsty Gallacher's?

No, and if I had it, I'd be the first one to use it. And by the way, Georgie's shorter than me, much shorter than me. She's tiny.

Here, Jeff, what's the strangest rumour you've heard about yourself?

Danny Baker wrote in one of his newspaper columns that I had six toes on each foot, which I couldn't believe. I don't know where he got that one from. I can confirm that I have the regulation number of toes.

Here, Jeff, if you hadn't become a TV anchorman, what would you have done?

I don't know, I would have been useless. If I could still work in TV, I would have loved to do something like *MasterChef* because you get to taste all the food. Away from TV, I would probably have been a teacher or something like that.

Here, Jeff, what are all those people doing behind you in the studio?

Well, they're making a hell of a lot of noise, to be honest. Actually, they're all working on Sky Sports News, so they're researchers and reporters. Some of them are working on all the things you see on the *Soccer Saturday* screen – the scores, the goalscorers, the league tables and the ticker tape stuff. I never look at that as being part of our programme; I see us as being the stuff that goes on in the middle. There's a lot of them, because it's a 24-hour news service. There's a lot of time to fill and it's a big and expensive operation.

What's the idea of having them exposed to the viewers? I guess it's a way of making the show seem less sterile. It creates a hive-of-activity atmosphere. It can drive you up the wall when there's a Grand Prix or a Grand National going on because they make a right royal racket. There will be roars of excitement going up in the background and there have been occasions where I've had to stand up and shout, 'Will you lot shut up?!' It's noisier than it is in the Emirates in there, though that's not hard, to be fair.

Here, Jeff, is Mrs Stelling an understanding woman?

Yes, extremely, and she's had to be throughout her life because she was Vic Wakeling's PA, so she had to be extremely understanding there, too. And tactful. Before we were married she would ring me and say, 'Vic wants to see you and Kamara in his office; make sure you look smart, he's going to ask you to close the door.' Now, closing the door meant you were in for a bollocking. Good news is delivered when the door is open. It was good to have her on my side, like today.

But yes, she's understanding because she knows I'm going to be working a lot of crazy hours. She knows we're never going to go out on a Friday or Saturday night when the show is on and generally on a Sunday I'm too tired to do anything, so that makes us very antisocial animals. I'm fortunate that on the days I don't work, I can help with the school runs and things like that. I remember last year we arranged to go to Lapland for a holiday with the kids to see Santa. I booked it, then when I checked my diary I realized that

I'd mixed up my dates and it was a Carling Cup week and I had to do the show. It was my gig and there was no way I could get out of it. Lizzie had to take the kids on her own. It was a nightmare.

Here, Jeff, why can't you be nice to Phil Thompson? What's he ever done?

That's a rhetorical question, isn't it? Why should I be nice to Thommo? I'm as nice to him as I could possibly be. I love Thommo, really, but people genuinely believe that we don't get on. I was at Dublin Airport recently and a scouser came up to me and said, 'Why don't you like Phil? He's a lovely bloke!' I have to explain it's just banter. People have to understand that not everything you see on TV is true and accurate. In the same way, if you were to watch *Superman*, would you believe people could really fly?

Here, Jeff, has the videprinter ever gone down on air?

Oh yes, it has. It's a nightmare, but there's nothing we can do about it because it's completely out of our control. We're lucky because we have reporters here, there and everywhere, so we can rely on them for info. But if the videprinter goes down for 15 minutes or so, all the scores come in at once when it starts running again. It's impossible to keep up with them. Every weekend I pray it doesn't happen.

FREQUENTLY ASKED QUESTIONS

Here, Jeff, who would be your dream panel, alive or dead?

They'd have to be greats in the game. So I would go for Jose Mourinho because he's highly respected and very articulate. I'd also go for Fergie, because you'd get an opinion. Forcefully. And I know from sitting with him at various functions that he is a fount of fantastic stories, a lot of which are not for broadcasting. Arsène Wenger would be great next to him! And to finish off, Brian Clough, though he'd probably end up presenting the show. I wouldn't get a word in edgeways, would I?

Here, Jeff, who were your TV heroes as a kid?

During my time at the BBC, I was lucky enough to meet with one of my heroes: Des Lynam. I remember one of my first brushes with Des came when I was a reporter at Aintree. We were covering the Grand National, and I didn't have to be there until the Thursday. I was reporting to the course at nine in the morning and got there quite late, and there was nobody I knew there apart from the familiar figure of Des Lynam who was sitting with a lady about five or six tables away. I had never met him before, but he called me over – he was a big star at that time as he was the anchorman for *Grandstand*. He said, 'Don't sit over there on your own, come and have breakfast with me and my wife.' I thought it was a class act from such a respected figure and somebody who was an idol for me.

I didn't bump into him very often after that, but whenever I saw him, we always had a laugh and a joke and he was always lovely to me. He was a real charmer and very witty. I remember even when I went to Sky, I bumped into him and he said, 'I used to think you had a future,' with a smile on his face. He was absolutely brilliant, and as a TV figure he was second to none.

The thing that made Des such a great presenter was that he was incredibly relaxed on air. The tendency these days is for a presenter to blast everything out to the audience and I work with a lot of producers who want me to get more excitable, but I tend to keep it calm. I don't want to give it 'more oomph'. Certainly, Des never did. But his biggest asset was his humour: it's what made him a star. There was one legendary tale when he was on *Grandstand* and announced to the nation that 'there will be football later, but first the Scottish FA Cup'.

To me, he might have been panicking internally, but on the exterior he was all urbane charm. I guess I probably learned subconsciously from watching people like Des on the telly. Certainly, when working on *Soccer Saturday* I always try to be a bit lower-key, which Des always was. I want to present in a normal, conversational tone without shouting at the camera. I don't want people shouting at me from the telly. Sometimes I'll be sitting there watching the telly and I'll be thinking, 'For crying out loud, stop shouting at me!' If I do get carried away on a Saturday it's through sheer excitement, but I won't be like that in the first three hours of the show when it's a lot quieter.

I admired Des as a broadcaster and I liked him as a person. They say you should never meet your heroes, but this was a case where it was definitely the right thing to do.

There was also a broadcaster from the north-east – who is still working today – called Mike Neville. He was and still is a massive star up there. The thing that appealed to me was his sense of humour. He used to present a half-hour news show and it was like he was telling you funny stories in your living room. He looked like he was enjoying himself when he was on the telly and I think that was the key with a lot of the more successful broadcasters – all of them looked like they were having a good time. Like I've said before, TV presenting ain't brain surgery and it certainly isn't a matter of life and death. You should have professional pride in your performance, but nobody is going to get hurt by it.

Here, Jeff, what was your first football TV memory?

There wasn't much football on the telly when I was younger. I remember there were regional football magazine shows on the Sunday that would cover all the reports and the games the day after but not much more. You might get a bit of a Sunderland game or a bit of a Newcastle game. If you were lucky you might get a Boro goal or a Hartlepool goal and that was about it. It all looked like it had been shot on one camera and it was in black and white – I was a child of the black-and-white days.

You used to get the FA Cup on TV every year and that was probably the only live football you would see all year, which was why it was such a big deal. I guess this was why the coverage started at eight in the morning. For a football fan it was probably the second-biggest day of the year behind Christmas Day. You wouldn't dream of going on holiday on FA Cup Final day in those days, and you certainly wouldn't plan on having a wedding that day – nobody would turn up!

Here, Jeff, have any of your on-air gags ever offended anyone?

I don't think so, but there was a story about an old lady in Blackburn who was a Rovers fan. It was at a time when they were having some difficulty a few years back. This lady was apparently very religious and she was praying for their survival, but not only was she praying for their survival, she also lit a candle for them to urge them on.

Unfortunately, the house caught fire from the candle she had lit one night and burned the building down. Now, I tried to deliver this story and by the end there were tears of laughter rolling down my face, and it wasn't until afterwards that somebody said, 'Was she OK?' And I thought, 'Oh my god, I don't know.' As it was, she was OK, but for a moment I was horrified. Sometimes you do things and regret them afterwards. It didn't help that Blackburn lost that afternoon, too.

Here, Jeff, what celebrities watch the show?

I'm told that Ant and Dec are big fans. Alastair Campbell is a fan, too. Thommo tells a story in his autobiography, *Stand Up, Pinocchio*, about Alastair Campbell. I didn't realize that Thommo was such a political animal, but by all accounts he was at a Labour Party Conference in Liverpool and was asked to give a speech about what a nice place it was to live and work. Phil was sitting in the VIP room and Alastair Campbell, who is a big Burnley fan, apparently said, 'Phil, that programme with Jeff Stelling on Sky is absolutely fantastic. Jeff's a brilliant presenter, top class. Let me tell you, when we were starting to build our election plans, the top brass at Labour got together to plan a strategy. We had to come up with a saying or highlight a person as a symbol of what the Labour Party should be about. I asked for ideas. Some mentioned the sayings of great political leaders. Others mentioned top sportsmen. Some pointed to famous movie stars. Then it came to me and I said, "Jeff Stelling." They all said, "Who?" I said, "He's a symbol of solidity, solidarity and knowledge."'

I thought, 'Crikey, has he got me mixed up with Garth Crooks?'

He then told Phil that if I ever wanted to go down to the Labour Party conference and give a speech I only had to ask, but I quite like keeping things non-political. I have political views, but I don't want to foist them on anyone else. Football views are dangerous enough. If I came out with any political leanings I'd probably turn half the country off.

It was all tongue-in-cheek, but it did make a serious point. Thommo went on to say, 'Before I left, Tony Blair came up to me and told me how much he loved *Soccer Saturday*.' Thommo makes a point of saying that he didn't mention me!

Here, Jeff, do you watch Setanta?

Se-what? No, I don't watch Setanta, but they owe me a bloody fortune because I can't get a signal and I've been told that's because I don't have the right band space. So even though I pay my £9.99 a month or whatever, we can never get a satellite signal. So nobody in the house watches it, never, ever. Maybe they're just deliberately not piping it through to my house because they know I work for Sky. I have thought that occasionally, but I know some other people who have the same problem.

Here, Jeff, why do you hate Leeds/Chelsea/Man City/Scarborough/Crystal Palace/Spurs/MK Dons/Queen of the South ...?

I don't: I love you all! It's impossible to persuade people that you are impartial and unbiased. I get it all the time. Emails come in every weekend and not all of them are love letters. During the game between Sunderland and Arsenal in 2008, I got a stack of notes, one of which read: 'Stelling, you could hardly keep the grin of your face when Sunderland scored against us in the 86th minute.' Then when Arsenal equalized a couple of minutes later, I got an email reading, 'Stelling, you were really showing your allegiance as a Gooner there.' You can't win. But hopefully you'll keep coming back for more. Saturday is the greatest day of the week after all. And it's always good to have you there with me.

Hopefully see you next weekend ...

Index

INDEX